A LEAF IN TH[E]

C000142719

PETER HUDSON

A LEAF
IN THE WIND

Travels in the
Heart of Africa

Flamingo
Published by Fontana Paperbacks

First published in Great Britain
by Columbus Books Ltd, 1988

This Flamingo edition first published
in 1989 by Fontana Paperbacks

Flamingo is an imprint of
Fontana Paperbacks, part of
the Collins Publishing Group,
8 Grafton Street, London W1X 3LA

Copyright © Peter Hudson 1988

Printed and bound in Great Britain by
William Collins Sons & Co. Ltd, Glasgow

FOR MY PARENTS

ACKNOWLEDGEMENTS

I wish to thank deeply the people of Africa for having me as a guest to their continent and for the unfailing hospitality and kindness I received from them wherever I went. For reasons of security, however, the names of some people mentioned in my book have been changed.

I would also like to thank my father, Miles Hudson, without whose prompting I may never have written about Africa; Vikki Tate, whose hard work in typing what I did write made it legible; my sister, Veronica Hudson, for her drawings; Serafina Clarke, my agent, for accepting my manuscript and for finding Gill Gibbins, my editor, whose enthusiasm and stamina gave life to a book.

CONTENTS

PART THREE: SOMALIA

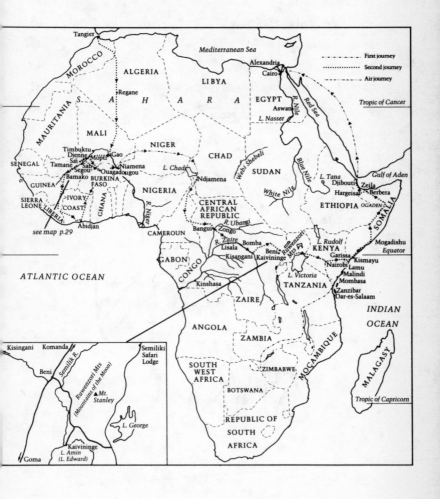

PREFACE

The Tuareg, a small man with his face tainted blue from the indigo head-dress he wore, was walking alone in the Sahara desert. He was a long way from anywhere but did not look surprised when we pulled up beside him and offered a lift.

'A lift to somewhere? Yes, that's a good idea,' he said. 'But first, how about some tea?'

The French people whose car I was travelling in looked as if they were in a hurry. They debated this idea of stopping for no reason except to have a cup of tea. The Tuareg laughed and continued to laugh, although the reason was lost to us in our car, until he rolled on his back and shook his legs in the air like an upturned beetle. Then up he jumped, and began collecting small bits of wood and bush. We joined him and soon had a little fire going.

It was the best time of day in the desert. The sun had sunk till it sat on the fine line of the horizon. The stinging heat of day had melted away and the soft colours of evening and the changing shades made it a scene of peace, a lull, a time to pause for thought. In fact, an ideal time for a cup of tea, as our friendly Tuareg knew very well.

He had nothing with him except a small goatskin bag which he proceeded to empty in front of the fire; its entire contents seemed to be for the sole purpose of making tea. First, out came a tiny teapot, then two small glasses, then a bag of sugar, then a bag of tea and other bags with herbs in them. There were a few dried dates which he passed around, and one or two ju-ju items – necklaces with small leather pouches that contained verses of the Koran written on scraps of paper, bracelets and a curved dagger. He showed us how to wear them and told us what they were for.

13

'This one will protect you from snakes all the time that you wear it. And this dagger will kill your enemies always with one stroke only.'

He asked if we wanted to buy them and when we said no, laughed and put them back in his sack.

The tea-making process was a long and exaggerated performance of pouring and mixing, pouring and mixing.

'*Trois fois*,' he said. '*Trois fois*. Three times I shall make tea from these leaves. The first time is strong and powerful. It will give you energy. The second time is weaker, but still with a taste of strength, and the third time, the weakest, is the time to really enjoy the sugar.'

I had just arrived in Mali and, like this Tuareg, I was travelling alone with a single small pack. I was lucky because I was free. I had money, enough to last me maybe a year, two healthy feet and the priceless vulnerability of youth. So I was able to throw myself to the wind, like a leaf, and see where it would take me. This was not the first time I had been to Africa. Two years earlier, in 1983, wishing to broaden my horizons which up till then had been restricted to developed Western countries, I had flown to Zambia where I had cousins who could find me a job. I soon realized that Africa had the space and freedom from convention I desired. I discovered that if you were kind to Africa, it was kind to you; much could be achieved with a smile. My cousins found me a job working as an overseer on a big white-owned farm and five months later I had taken a job building safari camps far out in the bush. This I greatly enjoyed, and I learned a few lessons in the realities of Africa, Africans and the veldt. I had then set out on a raw and naïve tour, heading south on my first African bus. No longer was I a white farmer and a boss. I was an insignificant traveller amongst the throng of bubbling, colourful Zambians.

My first night had been bad. At the town of Livingstone, by the Victoria Falls, I had been led to an expensive and very shabby hotel. There I had eaten a terrible European-style meal in a dirty, deserted restaurant and had sat alone and depressed in my dingy room, wondering if this was the right way to see

Africa. Next day I found, within earshot of the roar of the falls, a campsite inhabited by other European travellers with their backpacks and road-wise travellers' talk. It was so easy to slip into their stream and wrap myself up in their snugness of self-sufficiency abroad. Now I could go anywhere that followed the clan's well-trodden route and never once get bruised by the alien African world. Sometimes alone, and sometimes with these friendly people, I visited many countries. From the wild and beautiful Okavango swamps in Botswana, that place of clean, sand-lined water, of silthen otters, crocodiles, and birds of every hue and kind, I moved up through troubled Zimbabwe to Malawi, where I bathed in the sky-blue waters of its long, clear lake, camping on beaches with hippies, eating fish fresh in the morning. After that, to Tanzania, to lie lulled on the beach of Bagamoyo and smell the spices and weave my way in the snaking streets of Zanzibar.

By now I had seen many things of beauty, watched many scenes of quaint chaos and African urbanity. But as yet I had barely seen the inside of an African house and the only African friends I had were back on the farm in Zambia. Next I went to Kenya. Kenya has such a special beauty, such a feel of space and the essence of its wild life, that they almost compensate for the mass of tourists from whom, hard as you may try, it is difficult to escape. There I toured the parks and the coast and sat idle in Nairobi, and finished my year well pleased with all I had seen and done. I felt not a little changed since I had last seen England.

For the first time in my life I had seen that there were other people in the world who lived not unhappy lives despite the fact that they did not have the 'benefit' of our Western values and possessions, but it was not until later that I realized how shallow my experience of Africa had been. I knew now how Europeans lived in Africa and I had seen a lot of landscape, but of the local people, the villagers, the ordinary folk, I knew very little.

I had to go back. The few small things I had gleaned – the openness and simplicity of the smiles, the uncluttered, uninhibited lives – acted like a drug on me. I had to have more of it, try to understand it. But next time I was determined, if necessary, to shun my own kind in order to be just another ordinary person amongst ordinary, everyday Africans. Not superior, not too labelled. I wanted to lose myself in the vastness of the continent, let myself be open and vulnerable and be taken into the heart of Africa as much as any mere visitor can.

My second trip had started in Spain in the January of 1985. I had stood on a road on the south coast staring across the many-shipped Straits of Gibraltar to the bare, black mountain cliffs, draped so impressively into the sea, that were Africa. Behind them, I could think to myself, stretched that vast continent of so many different worlds, all those peoples, those plumed and painted lives so glamorously displayed in magazines and on television sets; they actually existed, in full scale, there, behind those cliffs. I was excited. I could go and see the realities for myself. That night I camped on a beach where I could see those cliffs, and when I woke in the morning they were still there, as solid as the Spain I stood on, beckoning me to them and beyond.

My trip lasted a year. In that time I visited many countries, some of which I passed only in transit, learning little except a picture of the landscape and blurred images of towns and cities where I was stuck for a few days, or even weeks. Those were always the most depressing times; two weeks stuck in Abijan, capital of the Ivory Coast, staying in the poorest but still expensive area, the infamous Triechville quarter, where I slept in a hotel-cum-brothel and did not see another European set foot all the time I was there. By day, the streets were like extended gutters littered with the round, brown forms of naked children playing in the refuse, baking in the harsh pitiless sun; by night, the doors of every alleyway partitioned by paper screens, with a candle and a prostitute behind them, like rows and rows of Chinese shadowshows. I was feverish in Niamey, capital of Niger, desperately trying to escape a heat so intense and thick that the bedstead in my room became almost too hot to touch; trapped in Ndjamena, capital of Chad, by wars and closed borders, the only foreseeable way out by

16

plane to France, meaning the end of my trip, and defeat.

Every day during that year had its incidents, some full of beauty, like a bicycle trip down the Nile valley in Egypt, and some exciting, like crossing Uganda two days after a coup.

About these experiences and many others – fishing with a Ghanaian fisherman in his dugout boat on the white-crested rollers of the Atlantic; attacks by hippos in the night, thieves by day; hailstorms and mad Frenchmen in the desert – I could write at length. And of course the everlasting game to be played with army, customs and immigration officials, and the trauma, intrigue or terror of every border crossing. Like, for example, the Liberian police officer on the Liberia–Guinea border.

Having been deposited by a fast-flying mini-bus in a remote and nameless forest, and asked to 'show my appreciation' to the Guinean customs men on their side, I had to negotiate a long tree-trunk spanning a river to find myself in Liberia. Climbing a small knoll cleared of trees, I came upon a group of mud huts. After a while a man appeared.

'Ya wanna caame to Liberia?' he asked, with that strange American drawl they use in Liberia.

'Yes,' I said.

'Well, if ya go inna tha' hu' ovar thy're, ya'll find a man who wants'a see ya,' he replied.

Stooping down to enter the low mud hut I came face to face with a large man in a shiny khaki uniform. His eyes were bloodshot and he was sweating profusely. In the dark, stuffy room, under the menacing eye of this man who somehow emitted a sense of power and unpredictability, I felt all the reality of vulnerability I could wish, and a shiver went down my spine. It was not so much that I feared for myself or my possessions but that I knew a whole world lay between me and this immigration chief. There could be no common ground between us, no overlap of understanding. In this remote corner of the world he was all-powerful. A rifle leant against the wall next to him. I smiled at him but he said nothing, just pointed to my bag with an angry scowl. Having extensively searched my own bag for him as he continued to sit there, dark and brooding with now a slight hint of a grin on his face, I heard him say, 'Watta you wan' in Liberia?'

'I'm a tourist. I want to see your country.'

'Who do ya work foor, thin?'

'No one. I'm just a tourist.'

'What college do ya teech at, thin?'

'None, I just want to see the country,' I said, realizing that 'tourist' was not a word he understood.

'We don' like pipple jist comin'a look a' our country fer now reason. We donna like spies an' we donna like meddlers. Ya look to mi like ya could be both.'

There was a silence while he stared at me through wary, bloodshot eyes. Then, simply: 'Gi ma so moey,' he said, with a broad, humourless grin. Meaning, I understood, 'Give me some money.' I gave him the equivalent of about half a dollar and he suddenly changed. Up he jumped and, putting a paternal hand on my shoulder, took me outside and started shouting, 'Somebody fine this boua soame transport. He wants'a go to Liberia.' And sure enough, transport was promptly found, and off I was dispatched, like an offering, to the many other horrors the country had to offer.

I could write the story of myself and my mental changes in that year, the loneliness, the happiness, the identity mix-ups, the loves and hates, and no doubt become a bore. But I do not wish to describe in detail or in fact my entire travels in Africa. The route, the number of countries visited, the distances travelled can be seen on the map, for what they are worth. And all those many experiences and sights, good or bad, sad or glad, that a year generates must take their chance and compete to be written down. In the same way that I travelled in Africa – with little or no foreknowledge, no pretension of aim and no ambition – so I shall write, giving only my first impressions, naïve as they may be, and trying to excise the effects of later reading and thought since my interest in Africa has developed.

Three countries especially struck me well and I liked them very much: Mali, Zaire and Somalia; and so mainly to these three I shall restrict my pen. All three are very undeveloped,

Zaire particularly. Mali is in the Sahel, that band of semi-desert, now beset by war and drought, on the southern fringe of the North African deserts, and Somalia is a land also of semi-desert, drought and regional conflicts. Both are on opposite sides of Africa and both have that wonderful blend of Islamic and Bantu culture. Zaire is the heart of the continent; a huge country of forested African lives, veiled in the mists of bad accessibility and rumour, but a country, like the other two, of open smiles.

Mali is where I met the lighthearted Tuareg with his teapot and trinkets. It was the first of these three countries I visited, so in Mali I shall begin. But first a few words in tribute to the Sahara Desert. To reach it I had passed through the chaotic intensity, the beauty and history of Morocco, where I was hustled and hassled and frozen in the north, and stayed with gentler people further south. I had passed through the serene sterility of bordering southern Algeria, where I found the people's generosity so extreme: one truck driver gave me the equivalent of twenty dollars because he felt sorry for me, and because as I was hitch-hiking he assumed I must be very poor and refused it back. And then I had crossed the Sahara driving a 1968 Peugeot, named by its owners – some Frenchmen driving other cars – 'le Tuareg bleu'. We got lost, broke down, got stuck and weathered any other disasters the Frenchmen could possibly engineer with their fatalistic ways.

To me, as it has to most people who have been there, the Sahara proved a moving experience. A belittling and a soothing. There had been no people, no hills, no trees and no animals. In fact I had seen only one mouse, one bird and one tree between leaving the last Algerian town and reaching Mali, some 1000 kilometres away. But the colours, the space and the shades of sand, the clockwork days, the wind, the sun and star-filled skies, that overpowering, almost mystical silence – these things and others less definable moved me deeply. Even now I feel a strong calling to return, to go back and regenerate what the Sahara, in all her harshness and her steely beauty, gives to those who go there: the blessing of a certain happiness and a calmness of spirit that can be found nowhere else.

PART ONE

MALI

1

Djenne and a Walk

The immediate change in atmosphere as one steps over the border between Algeria and Mali is very apparent, even so far in the depths of the Sahara. Here at last is 'Afrique noire', that place the Arabs of the more reserved and correct North so often warned me of.

'Beware of Black Africa, my friend. There, there are so many thieves you cannot walk the streets. There, the people are bad and drink much beer. And oh,oh, oh!! The women! They are big and black, unashamed and easy and will go with any man. There, you will drink yourself stupid, have your money stolen and be seduced by so many women you won't know what to do,' an Algerian customs man told me, envy in his eye.

In Mali begins that sprawling Africa of bright colours and markets selling anything that can be put to use, from old tin cans to old carcasses of cars. From here onwards there are ever more populous, ever greener lands where colours and costumes, customs and cultures change and deepen with every step you take towards the west African coast. Down through desert, through savanna, through forests you go, to jungles so lush they shock your desert-worn eyes; down into sticky cities and then out to splash into the cooling blue sea, and lay yourself down on the west-coast sands thinking back to all those countries and towns, so steamy and slow, living in self-wrapped worlds all of their own, that you've left behind.

Having arrived in Mali, I first visited the towns of Mopti and Gao on the banks of the Niger. The Niger, on the journey north from its source in the highlands of Guinea, forms an inland delta in the heart of Mali and at Timbuktu reaches the desert before turning first east, then south-east, then heading south again, to the ocean.

This region in which Mopti and Gao are placed was once very important strategically. Since as far back as the days of ancient Egypt there was much trading across the Sahara. In the Middle Ages the primary trade was in gold from the Western Sudan where it was plentiful to the North African coast and the Middle East. The towns such as Gao and Mopti, and their riverside brothers Djenne, Timbuktu, Bamako and others, in time grew wealthy and powerful from the taxes they could levy on this trade. Between the third and fourteenth centuries the great empires of Ghana, Mali and Songhai rose up, and with the introduction of the Islamic faith there came political and economic stability and so a brilliance of culture. The series of these empires only ended with the Moroccan invasion in the sixteenth century, followed by the breaking of Muslim trade monopoly by the European maritime nations. Never again was Mali to shine in prosperity and wealth as it had. Perhaps this golden era of African history was best depicted by the pilgrimage to Mecca of Mansa Musa, the greatest king of the Mali empire in 1324.

Preceded by 500 slaves, each bearing a staff of gold, and with nearly 100 camel-loads of gold each weighing 300 pounds, Mansa Musa appeared from the Sahara desert mounted on a horse. This negro king, from a land still regarded as barbaric, surrounded in mystery and myth, astounded all who saw him not only by the splendour of his entourage and the extent of his wealth, but also by his piety and open-handed generosity.

Mali is now one of the world's poorest countries. The most populated region is the southern savannah, where people of the Songhai, Malinki, Senoulou, Dogon and Bambura ethnic groups live. In the north there is true desert, where a few Tuareg nomads still remain to eke out a living. Further south is the Western Sudan, part of the Sahel which day by day becomes more like desert due to the effects of drought and bad land management. The Sahara trade has virtually ceased and because the Niger now floods only rarely, its inland delta is often dry and barren.

Mopti and Gao had a friendly atmosphere of seediness and dilapidation now, full of crusty old colonial buildings, rows and rows of tin shacks and elegant pirogues, slim wooden boats, with flags and families moored at their sides. It was the time of year for the big winds, winds that gathered sand and dust from the desert and held them high up in the sky, obliterating the sun. It was like living in a land of dusk.

I left Mali after only a few days to spend a month in Burkina Faso, a neighbouring country of friendly people, poverty and regular coups. When I returned the skies had cleared. I spent two days in the sweltering town of San, laughing with locals under a thatch, waiting for a ride on a truck to the old town of Djenne.

Situated in the heart of the Sahel within the arch of the Niger, Djenne, though no longer a rich and powerful kingdom, still has one of the largest and most interesting markets in the area, and people come to it from far and wide. The town is very beautiful, shaped out of smooth, weathered mud and sand, an intricate maze of twisty alleyways and secretive, donkey- and dust-filled squares. Its main feature is a huge and magnificent mosque – built entirely of compacted sand on a frame of wood, dominating the whole town, rising sheer and strong from the heart of the community. It is famous as one of the best examples of twelfth-century Sudanese architecture and the people of Djenne are very proud of it.

Approaching from the dry desert-like plains of the Sahel, the town appears as an island, showing prominently above a sea of packed, flat sand: closer to, dry riverbeds encircle it like a moat. The whole island is neatly finished off with a green petticoat of cultivated plots hemmed in by walls of yellow matted grass backing right up to the clustered houses. In the rainy season, if the nearby Niger floods, Djenne truly becomes an island in a glistening lake of water. If not, the wells on the bottom of the dry riverbeds have to be sunk up to ten metres before they find water.

The market takes place in Djenne once a week in the large

open space in front of the mosque. As the morning advances, it becomes more and more packed as people steadily pour in from towns like San and Mopti, and all the surrounding villages. Soon the market overflows into the hot streets and down the alleyways leading from them, commotion and colour everywhere. On every inch of ground there are people squatting in front of their piles of merchandise, mostly some kind of food. Brown lumps of peanut paste; gooey mixtures of red and green; hard balls of nut and honey; heaps of pungent herbs and spices; sacks of yellow and white maize; sacks of coarse sugar; rocks of salt; pyramids of watermelons like green cannonballs; fresh and old vegetables; succulent grass for the donkeys – all gently stewing in the heat, coated with a thin icing of dust and decorated with black flies like raisins. By afternoon the market works up to a frantic climax of hustling and bustling, buying and bargaining, everyone trying to make enough profit to buy supplies to take back to their villages. As evening creeps in, slowly the tired people leave town to start the walk home, long lines of them stretching like tentacles out into the shining white country; donkeys and carts laden with the day's bounty; women swathed with colourful cloths, balancing steeples of pots on their heads, swaying their hips with their necks straight and jutting like sea lions; and all the men and boys pulling and herding, cursing and whipping the animals they have bought or failed to sell. The sun drops from the sky like a stone and disappears into watery haze a long time before reaching the horizon, leaving a lucent and pearly light. A tranquillity descends upon the town like that of a deserted battlefield. All that is left are a few determined villagers hoping to sell their remaining goods, boys and goats competing for the leftovers and draped men drifting into the mosque, as if on an unseen current, for their evening prayers.

But there is another aspect of Djenne which is not so pleasant. The local Malian tourist authority, a cowboy agency called SMERT, promotes it as a tourist attraction on the scale of Timbuktu, and a continuous flow of camera-clad tourists inundates the town. They wander around for a few hours, snapping madly, and then leave. Inevitably, the locals have learned either to ignore all foreigners and dislike them, as mainly the elders do, because of their lack of tact and predatory attitudes; or to hustle them to see how much can be got out of them in the short amount of time available, as the younger men tend to do. This is very sad, as it is quite contrary to the usual custom of Muslim people. Theirs is a dignified and very hospitable creed, but it is quite impossible for them to be hospitable with dignity towards people who do not have the time or the wish to try to understand and respect any other culture than their own.

I did not get on well with Djenne; like the other tourists, I was too conspicuous and not much liked. I spent a few days there, sleeping on the hotel roof and sneaking around the town, diving down alleyways to avoid the hordes of boys, or walking out into the surrounding desert to watch the town prickling in the heat of day and softening in the haze of sunset. I decided I would leave and, to everyone's horror, walk to a village called Sai, about 70 kilometres away across the desert: there were plenty of small villages on the way where I could stay and perhaps be accepted a little more readily. I chose a guide from the ever-present young men offering their services for outrageous prices, eventually taking one who felt he could lower his fee a little. His name was Nouhoum Dio but, like many of the lads in Djenne, he had adopted a Western name for the sake of tourism. His was Bill. He had friends and family in many of the villages we would be passing, he said, and he could speak French and all the local dialects.

He was an obviously intelligent lad even among this sharp-witted crowd. He was also enthusiastic, taking up any idea I put to him and embellishing it with great imagination. He was about sixteen years old and tall for his age, with a cheeky, light brown face. Very proudly he took me to his home: ordering his mother and sisters around in a way I'm sure he wouldn't have had I not been there, he had a meal prepared for me. He seemed a bit jumpy, and now and again a frown clouded his forehead in a way that worried me; but I had to have somebody as guide and when he smiled it was a nice smile.

We set off in the late afternoon, after the main heat of the day, I with my rucksack, Bill with a small shoulder bag and a smart pair of walking shoes. The evening was beautiful and calm. We quickly left Djenne behind us, fragmenting into the shimmering atmosphere. The plain, except for the occasional dry riverbed littered with stones and cattle dung, and a few sporadic, starchy trees, was endless and featureless, falling away before us like a sheer drop to the thin white line of the horizon that despairingly inched its way forwards, unreachable and uninterrupted.

After three hours we spotted our destination for that day, a village called Gomitogo. At first it was just a black dot. As we drew nearer, though, I saw what looked like a medieval castle of turrets and high defensive walls silhouetted against the evening sky. I had been expecting only small scrubby villages out here, so finding this grand and majestic apparition was like

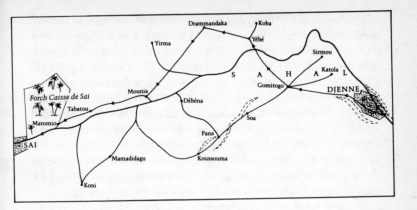

discovering a hidden kingdom, as indeed in its past it may have been, being a satellite to the kingdom of Djenne. As I stood amongst the outlying fields of cracked earth and scarecrow maize stalks, I could just make out a movement of people winding their way back into the intricacy of mud dwellings clustered round a tall mosque rising out of their midst like a hub on a cartwheel. It peered over the desert, drawing all towards it like a magnet.

The sun was setting when we arrived. Long shadows crossed the ruddy sand to make black holes of the alleyway entrances. I half expected to hear a fanfare of trumpets and see shining Arabian knights bear down upon us to demand what we wanted of the king, but instead, as we climbed up to the first houses, a man in white robes appeared. He politely went through the ritual greetings.

'*Koniamé . . . Arratigé . . . Kouneisamé,*' to which we replied each time: '*Adamagana.*'

Bill said, 'This white man is a tourist and would like to stay in your village.'

'Follow me and we shall go to the chief who will give you both a place to sleep.'

As we followed him along the twisting ways, curious faces peered at us out of doors and windows, the whites of their eyes

29

and teeth starting out of the darkness, and women snatched toddling children out of our way. The village was silent except for the soft padding of many little feet from a posse of boys and girls following us like stealthy cats. The chief was just as I had always imagined chiefs to be – old, wise, a bit eccentric and surrounded by his wives, children and grandchildren. He did not say very much but looked a kind old man. We sat for a while in his courtyard, making sporadic conversation and smiling at each other whilst his wives prepared some food. Bill, in an important and nonchalant way, entertained the children by drawing pictures of the mosque. Later on the old man made a place for us to sleep on his roof. I lay awake for a long time, looking up at the clear sky, trying to pick out the Southern Cross from the milk of stars while Bill rolled himself up in his sheet and went to sleep.

All around me the stark silhouettes of jumbled houses and the towering mosque framed the bright night sky. The smell of smoke and cooking wafted over and I could hear the soporific sounds of a village preparing for bed: the clatter of pots and pans being washed, the hum and mumble of sleepy talk, the occasional cry of a baby and yelp of a dog, the agonized shriek of a distant donkey, the creak and shift of the earthen village settling into the cool of the night.

The difference between this place and Djenne was very real. I could feel it even in the atmosphere swirling around me on my rooftop like a breath of fresh air. When people had smiled at me, it had been a free and open smile like that of a child. The children, although they stared and followed as would be expected, instead of shouting the inevitable, '*Donnez-moi, donnez-moi*' that mothers taught their children in towns like Djenne, chanted, '*Sava, sava, sava*' – how are you, and welcome.

Whenever I met an old man round a corner he would stop and shake my hand and say, 'Your health is good . . . yes? The health of your brothers and sisters is good . . . yes? The health of your mother and father is good . . . yes? And your country is prosperous and very happy . . . yes?' Everywhere women and children, giggling shyly, would brush my skin softly like the caress of butterfly wings, and babies would be egged into howls of terror at my ugly white face as a playful game by their mothers and sisters. There was a feeling of contentment and peace that seeped out of the very walls and substance of the village. The people were all devoted Muslims. Their lives revolved round their religion and their mosque, both spiritually and physically. They were full of gentleness and disarming hospitality.

Climbing to the top of the mosque in Gomitogo gave a spectacular view and was a wonderful sensation, like being a shrimp in a sandcastle constructed by an ingenious child. It was a big mosque, though not as large as the one in Djenne, again made wholly of compacted sand on a frame of huge wooden crossbeams which stuck out of the walls all the way along the top like the sleepers on a railway line. Minarets, patios and balconies appeared here and there, seemingly haphazardly, but the whole fitted together very well, smoothed over by wind and sun. Through the grand carved wooden doors at the front was an open tiled courtyard. Next to it was a tall room, quiet and in a world of its own coolness and peace, criss-crossed by sturdy pillars stretching up to the ceiling, and there were many straw prayer mats on the ground. A narrow stairway wound itself round the room, curling up a small tower, appearing on windowed balconies and disappearing again into thick walls, gradually making its way out on to the roof and then up the main minaret. Up here on top one had the same feeling as on a mountain. Silence, wind and the world spread out below you like a map, in this case a fine view of the higgledy-piggledy village directly below, flattened out into a jigsaw of square yards and oblong houses, threaded through by winding, walled-in alleyways and dotted here and there by the scurrying people. Everywhere I looked I saw their oval faces turned up towards me, like little moons, full of curiosity and wonder at my presence on the minaret. The huge desert plain, an undulating surface of hardened sand and rounded pebbles, stretched away from the outside walls of the village to a horizon, blurred with the furze of scanty trees. It was a clear, crisp morning of crystalline blue and snow white, with a strong wind whistling and whisking through the arches and craggy conicals of the mosque. The only inhabitants up here, high over the village, were proud and elegant harriers soaring on the wind; small, twittering sparrows hopping about on the worn, warm walls; gurgling, cooing doves looking for love and, of course, the inevitable multi-coloured lizards scratching around each other and rearing their fierce orange heads. And there was myself and the two mosque-keepers who had brought me up here, as craggy and sandy as the mosque they loved.

Beaming with pride, they told me, 'This mosque is very, very old, older than us, older than our fathers and older than their fathers. It is so old, in fact, we do not know how old it is.'

'Don't the wind and rain wear it down and wash away the sand?' I asked.

'Yes,' they said. 'Many times we have to re-build it, or part of it, but the beams and foundations are the same as those our forefathers laid.' Those were their roots, the roots of their village, that anchored them to the wind and time-swept earth.

'When did you last have to do this?' I asked.

'Not for many, many years,' they replied. 'We wish we did, because that would mean the rains once again fell as they should.' Drought would destroy and uproot this mosque in a way rain never could.

Before I left Gomitogo I shook hands again with all the elders who had congregated outside the mosque, and gave the chief a bag of kola nuts, small, red, bitter nuts that all the old men like to chew as a mild stimulant, similar to the qat and mira of eastern Africa. In these remote villages they are hard to to get and consequently expensive, so they make a good parting gift.

Bill and I followed a trail of village folk making their way across the plains with carts and oxen to market at a nearby village called Yébé. On the outskirts of Gomitogo we passed a few dilapidated dugout boats moored in the sand, sad re- membrances of the times when even here the flooding Niger would turn the surrounding sea of desert into a sea of water.

32

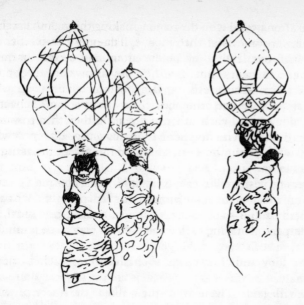

As we marched along in the happy morning air, following the villagers, Bill and I talked continually. He was nearly always cheerful and chatty when we were walking. We would be alone, away from the local people, and he seemed relaxed and confident. And he seemed to like walking, though he did flag now and again because his smart shoes chafed him badly; but he endured the pain because he was very proud to own them.

A sort of contest of wills was slowly building up between us as we walked. Bill would incessantly ply me with eager, naïve questions about the West and its culture, and I would counter with questions, probably equally naïve, about the local people and their way of life. He would wander along behind me, dogging my steps, trying hard to think of a new question.

'What do the people in London do when . . . when . . .?' Or, 'When I come to London you will find a girl for me to marry, won't you? They are pretty and anyone can have them!'

Bill was not particularly interested in the answers, he just liked to hear me talk about the West, and whatever I said never dampened his idyllic view of it. The more he heard the better he felt. My attempts to divert the subject to him and his own people were answered with monosyllables and before I could draw him out further, he produced another stream of questions and fantasies. But then I, in my turn, defeated by his stamina, would also resort to flagging, monosyllabic answers until he gave up, and a silence fell between us. Now he would walk along for a while, a little behind me, with a frown of concentration on his forehead until suddenly some new idea would overpower him. Then he would run up enthusiastically to tackle me again, and I would laugh and give him the answers he desired. We had difficulty finding common ground as he only wanted to gorge himself on the wonderful West and I wanted to know about the local area and culture which he was desperately trying to flee and did not want to be reminded of. But we both enjoyed this gentle sparring; it passed the time on the long walks and was a challenge for each of us to dominate.

The villagers we were following walked fast. A woman with a child swathed onto her back in a cotton shawl, a full basket of gourds on her head and one in her hand could march for hours on end at a rate that had me puffing with only my meagre sack to carry. It took us four hours to reach Yébé and we only stopped once under a tree where I gulped down my water, but was surprised to see that no one else drank anything. The walk was strangely invigorating, the empty lands, beautiful and pure, undisturbed by any noise but the wind and our hastening feet.

As we drew near to the market of Yébé we were met by a hum of noise, like a disturbed bees' nest, of people hawking their goods, meeting, greeting and arguing: there was an excited market-day feeling in the air; already there was a hectic throng of people and their merchandise. This market, though, seemed different from the one in Djenne: all the people were local village folk. There were no pick-ups or trucks from the towns, and selling was more relaxed, not such a hard, serious business.

The market was out in front of a low, soft-sand village that seemed almost part of the landscape, dominated by a big sandy mosque quivering in the heated air over the glaring houses. Surrounding the market, like a kraal, were discarded carts and tethered donkeys, clusters of frisky goats waiting to be sold, piles of straw, boxes and bags, and small boys teasing and tending their fathers' oxen. The market was a jumble of colour and bodies mingling and sitting, smiling and friendly. I did not feel at all conspicuous or a stranger. As I wandered along the lines of women squatting amongst their nests of wares, people smiled at me and I felt welcome. The harsh sun beat down all day, condensing the dusty air into a thick soup by the afternoon.

At midday Bill and I had a large and sweaty meal of rice and sauce in a little market restaurant. In the afternoon Bill drifted off with some friends he had met and I found a tree a bit away, crawled under it and, lulled by the comforting drone of noise, dozed until I was woken by a tentative poking on my legs and the chatter of a small boy squatting at my feet. These little men of Africa, with their stern faces and piercing questions, are so independent and well co-ordinated that you soon learn to treat them on equal terms, or they will treat you as a fool. This boy talked away happily, asking me questions and making concise little mimes of words I did not understand, amusing me and himself for a while. Then he walked away lightly, back to the hub of excitement. He was a sweet change from the hustling, nagging, swarming children encountered in some cities and towns.

In the evening when once again I felt like joining the land of the living, I wandered round the now packing-up market, vaguely looking for Bill. I sat on a wall in a line of children, tired and scruffy after a long, exciting day at market, and with them watched battle commence between some oxen and their owners who were trying to stir them from lethargy brought on by a day of stagnant heat and messy flies. The oxen, when once risen to their feet, were irate and frisky; the owners were tired and determined to hitch them to their carts. Each time they lined two of the beasts up and tried lifting the yoke on to their necks, the oxen moved forward and veered round in circles, flinching away from the pain inflicted as their owners pulled a

35

string attached to the side of their nostrils. Around and around they went, like a merry-go-round, their owners humping the carts after them, boys frantically whipping them, and the oxen stamping their feet and bellowing. This battle of wills continued until eventually the oxen were beaten into submission and had the yoke strapped on with leather thongs like iron girders.

The sun by now was slowly melting into evening. The heat oozed out of the day, leaving a breathing space of clear and gentle tranquillity. One of the oxen owners noticed me on my wall amongst the children and came over to ask what I was doing, sitting on a wall in Mali. He spoke a little English, learned from years as a young man earning a wage in Ghana, and was very friendly. His name was Konumé. He looked tough and weathered in rags of modern clothes and could boast no shoes to wear on market day.

'How is it you have come to this village of Yébé, Mr Peter?' he asked me.

'I've walked here,' I said.

'But why?' he said, with concern. 'Why have you walked here? Surely you could rent a car. I have seen other white men pass here in rented cars. You can rent cars in Bamako, Mopti or anywhere. What is the job that you do here that makes you walk when you could rent a car?'

'I don't have one,' I said. 'I walk because I want to walk, so that I can see the country better. I am a tourist.'

'So who pays you to do your tourism?'

Hoping my explanation would suffice, I told him I was on holiday, paid for by myself.

'But why, then,' he persevered, 'if you are on holiday, do you not go somewhere comfortable and beautiful? You could go to Ghana. There, there are long beaches where all the white men lie down in the sun, and very big hotels you can stay in. I know this because I have seen it with my very own eyes when I was working there. Now, though, I am glad to be back with my own people. There are many bad men in Ghana.'

Each answer I gave him seemed to lead into deeper water, until eventually he gave up and put it down, quite rightly, to the strange, inexplicable behaviour of Westerners. He asked if I would like to go and stay in his village, Drammandaka. When I eagerly agreed, he went to the find the village chief so that I could be introduced to him and officially invited. The chief, when he arrived, was a thin, watery-eyed old man. He was very shy of me but told me I was welcome to stay in his village and that I could travel there with my new friend, Konumé, the village carrier; he would go ahead of us and so be there to welcome me. Konumé and I waited by the cart while it was loaded by a team of boys with the day's purchases. Bill appeared. When I told him the plan of going to Drammandaka he shrugged his shoulders and said 'You won't find anything there, these people are as poor as dirt.'

The journey was very pleasant and slow. The country we passed had changed little, still a sand-packed plain undulating gently and dotted here and there with a few big, gnarled trees that had escaped the villagers' axes. Sitting on top of the rumbling cart amongst a throng of women and baskets, I watched the villagers amble back home after their hard day's bargaining and merry-making, singing and laughing as they went along. Each time I looked around me the landscape had changed colour and the shadows had changed shape. Now and again Konumé, perched in front with legs dangling over, a small stick in his hand, whipped the oxen into a trot. Then the world would swoop and heave like an ocean as the cart lurched to and fro, but the oxen would always drop back into their stubborn, interminable, plod-plodding that would barely out-strip a weary snail.

Drammandaka, when eventually we arrived at dusk, was small and bedraggled, but it throbbed with life. In the middle of the village, in a clearing of dust and scraps, we found the chief waiting to welcome us. He took me, Bill and my bag to a hut belonging to his brother, who was away. Someone fetched the village chair and, placing it in the middle of the earthen hut, had me sit on it. Then, one by one, all the men of the village came in, formally and politely greeted me, and sat down on the floor. Before long there were many bodies in the close, stuffy room. Looking down from my elevated position I saw their friendly and expectant faces turned up to me. I asked them questions about themselves and their village and they told me of their families and their troubles.

'The rain fails year after year. The crops wilt or do not even germinate,' they said.

Pointing to the desert surrounding the village, the chief, with outstretched arms and a forlorn face, said, 'This, this used to be all water in the rainy season. It even used to flow into the village and flood the houses. But now I can hardly remember the last time it happened. The young men have never seen it so,' and all the men nodded, and smiled in happy recollection, laughing at the thought of water actually in the houses.

'We have to send all our sons away for many years to earn money to bring back to us so we can survive. Now the village is left with only old men, women and children.'

They did not want to be defeated and have to leave their village where their fathers and grandfathers were buried; to do so would be like uprooting a flower. The village would wilt and die. But what could they do when the rains never came? As they looked at me and told me these things, I sensed a feeling of relief, and expectation, and happiness that I was there with them. I, a representative of the mysterious and knowledgeable outside world, had come to them in their small, insignificant village to hear their problems and help.

'Tell us, please, when will the next rains come and, if not, why not?' they asked.

They had a deep, desperate trust in me, or rather in what I stood for. I knew they would not believe that I had gone there out of inquisitiveness or even pleasure, so I did not tell them. I felt helpless and inadequate. They were kind, unselfish people but I had no answers and when this showed in my face, they told me with deep compassion, one after the other, that they were happy just to have me there as a guest amongst them: my presence alone gave them confidence and hope; they felt they were no longer ignored or forgotten. They did not want me to feel uncomfortable.

We went to sit outside the hut when the darkness of night was complete, laughing and joking round the fire, each content in the presence of the others. They killed a goat from their small herd and fed me like a king. They brought buckets of water for me to wash in and they sent away the curious children and women who stood in a circle around us. They looked after me with an understanding and care that made my heart lurch. Maybe it was their apparent total lack of selfishness which, as we know it, they do not even understand. In a life where there is little or no privacy and therefore less consciousness of the self, and where, from the moment of birth, people eat, sleep, reproduce and die in very close proximity to others, they learn to share and have patience with others as naturally as drawing breath.

Since arriving in the village I had noticed a startling change come over Bill, something I had noticed before once in the presence of others. He was strutting around like a young cock, full of superiority and insolence, shaming me many times with his sharp and cynical treatment of the gentle old men, completely against the custom of his people. He was fighting his own lack of confidence and emptiness because he was just a town johnny in the presence of humble and genuine people, losing his bid to be something different from what he was born to be because he came from a town where the pure strand of his culture was twisted and stained. But the old men smiled at his insolence, and their pity closed him up like a clam. I could not help feeling sorry for him, though, because the pain on his face was there for all to see. He was proud of his modern clothes and Western knowledge in the same way that a child is proud of a shiny toy car. He could not understand why it did not always work as it should and have the same effect on other people. More and more he plied me with questions about Michael Jackson and cigarette brands, thinking maybe it was just his technique and knowledge that were failing him. Poor Bill, losing touch with his true culture and never really able to reach the dream of the West, left in a no-man's land of insecurity and uncertainty. But still, he was an African. He was born with his ancestors' resilience and stubborn happiness. I hoped they would see him through.

In the morning another huge meal, of rice and manioc-leaf sauce, was brought to me in the hut. The skinny old chief sat watching me eat it with a satisfied but tired look on his face. He was a tough old man bearing the burden of responsibility for his village. In a community such as this, the whole village lives as one family and the head of the family, the chief, acts as manager, tax man, banker, spiritual leader, judge and father. He is reponsible for the survival of all.

The whole village assembled for our departure and asked me to take their photograph. They stood in a huddled group, the men self-conscious and stony-faced, mothers proudly holding their wriggling babies, and small boys and girls hopping up and down at the back to get in the picture. When we left they followed us out to their sad fields of maize, shook my hand in turn and asked me to come back some day. I handed round kola nuts to the old men, sweets to the women and children, and I gave the chief some money, telling him to buy something for the village. He accepted it, only, I think, to satisfy my need to show gratitude and to give something, no matter how inadequate, in return, not because he wanted any payment for my stay.

With the chief leading, an ancient gun over his shoulder like an old campaigner, and a boy carrying my pack on his head, I walked away. It was a poor, dusty little village with no beauty and no walls to protect it from the outside world, but still I felt I was leaving a haven of something pure, I cannot be sure exactly what, but I knew it was something truly humble and great; something that is disappearing as fast as the world is developing. They waved until we were out of sight and they were just small dots framed against the mud walls of their homes, insignificant under the indifferent blue sky.

When we found the main track again, some distance from the village, the chief and the boy left us. With Bill back to his normal, cheerful and chatty self we set a good pace for two or three hours until we came upon a small cluster of red mud brick houses, like chameleons on the red mud earth. We could not just walk on through the village without seeming impolite, so we went to find the chief, who insisted that we stay a while. We were taken into a pitch-dark house but soon our eyes adjusted from the searing glare. Inside, the house was like a cave, with smooth mud walls curving down to a trodden earth floor. There were mats and a bank of sumptuous cushions to lean back on, but again the village chair was brought for me to sit on, leaving Bill and the chief to enjoy the cushions. All the elders came in, greeted me and sat down, but there were not so many here as at Drammandaka, so the room remained quite pleasant. Soon the door and window were clogged with the faces of children, like bunches of sunflowers, curious, staring and beautiful.

Perhaps it was because of the time of day and the heat that, although this chief told me all the same problems I had heard at Drammandaka, he and the old men seemed somehow disinterested in them, talking as though about some other place, and other people. It was hot and oppressive. This time of day was for getting through only. Important subjects must be left for the evening when all men are free, and the air and the head are cool and clear.

I soon promoted myself from the chair to the cushions and sat next to the chief, a playful man, full of mirth and inquisitiveness. The afternoon passed in laughter or languid talk, smoking and dozing. Bill made sweet coffee in the corner, handing it round reluctantly, but even he was drawn in by the humorous chief and sketched more pictures of mosques for the children. Later on the chief's wife brought buckets of water and Bill and I took it in turns to go behind a grass screen to have a thorough wash. Afterwards we sat around a big bowl of rice and chicken. The chief carefully pushed all the juiciest morsels over to my side of the plate, making sure I ate them. Hands were washed before and after the meal in a bowl, with his wife pouring water from a kettle. I was always impressed by the cleanliness of these Muslims. They kept themselves and their clothes meticulously clean. Before the sun was up the first to stir were always the women, bent double like rag dolls with one hand on a hip and the other clasping a small reed brush, shuffling round the huts and the yard sweeping the dust and the debris of the day before into a pile, carefully and

41

thoroughly. Only the children were scruffy and dirty, as children usually are only minutes after their daily scrubbing.

When we left towards evening the men took us to the outskirts to say goodbye, and the still curious children followed us down the road at a safe distance, like inquisitive dogs, then stopped and silently watched us dwindle out of sight.

The country had changed. It was less barren and in the afternoon light, gentler to the eye. We passed through a grove of tough, gnarled trees with big canopies of thorn and leaf, and high banks of soft sand, woven with coarse grasses on their leeward side. Mounia, the next village, was not far away, so the sun was still up when we arrived: large, spread out with proper streets and shops, it was bigger than any I had so far seen. Bill had some relations here so we went to stay with them, a sizeable family who lived with their animals in a courtyard surrounded by a tall wall, a wonderful display of order amongst chaos. At one end of the courtyard, by the doorway into the street, was a big shabby tree; at the other, a selection of mud huts and lean-tos that were the family quarters. In between teemed a melange of cattle, goats, sheep, guineafowl, chickens and children, with water troughs littered about and stick pens lining the walls. The cattle bumped into or trod on the goats and sheep, who bleated incessantly. The scampering, scavenging chickens and guineafowl and the playing children clambered in and out of their legs. There were yelps of excitement from the children when I walked in. Their little faces grinned mischievously. Here was something to really keep them entertained for a while.

I was surprised by the striking difference in the people of Mounia from all the poorer villages I had visited. The women, of whom there were maybe six within this family, seemed more gentle, with fairer, smoother complexions; when they moved they did so with elegance and poise. Their faces were more rounded, more open, with sharper noses and chins, and their expressions told something of a slight, subtle humour, as did the glint in their eyes. Their lower lips were dyed indigo and jutted out sensually. The soles of their feet were dyed black, like little Chinese slippers, and they wore bracelets and necklaces of bright-coloured beads and clothes of thin, silky material, flowing and loose. They were very beautiful. The men were hawk-like, handsome and stern with more elusive characters; quiet, but you felt they would make valuable companions.

Our arrival coincided with feeding time for the animals, so I was sat down on a mat with a big jug of water to quench my thirst. As the evening deepened with its play of colours, piles of dry grass were pulled down off the roofs and thrown amongst the cattle, goats and sheep. The cattle were very greedy and selfish, heartily butting the sheep and goats out of the way whenever they had the cheek to try and grab some. They in their turn, though, bullied the guineafowl and chickens who darted in and out trying to find juicy morsels and seeds. The children had been disentangled before the scrum started, and were fed in the corner.

When it was all finished the cattle were pegged down and the sheep were threaded through long ropes with nooses in them, wriggling like mackerel. The guineafowl made their way along the top of the wall to the tree. There they stood in a row, tottering, trying to pluck up courage to fly up into the tree to roost. Experimentally flapping their stubby wings, shifting their feet and cocking their heads idiotically backwards and forwards, they eyed the tree, trying to pick a route through the thorny branches to a good spot, like navigators planning their way through a fog. One by one, with a great swoosh of feathers, they leapt into the air, desperately beating their wings, and rose, slowly and uncertainly like balloons, to crash into the branches, snapping twigs and pummelling their wings on the foliage. Not a very elegant affair, this bedtime ordeal. But it had to be done, and once safe and sound on a cosy bough, they shook out their feathers, dusting themselves down like old women straightening their skirts, and settled into the night with regained dignity, gurgling *'pourquoi, pourquoi'* (why indeed) as the sun disappeared behind the wall.

The animals having gone to bed, the children shifted their attention to me, coming to sit on my mat next to me, silently studying my every move. The women busied themselves over fires, cooking, and the men laid out their prayer mats, facing east. They washed their hands and feet, gargled their mouths and rinsed their faces before bowing down and paying homage to Allah. Bill didn't pray with them. Although he went to the mosque in Djenne now and again, he was not very interested in religion, he told me. He was happier this evening, because this family was more 'civilized'.

Later, when the food was ready, all the men gathered round a big bowl of rice with a peanut sauce poured over it, daintily picking at it because it was too hot, and fanning it with a straw fan. When it was cool enough each expertly rolled the rice into a ball in the palm of his left hand, and popped it into his mouth. As had often happened when I ate with Muslims, I found, suddenly, that they had all finished and were sitting back, leaving a huge amount still in the bowl for me, and with contented looks on their faces watched me struggle to finish it off. If I made signs that I might be going to give up, they gave heartfelt and serious encouragement until the bowl was clean. It is a kind gesture, but I soon learnt not to be the last one to finish, whether still hungry or not, because when you are offered something you must accept. To the Muslims the giving is a privilege to the giver in the same way that receiving is to the receiver in the West. So in turning something down you are doing them, not yourself, an injustice.

The women ate separately, out of sight, after taking away our plates and bringing water for us to drink and to wash our hands. Late into the night I sat with the young men outside in the village street, listening to their talk.

'Who is it that has to take the goats out tomorrow morning? It's your turn, Mohammed.'

'No, no, it's not me. Who was it who spent all afternoon and half the evening looking for that lost ewe? And who was it who cut all that new grass?'

'Ah, well then, it must be your turn, Ali, little brother. It's your turn to take the goats first in the morning.'

'Me? Aah, no. I can't take the goats out tomorrow. Father wants me to help him put up the new sheep pen.'

44

'By God, so it must be my turn. I shall take them, and go to the gully far, far on the other side of the great baobab by the pond. There I will find some good grazing, *in sha'allah*.'

'Ali, why is it you want to buy those sun-glasses Hussein is selling in his shop? What do you need to waste your money on sun-glasses for?'

'Oooh. Aah. They will look good, brother,' came Ali's sing-song voice. 'You wait and see. When I have them you will always be borrowing them from me. Oooh, yes. They are a good pair of sun-glasses. Yes. Aaah, they are special.'

'But you're too small for them, little Ali. They will sit on the end of your nose and make you look a fool. And Father will think you look foolish as well.'

'Ah, you only say that, big brother, because I thought of buying them first. Oooh, you would buy them if I did not.'

'Ha! Me, little brother? Never. I have strong eyes. I have no need of such things.'

They talked sporadically and vaguely, on and on, small voices under the well of space, until one by one we crept back into the dark, sleeping yard and lay down on our mats amongst the animals.

The cockerels around Mounia had a tendency to start their crowing a long time before the sun was due. So in a village where every household had two or three, somewhere around four or five in the morning the air was filled with a chorus of shrieks as the restless cocks beckoned the dawn. Even if you managed to sleep through this, the morning wails of the pourquoi-ing guineafowl, or the eating, bleating goats and sheep, or the tireless buzz of flies would wake you well before sun-up. As it was, I was woken by the sleepless children who, like little wraiths in the pre-dawn dusk, surrounded my corpse-like form in a vigil of whispering and giggling. After all, it is not every day you find the inert body of a European stretched out in your yard.

Before the sun was high we had a breakfast of millet cake, then the boys and men took the animals out to the bush to graze, and Bill and I set off for the long walk to Matomio. It turned out to be a staggering day's walk of bleaching sun that seared the senses to raw edges and made each step a monumental task of will. We walked and walked, through a land featureless except for the interminable track gleaming like white-hot steel, leading into a world blank and without form, a sheet of cruel, glittering heat and glare that could only be glimpsed at with watery eyes. Now and again we crouched under scanty trees, lapping up the feeble shade and sipping our precious water. During the whole day we came upon only one village, of one family and two houses, oppressed and flattened by a sun that filled the entire sky. They gave us some water and let us join them in the shade of a lean-to. They had just moved there and were still in the process of building the second house. I could not think why they had chosen a place so devoid of growth or distraction, unless it was because they had been forced to move from an area that had become even more desolate than here.

In the afternoon we met an old man wearily plodding his way through the inhospitable country, winding amongst the clumps of thick thorn and gorse, coming in our direction. All he had with him was his stick and a bundle of clothes on his head that kept off the sun. Eagerly he accepted our water bottle and drank deeply. Somehow it seemed completely natural when he drained it to the last drop, although that left us with nothing. He was old and we were young, and the old are privileged and free to take advantage.

2

Matomio

Arriving in Matomio in the evening was like entering a different world: a forest of shady palms surrounding a small valley dotted with sandy banks of tufted gorse and big, solitary trees. Little herds of goats, tended by boys, grazed around the perimeter, and men drove their cattle along the paths, lightly tapping their flanks with sticks.

The village was a mixture of the more traditional round mud huts with thatched roofs and bigger, square houses of mud brick, some with corrugated-iron roofs. Tall walls of golden matted grass and low, broken-down, brick walls surrounded the family homesteads. Each one was like a little village on its own, but they all fitted together in a jigsaw, threaded by skinny alleyways, twisting and turning so that you could quickly become lost down them, and end up in someone's yard. Wide thoroughfares of dust and strolling donkeys led between the separate areas of homesteads, like knives dividing a cake, leading to the centre of the village, a big marketplace, quiet and unused today. Next to it was a deep, dry pond full of sheep and rubbish, and the main and only street which was an extension of the road leading to Sai, my destination. This street had a few shops in it. There was a bicycle shop, a cluttered shed full of the skeletons and rusty limbs of ancient, cannibalized bikes. There were occasional doorway-stalls of sugar, sweets, and cigarettes being sold one by one. One piece of road was enclosed by a grass screen, behind which a large lady stirred a pot of millet and slapped

47

some on to a plate for a few coppers. And there were a couple of more substantial stores selling big business items, such as sacks of maize and rice, oil and salt.

When we walked into the village in the evening sun, exhausted and dirty, it was a hive of activity. Women with arms like pistons pounded grain with huge spatulas into wooden toadstool pots. Animals idled up the streets like pedestrians. Groups of children ran round and round like fighter squadrons. Clusters of young men chatted on corners and old men sat in wicker chairs. To me it looked like one of those pictures in children's books depicting a typical, idyllic African village. All the colours were vivid in the low sunlight, contrasting with the black shadows stretching across the roads like railings. Sheep dotted the landscape like puffs of cotton wool and the cattle, red with dust, looked healthy and tranquil.

As we walked on, the call to evening prayers drifted from the mosque, chanting in a thin, wailing voice the faraway words of the Koran. It was a homely and comforting sound. People who noticed me called me over to ask what I wanted, and a flock of children followed me like a wake, frothing and bubbling with evening energy and mirth. A small blacksmith with a gentle face and squeaky voice gave us directions to some distant relations of Bill, with whom we were going to stay.

Their home was much the same as the one I had stayed in the previous night, a big closed yard where animals and family lived together. At the door we were met by a clutch of women and girls who were very forthcoming and lively, surrounding me, cooing and gurgling with delight, totally uninhibited, the same breed of people as those in Mounia, with the rounded, smooth look and the blue-dyed underlips. They chatted to me continually, not put off by the fact that we had no single word of common tongue. They told me long stories and asked many questions with shrieks of laughter that became all the more intense when I looked helplessly dumb. They pointed to objects, saying their word for them slowly and deliberately, getting me to repeat them over and over again, and they asked

Bill many questions about me, looking serious at the answers. They made me feel very welcome and at ease, and treated me kindly but with fun.

There were only two men present; whether there were more who had gone away for a time I did not know. All the rest of the family were an assortment of women and girls whose relationships with each other I had difficulty in determining. I think two of them were wives of the head of the family, and the others were sisters or sisters-in-law, and daughters and grand-daughters. The father of the family was a quiet, reclusive man, dignified and serious; he lived at the end of a yard in a separate, screened-off enclosure, but came out and greeted me warmly, and bade me stay in his house for as long as I wished. There was one son, a boy of about fifteen, who was also quiet and serious. He studied at the local Koranic school, the only school in the village, which taught solely Arabic and the Koran. He would often come up to me, sit down on my mat, and ask me earnest questions in his tortuous French.

Life in the yard was full and simple. Everybody went about it with a slow, purposeful detachment so that daily life passed in an unhurried, dream-like way. The day always started before the sun was up, when the first faint sign of dawn stained the horizon. The women sleepily shifted around in the early light like shadows, sweeping the ground and rattling pots and pans before anyone else had stirred. Soon, though, everybody would be up, looking glum and uncommunicative at first. One by one they would go to the well to wash. They scrubbed thoroughly with soap, behind the ears and between the toes, perched on a small stool, taking their time and gradually becoming alive again. They squeezed water down their faces and arms and swilled out their mouths. Then they popped in a short fibrous stick that for the next hour or so they used to scrub their teeth, now and again emitting long jets of spittle like cobras.

The sleeping mats were shaken out and rolled up. The embers in the fire were brought back to life with a few puffs and some dry kindling, and the lambs were loosed from their tethers. As soon as they were free they rushed for their

49

mothers and vigorously butted their udders, loosening them up before suckling, fighting amongst each other for the teats. A meal of liquid millet, a bit like porridge, sometimes with sugar and sometimes without, was prepared for us, and sipped out of baby calabashes split in half for spoons. The father made it his job to give me my food and see that I was happy. Then he made coffee behind his screen in a big metal cup that was passed around the whole family. Before the sun was too high, every-one went out to do the business of the day: boys came and took the goats out to graze; the women went into the village to buy, sell and exchange goods; and the men went to the mosque to meet friends, to discuss business and religion. Once again the village was alive with activity.

A hub of women stayed back in the home to look after the babies and do the washing, pounding and cooking for the day. They did not work too strenuously, though, as there was plenty of time and no point in exhausting themselves in the heat. They would spend hours squatting over a pot of peanuts, methodically shelling them and continually chatting about the village, exclaiming at scandals and laughing about people who had made fools of themselves or were just hopeless characters.

'Ah, Fatima,' an old lady would say, 'did you hear about that bad man, Mahamadu, who sells the meat which is always too old? His wife got fed up with him beating her so she went to stay with her brother on the other side of the village by the palmerie. When Mahamadu came back and saw that she had gone he went into a rage. He thought she had gone to make a rendezvous with a lover at her brother's house. Ah, yes, can you believe it, Fatima? That woman who has given birth to so many children she could be a grandmother to the whole village.'

'Ha, ha. Yes, that old fool. He is always thinking everybody is after his wife, or that daughter of his, who has known nearly as many men as her old mother has.'

'Yes, yes, aah. And you know he went round to the brother's house with a big stick and shouted outside, "Come out of there, woman, I know what you're doing. Come out now or I will come and drag you out," so loudly that everybody could hear. Oh, the shame of it. And of course the poor woman came out, but only after a long time of shouting and arguing and that brother of hers always standing at the door denouncing poor foolish Mahamadu as a man who does not know how to treat women properly. But the joke is that, whilst Mahamadu was there shouting and cursing after his wife, his daughter, so I'm told, was seeing that boy, the cotton merchant's son, right in his house. Ha, ha, yes. Can you believe it? What a fool he made of himself.'

'And that man, the bicycle mender. Yes, he was so proud of a new bicycle he had, so proud. He rode right down the main street with his head so high, and on down the hill he went, but his pride was so big he forgot he had not fixed the brakes on yet, so down he went and crashed straight into old man Ahmed's goat pen. Ha, ha, ha, you can't believe it! Oooh, yes, it looked so funny. Yes, he was a fool as well, and old man Ahmed gave him some sharp talk and took him down a peg or two.'

By nine o'clock it was already getting quite hot. By eleven it was very hot, the sun like a battering ram, the village glaring and inhospitable. And by midday everyone had given up work and returned home to eat some maize or rice. The heat was a very dry heat, but the air became so hot it was an effort to breathe. The only way to bear it was not to try and fight it, but to reconcile yourself to it. So after the meal everybody crawled into dark huts to lie down and sweat it out. In our family everybody, except the old man, squeezed into one small mud hut. In cosy confusion we lay on mats, mingling sweat and sharing the heat. Another mat was draped over the doorway to cut out the stinging blast of light from a courtyard that was now unapproachable, shimmering with heat waves. The clogged atmosphere of bodies and minds and the dark, dank heat in the hut drugged me into sleep. The only other activities that took place at this time of day were knitting, sewing, weaving mats or plaiting hair – all slow, soporific exercises that lulled the mind.

Tea was continually made in the customary tiny tin teapot,

51

a long and almost fruitless process that produced a few thimble-sized cups of extremely strong and sweet tea. Mainly, though, tea-making was a ritual of mixing and pouring with great dexterity and show that was pleasant to watch and prestigious to do. It was a process that could take up to an hour. The maker, generally a man or a boy – tea-making being regarded as hospitality and hospitality being the duty of men – transfixed everyone with his daring and method: at any moment you expected the fast hands to make a mistake as they poured the tea into a cup from an ever greater height and then mixed it back into the pot, over and over again. It passed the time very well.

The women and children took a great fancy to my feet. They stroked them all afternoon, like delicate pieces of china, wriggling the toes and exclaiming at their white softness and angular shape; their feet were all flat, cracked and hard, like worn-out shoes. The hut became like a seething lair of fox cubs, wriggling and winding themselves around each other as more people squeezed in.

By four-thirty the children became restless, running in and out of the door into the yard. Slowly they roused the grown-ups who, like drunks, stumbled outside and over to the well to freshen themselves up. As the sun sank low, the air again became bearable and the deserted village came back to life. People were free to mingle and enjoy themselves now. In the yard the women were in fine fettle, laughing and joking whilst they cooked the evening meal, washed the children and socialized with friends who dropped in. Once again the men went to the mosque to pray or perhaps just to lay out their prayer mats in the yard and prostrate themselves, facing Mecca, and the young boys went to the Koranic school.

When darkness started to creep over the village people returned home, ate their evening meal and talked about the day. Straw mats were pulled out into the yard and everyone settled down to a long evening sitting under the stars, chatting and making more tea.

One evening while I was there one of the small girls was ill with a fever; her mother came and asked me if I had any pills I could give her. I went to have a look at her and she did indeed look very ill, white and sweating. Her mother, though, thought it quite a joke when I felt her forehead and gave her some aspirin, calling everyone over to have a look at what I was doing. I felt very sorry for the poor girl, who was poked and pushed around as everyone suddenly took an interest in her. When they saw the pills, of course, they all wanted some, for any sort of ailment. To them it was really just a big game; the pills were like sweets, extra luxuries that were not really necessary but certainly good if you could get hold of them. One old lady came up to me and pointed at her pancake flat feet, hard, brown and calloused, with big spatulate toes and deep cracks in the leathery skin. I asked Bill what she was saying and when she repeated it everyone rolled on the ground in paroxysms of laughter. She wanted some pills to make her feet pretty again. Looking at her little mischievous face, I could not tell whether she was serious or not, so I told her to go and buy some shoes if she wanted to have nice feet again, which sent everyone off into even more fits of laughter. Now they were all asking me for pills to make their hair longer, cream to lighten their skin and shoes to put on their feet. The little girl was forgotten, wrapped up in a blanket, eyeing me with suspicion.

The evenings were the time for merriment and fooling around. Any distraction, no matter how small, was seized on. Maybe one of the women had another story to tell about a man arguing with his wife, or someone treading on a snake. Then everyone would surround her on her mat and listen and make jokes about it. But as the night deepened people became quieter, huddling together on their mats, whispering and sharing each other's warmth and touch under the coal-black sky. There was a close and intimate feeling amongst them; the atmosphere was charged with companionship, love and poetry. We lay on our backs watching the stars winking at us as, imperceptibly, silence overcame the sporadic talk. We pulled our sheets over our heads and slept; children in the arms of mothers, brothers curled up together like puppies and sisters cradling baby sisters.

53

I stayed in Matomio for five days. Sometimes in the evenings, before the sun went down, I would go and sit in the palmerie just outside the village, leaning against a big palm tree amongst the ants and spiders. I would watch the sun sinking like the hand of a clock, lower and lower, until the shadows became infinite in the amber glow and the dark velvet sky was strewn with tatters of red and yellow. Scrawny sheep and long-horned cattle appeared out of the greying bush and made their way towards the village, stopping here and there to nibble a juicy leaf. Oxen, pulling carts piled high with wood, moved wearily along the fading track, nearly home but still urged along by their brown, leathery owners. In deep pits of their own making, the brickmakers laboured on, making use of the last light and the cool air, their bricks stacked around them in zigzagging patterns, slowly drying and hardening from brown to grey. There were so many brickmakers around the village that all their excavations had begun to join together, making a moat with only skinny walkways of earth left crossing it.

The solid wall of mud huts and grass enclosures that were the village started to lose its starkness of day as dusk turned to dark. A curtain of stars hung over the village and the air quavered with the chanting of the Koran by the harmonious young voices in the school. Cooking fires glinted in the dark, and as the silence of pure darkness eased its way round me, I would know it was time to return to the warmth of my family.

I had one particular friend in the village, the squeaky blacksmith I had met on the first day. As he could speak no word of French and I was still struggling with hello and goodbye in his tongue, we had virtually no means of verbal communication; but despite that I felt very close to him. Whenever I walked past his small workshop he would call me over. Smiling deeply, he would bid me sit down whilst he went on working, now and again looking up to see if I was happy.

I could sit there for hours watching the skill and dexterity of his hands working the metal, heating it up with a small pair of goatskin bellows between his legs and piling charcoal on top until it glowed white. Next to him he had part of a car axle planted in the ground to act as his anvil. On this he would hammer and tap-tap, hammer and tap-tap a perfect edge to a knife or an axehead, turning it over and over, re-heating it, and gradually working the metal to a hair-line sharpness. Dipping it into a bucket of water, he would momentarily disappear in a cloud of steam, only his eyes peering out at me, full of meaning and silent talk. Sometimes he punched holes for bolts in cart drawbars, and sometimes he made fine delicate copper bracelets. These were his pleasure and his art. He would spend a long time over one, creating a perfectly round and smooth bangle, shiny and fine, from the original square lump of metal, like the metamorphosis of a caterpillar to a butterfly. He was one of the few men in the village who worked all day, only occasionally dropping off at his post, curled up, dozing amongst his tools and pieces of scrap metal, like a child amongst his toys.

On my last night in the village he took me to his house where his wife had prepared some coffee for us. He loved her very much and was very proud to show her to me, and she was proud to show me how well she loved and looked after him. We did not say much as we sat and watched her stir in luxurious amounts of sugar to the hot black coffee, because we were unable to. But the few simple things we communicated were all that was necessary. When we said goodbye it was not a real goodbye. I, for one, felt that part of him would always be with me. I had learnt something valuable from his unhurried and trustful manner, and felt a bond between us that distance would not break.

During the time we were in Matomio, Bill and I had been fairly independent of each other, only meeting in the after-noons and nights when we were with the family. He had been quiet and well mannered in the village. Towards the end of our time there, he asked me where I was going after Sai. When I told him I was going to Segou and then Bamako he got very excited:

'Ah, Bamako, the capital, yes, that is a good place to go. I shall come with you and show you around; there are many things to see in Bamako. We will make a grand team and then I can find a job.'

'But what about your mother and sisters?' I asked. 'You haven't even finished your education yet, you should go back to Djenne.'

'No, no, Djenne is a stupid town, a small town. I must go to Bamako and get a job and make money and then I can go home and my family will be proud of me. You have brought me this far – you must take me to Bamako.'

I didn't want to take Bill with me: besides other reasons, I couldn't afford to. I told him I might be a long time in getting to Bamako; it would be better to travel separately. At this he became surly. In Djenne, Bill had seen much of the outside world passing through and he liked what he saw. He was bright and enthusiastic. He wanted 'out' of small-time Djenne but he was still too young and did not have the means to strike off on his own.

The village of Sai was only a short way from Matomio. One day we packed our bags and, having said our farewells, set off for it. The walk was gentle and easy, along an avenue of palms, and by midday we had arrived. Bill had brooded the whole way and hadn't spoken to me once. There was nothing much to Sai, and it quickly became apparent that we would find nowhere to stay and no transport to take me to Segou. I told Bill we would return to Matomio as the next day was market day, and the pick-up trucks that came to the market would be my only opportunity of a lift for a week. Bill refused to move. He said that as I wouldn't take him with me to Bamako, and as we had arrived in Sai, our agreed destination, I should pay him now and we would part. I paid him our agreed price plus a good tip, but he became angry.

'Is this all you can give me?' he shouted. 'We've been away far longer than you said we'd be. How shall I get back home? Why did you deceive me and then offer me this pathetic amount of money?'

'But that's more than we agreed on,' I said.

'Huh! You know nothing. I have friends here. I could have

them rob you of all your money. There are no police for miles. We could even kill you and no one would know because no one knows you're here.'

This was all getting a bit out of hand, I thought. Bill was a nice boy. Had I made some terrible mistake with him somewhere, or was he just trying to regain his dignity after his elaborate plans had come to nothing? Was he ashamed to go back home without more to show for his excursion, or was he just trying it on? I wasn't sure.

I said, 'Bill, I know you too well now. You're a nice person and it's not in you to do that sort of thing.' At least I hoped I did and it wasn't. It was true nobody knew I was here, that I was in the hands of Bill and his friends; and Bill was a complex person. He seemed to accept what I said but we walked in uneasy silence back to Matomio. Bill took a truck going to Djenne that same day. We said goodbye pleasantly enough, but he couldn't look me in the eye as he always had done before. I felt sad. I had liked Bill, we had had some good laughs. I always remember him referring to me, as he often did with that mischievious glint in his eye, as 'the big white boss who must carry his own bag and walk'.

When I woke next morning I immediately noticed a different atmosphere. There was a buzz of excitement and anticipation. It was the one day in the week when the routine and monotony of everyday life would be broken, when people could let their hair down and really enjoy themselves.

In my household the women were busy and pre-occupied and had no time for the normal daily ordeal of caring for the family: they were absorbed in making themselves beautiful and preparing their bits and pieces to be sold in the market. The men kept out of their way. All morning in the village the same was happening, a pent-up hum of activity and preparation sang in the air like electricity, an atmosphere of summer fêtes and tea parties, a controlled and dignified indulgence. Village folk, perched on ox-drawn carts, walking, bicycling or riding donkeys, poured into the village. Jingling, juddering pick-ups, rusting on their axles, shuttled back and forth from more distant villages, swaying alarmingly with their precarious loads of technicolour women and baskets strapped firmly on to the back in a single, towering heap of struggling limbs and compressed wares.

The market place itself was a vast canopy of thatch and sticks, the roofs of hundreds of small lean-to shacks resting on a forest of wooden supports. There was a grid of tiny passageways slicing in between them, down which you had to walk at a stoop to avoid the crossbeams sticking out treacherously, and in order to see below the sea of roofs across the sprawl of the market beneath. Around the edge all the shops and houses had opened their double doors. In these, the professional marketgoers were the first to set up their stalls of goods, mostly imported things: shiny plastic shoes, small decorative mirrors, bags of coffee and tea, dates and sweets, cigarettes and matches, candles, lamps, combs, pocket knives, shoe-laces and many other miscellaneous but useful items. The local people sat down under the lean-tos in ordered confusion, forming districts of similar items of locally made and grown goods. Lines of men with silver-coated hands, working away at sheets of aluminium, squatted amid walls of roughly made pots and pans. Other men displayed long straw mats, yellow and fresh, woven with patterns of red and blue, hanging from the eaves or laid out on the ground. Huge piles of golden-grass scrubbing sponges tumbled into the alleyways. Car-tyre sandals stood proudly in rows of pairs, with still rounded soles from the curvature of the wheels and displaying the trade names of Dunlop or Michelin. Watermelons cut in two, dusty dried fish and fly-speckled animal intestines swaying on strings, all crowded under the stalls with their patient owners who idly waited for custom, brewing tea and socializing with friends.

Before long the whole market square and all the streets running off it were bulging with bustling people, jostling and nudging in the crowded, congealed ways, mingling and parting like a stream of eddies, whirlpools and rapids. It was an exciting market, international with its many different peoples. There were Tuaregs, Bambara and Peul, in-betweens and

imports from all the surrounding districts. Some of them were pitch-black, some fair, some tall and slender with eagle noses and flowing robes, and some stocky with flat noses and skin-tight clothes. Everybody was dressed magnificently in their market-day best. Stunning, tall ladies with spotless flowing dresses of goddess white or devil red, with every hue and pattern in between, would suddenly loom out of the surrounding mass of bodies like queens, rings through their noses and dainty shoes on their feet. Dangling, jangling necklaces and bracelets adorned their richly oiled, ebony skin. In the dry, dusty villages it was a wonder to me how they attained such perfect cleanliness and beauty. Heavily sashed Tuaregs, in from the desert, with long lethal knives, wandered round hawking the materials piled on their heads and under their arms, drifting sadly among the crowds like wraiths. Rich patrons with big bellies draped with expensive clothes strolled leisurely, accepting respect. Holy men with worn and precious sticks in their hands and white caps on their heads, teeth red and rotten from the kola nuts they chewed, greeted friends with long formal rituals of wishing health and happiness that went on and on until they were satisfied or thought of something else to say.

Shrieking, squeaking, squawking children swam in and out of the crowds like shoals of flickery fish. The young men, looking spick and handsome in their natty modern dress, lounged about very 'nicely', eyeing the girls and talking in secretive whispers. And young girls, bare-breasted, with wreaths of coloured beads about their slender necks, were on display for eligible bachelors or rich married men on the lookout for a new bride. Girls, boys, women and men alike carried things on their heads as if they were extensions of their bodies. Unbelievable tiers of baskets and calabashes towered above the crowds, swaying from side to side like pendulums upside down. Interspersed between all these glorious people were the old women, wrinkled like prunes and ugly, their dresses untended and their feet un-shod, yet frantically doing the most energetic business of all. Very poor people, broken and without a home, came to be amongst the wealth of market day and to beg for scraps. And there were the blind and the crippled, and small boys prompted and trained to ask money off likely-looking people, who gave freely and made their friends do so as well.

On this day there was no sleeping away the afternoon. Every minute of the show had to be savoured to keep them going until next week. All those long hours of careful matting, weaving and sewing, and those small amounts of money secretly saved up, all paid off now. With the heady freedom of the planner who has already accounted for the sack of maize or the rock of salt, they could throw away what remained on little luxuries like scented soap or peanut paste, or on more extravagant things that would ease life a bit, some lovely new material for a dress, perhaps, or a bigger and better pot for the fire. They could be like children with pocket money, spend-thrift and carefree with what they had. The men would buy a new pair of shoes or some good chewing tobacco. And those piles of big, shiny tin bowls with flowers decorating the sides and pure white enamel on the inside were irresistible, so maybe they would buy one for the wife. The mounds of gourds and sieves and herbs and spices diminished as they spent, and the patient sellers could then go and buy in their turn that small item that had caught their eye earlier on. Everybody was happy and handsome in their preened and primed condition on this day – the market day. Even for those with no money or merchandise it was enjoyable, as they could hawk and hustle or wheel and deal on someone else's behalf, or just feel part of the throng of intoxicating high life. The day went on and on with a squabble here, some singing there; always something to see or do. The old men could sit in their chairs and watch it happen as it passed and the young men could go and find it.

For me, though, it was the end and time to leave. My pick-up truck taking me to Segou was at last ready to go, having been packed for maximum profit if not maximum comfort. Reluctantly I climbed on board, said goodbye again to my family and friends. I left the market in full swing with a buzz in my head of unique images and seductive feelings and when, after many hours' driving through a hinterland of shrouded soft sand and bush, I glimpsed the twinkle of electric lights ahead of me in the night, I felt as though I were waking from a dream.

Segou was a lovely town on the banks of the Niger, a day's drive to the west. Like Mopti and Gao, it was a town of gaiety and dilapidation, carefree with cobwebs, a comforting town of soft edges and slow, village lives. I stayed there for about a week with a student called Michael and his family. They lived on a long, straight avenue pretty with mango trees, whose brown boughs shaded the red earth road. On each side huddled low mud houses with corrugated-iron roofs, their many worn windows and doors alive with peeking faces and family noise. Football games traversed the street and mobilettes buzzed like clockwork toys in and out of the taxi bashés and the rusty cars which sat embedded in the red earth, back into which they were slowly being absorbed.

Michael studied French in Bamako and was home for his holidays. He had picked me up wandering the streets on the day I arrived, trying to find somewhere to stay. He took my bag and me on the back of his mobilette to find a hotel, but stopped off in his street to give me some tea. As we sat outside his house, his friends quickly gathered round and started plying me with questions about Bob Marley. I seemed a good 'find'. Michael invited me to stay.

He lived with his grandfather and a large, indefinable family of women and girls. His grandfather was a gentle, dignified old man who sat all day on the verandah in his yard. He told me I was welcome to stay. Michael's small room adjoined the yard; it was dark and dank, with draped curtains, a bed thin and low, a chair and all the oddments of his life: photographs of faded friends, magazine cuttings of cars and places to be desired, and of course, football teams, bleached with age. I had his bed and he had the floor, and there I lay in the afternoons and nights, a-drip with sweat, my belly a balloon from the vast amounts of rice they liked me to eat.

I walked the town in the mornings and ends of days while Michael was off playing his sports. There was music and dancing somewhere in Segou on most evenings. One day I found a big dance taking place on a wide street of earth, watched entranced by a large circle of people pressed very tight, some standing on buses and cars and some on rostrums at the back. The sun was low and cast rays of gold upon the tiers of round faces. At the front of the circle sat the children, all clean and beautiful, their honey eyes wide and staring at the spectacle before them. At one side were some chairs where the mayor and other town dignitaries sat in robed splendour with their well-built wives. I came amongst them as if unseen. God, how they looked happy and serene, these people of Segou, I thought. In the circle drummers beat a frantic rhythm, and lines of wobbly women with costumes bright-coloured and all the same, the work of clever hands and many an hour, jogged and swooped, shook their turbaned heads and sang as they chug-chugged round like a train. Two strong, muscled men, naked but for a piece of cloth, threw each other in somersaults and cartwheeled in the open space, their hard calloused feet sending up puffs of dust. As the glistening drummers increased their beat, hands a-blurr, these two men lost themselves in the heat of sound. Their limbs took on a life of their own. Every bone and muscle tensed and twisted as if in a fit; they became at one with the beat, their animal involvement was mesmeric. I became aware of another man, spurting fire from his mouth, and another juggling with knives. For many hours the dance went on, long after the sun had sunk. The crowd swayed and sang, people jumped up and joined in, giving a performance of their own. Fools and jokers jested to applause, and on and on they went.

I left Segou by boat and went up the Niger to a village called

63

Tamane. The boat I took was an especially large and beautiful pirogue, her wooden sides painted in designs of blue and green and red, flags fluttering at prow and stern. She was covered by a fixed awning of bamboo and reed and on the top of this many calabashes, smooth, rounded and tight-packed, crowned her with a dashing strip of gold.

The captain was a very fat man with an arm like an ox's leg. With his equally large twin brother, he ran the boat with an iron rule. Their size did not inhibit their mobility and they moved with the agility of a couple of gorillas. The boat was propelled by two Peugeot 303 car engines in the stern, in a puddle of black, greasy water in which paddled the soot-stained engine man.

'Get that engine going, you heathen!' one brother would shout. 'Stop the valve, give it some choke. No more sacks of salt up that end! Here, put them here,' and a brood of women would be dislodged a moment while the sacks were placed beneath them and they would be raised yet another level so that their heads now pressed against the awning.

When the time came to depart, and that half of the Segou market which was not to come with us had been encouraged overboard by the brothers, attempts were made to push the boat off. It had become firmly stuck due to a case of extreme overloading, so all attempts were in vain until a brother lent a hand, and with an almighty grunt had us floating freely.

'Hey, old man,' one brother let forth to a passenger, 'why is that sack you're sitting on whining and kicking so? That's the first time I've seen such a lively sack of rice. I don't suppose it might be a goat, old man? I told you, no goats on this craft. That will be an extra half fare, please.'

64

'But he's dead,' pleaded the old man, as the sack suddenly gave a particularly large kick. 'By God, at least he was dead! I cut his throat myself not long ago.'

'Whether he's risen from the dead or so long dead he's rising, I don't care, old man. Half an extra fare for any goat that moves, please!' and the whole boat-load of 50 or so passengers, all hugger-mugger with their wares, had a great laugh at the old man's expense.

Unfortunately at this time of year, which was March, the Niger was very low, and as our splendid boat was so large and overloaded, after only a few hours' motoring up-river there came a meeting between the bottom of the boat and the riverbed. This meant that all passengers were unceremoniously herded over the side chest-deep and, under the orders from the brothers, began to push. For the better part of 60 kilometres we became little more than a troop of slaves, pushing the boat off one sandbank to another with the ever humorous brothers at our backs to make sure we didn't slack.

'Push, people, push, or shall we settle and make our lives here in the middle of the river and forget our families and jobs and homes? We could be happy, we could make good lives. What are families and homes and comfort? Nothing, I tell you. Yes, we could be happy here, living like all the little fishes in the stream. Is that what you want? Is it? Because if it isn't, push, push, or here we shall remain.'

From Tamane I took a bus to Bamako, and stayed there until I could get a visa to Guinea, my next destination. The time passed slowly, the mosquitoes were bad and each evening I watched huge bats, nearly a metre in span, swoop and fly in the sky with the swallows. I saw my first rain since leaving England, a sign that my course was south. And south I continued, through forgotten Guinea, to Liberia and the sophisticated Ivory Coast. For two months more I travelled and sweated and sometimes rested, through Burkina Faso once more, to hot Niger, to Chad and wars, through the green, rolling beauty of Cameroon and the poor, backward Central African Republic, and thence at last to Zaire.

PART TWO

ZAIRE

3

Zongo and an Official Encounter

Zaire is the Amazonia of Africa, mostly a basin of jungles and forests that drink from the great Zaire river, for so many years known as the Congo. It is one of those countries you can spend a lot of time looking at on a map. You trace that long, wide river from sea to source; you go up the tributaries and the sub-tributaries that spread out like the veins on a leaf, thin blue lines penetrating every part of the deep green country. You get lost in the blanks in between them and wonder what is there. The map-maker says nothing, just uniform green. But you know better. And all those little black dots scattered almost haphazardly with pleasing, rounded names like Boendi and Bomba. Who lives there? What sort of life do they live? It's all so enticing. And those rumours you always hear – the worst corruption, the worst thieving, the worst roads. How do they fit in? Sometimes they are true, but they can never be a deterrent. They are part of the country. If the map-makers could mark them down, they would, the same as they do the relief.

The country has had a complex, often bloody history. The original inhabitants were simple hunter-gatherers who lived in much the same way the pygmies there still do, without a social structure or kinship system. Then small communities settled on the riverbanks evolved into kingdoms, now expanding, now contracting as tribes came to power or faded. Then the Portuguese arrived in 1482, and Arabs came from the east, and both of them, with their excessive demands for slaves and

69

their trade networks, dominated and eclipsed the native kingdoms. The great explorers of the nineteenth century were the first Europeans to penetrate the interior of Zaire, and they, too, had far-reaching effects. David Livingstone with his journals inspired a huge influx of Protestant and Catholic missionaries who came to 'civilize' and 'educate' what he called the 'savages of darkest Africa'. Henry Stanley, who had originally come to look for Livingstone, was the first European to traverse central Africa from east to west; with his knowledge of the area he helped King Leopold II of the Belgians claim a large part of it in 1885, which became known as the 'Congo Free State'. This free state was then subjected to a most brutal era of 'pacification' and colonization, and was renamed in 1908 the Belgian Congo. In 1960 after great pressure of riots in Leopoldville and powerful independence movements, the country was reluctantly granted independence. Years of bloody power struggle followed between the country's many tribal and regional groups. Zaire has between 200 and 250 different ethnic groupings; with borders arbitrarily drawn at the Berlin conference in 1884, many tribes had their traditional lands partly in Zaire and partly in neighbouring areas, leading to constant border disputes as well as virtual civil war. In 1965 one powerful army general took control and, as President Mobutu, has continued to rule since. It has been neither an easy nor a peaceful rule, within his own borders or beyond them. About three-quarters of the rural population are subsistence farmers following traditional ways. The economy is weak, there is much dissent and poverty, but the autocratic régime maintains itself principally through Western financial and military support and a system of corruption and intimidation. But because this country is so large and its terrain so difficult, because it remains largely undeveloped and in some cases even untouched, and because my experience had so far taught me that the less developed a place the more gentle and genuine the people, I had been looking forward to coming to Zaire for a long time.

* * *

I stood in Bangui, capital of the Central African Republic, staring over a wide, lumbering river to Zaire on the other side. The river was the Ubangi, and it divided the two countries on the northern border of Zaire. The water looked dangerous and treacherous, a solid body, dark with mud and conflicting currents. The opposite bank was a mute, anonymous green line broken only by a village with a small sandy beach. That was Zaire, Conrad's 'heart of darkness'.

To change countries I took a pirogue, made from a dug-out tree. The owner of it was a skilled paddler. We did not just push off and cross, but made a long and laborious zig-zag pattern, using the whirlpools and currents to help us over. I was filled with excitement and a few nerves as I sat low in the water, the wind ruffling my hair. Zaire was coming closer, for better or worse.

We arrived at the village on the other side and pulled up on the beach. Here I met up again with Carsten and Nils, two Germans I had come across in Bangui, who were travelling across Africa in a truck. Together we walked up the small beach to a stone house that announced itself as the 'Zongo Immigration Post'. Inside the hot and sweaty little building were four hot and sweaty men. The scene fitted some of the less desirable rumours perfectly. Our entry evoked no sign of interest at all. The four vaguely uniformed men were arguing and shouting at a frieze of faces peering in at two big verandah windows. They were arguing about money, who should pay, how much, for what. The villagers wanted to go to Bangui for the day, or had come back without the correct stamp. They bargained and grumbled and stood defeated because they could not pay the money they were asked for. The four men looked harassed and bored, and made smudges in big books. We waited.

About half an hour later a very smart man in uniform entered. Immediately all were hushed. He looked even more bad-tempered than the four men. He shouted to the room at large and in between his shouting he said to us, 'The office is now closed. Come back in the morning.'

'But we've been here for a half an hour,' we said. 'Surely one

71

of you could stamp our passports so we can get on our way?'

'Impossible, quite impossible! Didn't you hear me say the office is closed? Where do you think you are, huh? What do you take us for? This is Zaire and here we do things strictly by the law. It's ten minutes after five so the office is closed. Of course,' he continued, 'if you wish to keep the office open to complete your formalities it can be arranged, but you'll have to pay for my men's overtime.'

Fortunately, Carsten, who was full of initiative, had anticipated something of the sort: in a trunk in his truck he had many mini-bottles of rum. What a transformation – within a minute the policeman had a bottle of rum in one hand, a huge grin on his face, and his other arm clasped round Carsten in token of eternal friendship. The formalities were forgotten; now the problem was to prevent him impounding all the other bottles and anything else in the truck that took his fancy. We made a rendezvous to meet him in the evening for a beer, were given permission to camp behind the office, and provided with a machine-gun-clad guard to look after us during the night.

Promptly on time Zarky, as our policeman–now–friend called himself, turned up in civilian clothes. A river boat had just arrived at Zongo amid raucous hooting, a complex affair of many barges and boats, rust and ropes, all muddled together and every inch alive with people. It was like a village afloat, complete with chickens and goats and open fires, and Zarky steered the way towards it for our drink. The party had started without us, the hooting drawing most of Zongo on board. We picked our way across a rotten plank and through a mass of bodies, dancing, singing, eating and mainly drinking. On the captain's verandah in the stern we perched on beer crates. His wife stirred a big pot over a charcoal fire nearby, his babies and miscellaneous goods littered all about. One clear bulb hung to give some light.

Zarky was now a different man. He was shy – mild, you might almost say. His uniform had obviously made a great difference. He changed us some money, at a bad black market rate, and bought us some beers. Accompanied by our friendly guard, we proceeded to get fairly tight. Zarky did not have much stamina, though, and before long he was out for the count, slouched in a chair with a young woman draped over him, cooing. Now our guard could hold forth without fear of intimidation; even in his milder form, he was obviously still scared of his boss.

'Oh, I'm not really a guard,' he said. 'I come from the Katang Province in the south. I have to come and do my military service up here in the north. But violence, you know, that is a fool man's game. You kill somebody and what do you gain? Someone kills your brother and what does he gain? We just go round in circles. I do not want to kill someone. But maybe I will have to because I have a gun. I shall become a doctor. I was studying before I was sent here and now I have no money to get out.'

He was a bright young man, who talked about things in theory, not in practice. He showed us the workings of his gun, and I hoped he would have no need to use it, the terrible state it was in.

That night, at about three o'clock, thieves struck in our camp. They cut out the truck's front windscreen and climbed in, to find my two sleeping friends. There was a lot of shouting and I scrambled out of my tent too late to see the men disappear with only the windscreen as bounty. Fortunately our guard was still fast asleep, so we were saved the possibility of randomly fired bullets, or even an exploding gun.

Because of this little incident, proceedings next day became highly complex. The formalities were manifold. Our policeman friend was back in uniform, so back to his officious self. We were not free to leave until quite late in the afternoon. But then Zaire lay before us.

4

Through Forests and Villages to a Big River

Nils and Carsten had a superb Unimog truck, converted to the ultimate in overland vehicles. It had everything from beds, a kitchen, air conditioning and a shower, to a fully fledged workshop that folded out of the back and, of course, a spare windscreen. I felt as though I was in the lap of luxury as I bounced around inside. We travelled together for about 500 kilometres to a small town called Bomba on the banks of the Zaire. It took us eight days and that was fast, because they were in a rush: they were short of money, having only enough to feed their vehicle with fuel and not enough to feed themselves, so they could not idle on the way.

At first the country we passed through was not wholly forest; there were wide open spaces of luxurious, tall green grass. Sometimes, on these plains, we saw hundreds of perfectly conical hills matted with grass, covering a large area. They looked like mini-Dolomites sitting in a field until the head of a villager popped up in a 'valley' and shattered the illusion, for they were only ant hills. The forests were full of palm fronds and short, twisted trees. They were clogged with jungles of undergrowth, dappled in sunlight, and they hid all animal life except the occasional flash of a brightly coloured bird. Wherever there was a stream, or a deep-gorged gully, they concentrated their strength, thick and impenetrable. At the bottom of these gullies were short wooden bridges. We always got out to check before we crossed them, having seen some trucks that didn't and had gone right through some rotten timbers.

The month was June and the land was cool and tranquil, its succulent, fresh vegetation tempering the equatorial climate which in most of Zaire means hot, wet and humid, varying little all year round. By day the bare earth of the road might be scorching hot, but amongst the fronds and ferns, with a trickle of a stream nearby and big boughs of taller trees well canopied with leaf hanging overhead, it remained cool and peaceful. The road was atrocious. Seemingly built entirely of mud, it cambered steeply into deep, sticky ditches on either side. When it had been raining, which it frequently had, staying on the top of the road and not sliding down the side was very difficult. Fortunately the Unimog was provided with a vast winch on the front with which we could pull ourselves out. But all along the way we came across many trucks well planted in that terrible mud. Around each one its occupants would be knee-deep, digging with their bare hands. As we rounded the corner and they saw our winch they cried out to us: '*Ndeko, ndeko,* brother, stop and pull us out.'

They would be very merry and shout and cheer as the mud reluctantly disgorged its victim. Sometimes they would give us pineapples and bananas and let us pass in front, for surely at the next corner, by the way they drove, they would be in the ditch again.

There were not many villages here, and those there were clung to the road, seeming to shy away from the forest pressing in behind them. The soil round about had been scratched clear of all vegetation so they had a bare, brown, breathing space. The houses were well constructed from frames of wooden struts packed with mud, with a perfect thatch on the roof.

Our first night in Zaire was spent in one of these villages. The people came out and welcomed us: we could camp in an area they had cleared to build a church, they said. Boys fetched us wood for a fire, and watched with deep fascination and round smiling faces as I pitched my tent and my friends unfolded their truck into tables, chairs and a stove. They wanted to help us do everything and joined us by our fire, but as the evening deepened they went back to their homes. In one of them a man had some crates of beer. A boy came running with a bottle for us and I went back with him to pay for it. In the hut, as in the village, there were only the bare essentials: a chair or two, a table, a bed of woven reeds and one or two household utensils. There was no superfluous ornament; the only 'art' lay in things of practical use, such as a carved stool or a colourful mat. There was though, surprisingly, a deep-freeze run off a car battery, and in the deep-freeze were the crates of beer. As I found throughout Zaire, no matter how poor a village, how malnourished the children, generally there would be a good supply of beer, very often kept in a deep-freeze.

The owner of the house was a middle-aged man who spoke some French.

'No, no – no money for the beer, please,' he said.

'Thank you. Have you lived in the village a long time?' I asked. He seemed educated.

'Yes, this is my village,' he replied, 'but I spent many years with the Non-conformist missionaries being educated. I am a minister now and that church being built is my church. It will be a good thing to have another church in the village. The villagers love to come to church. Have another beer. Yes, the Church has done much for our people. Whichever Church it is, it has done much good, teaching us how to live decently and to stop all our heathen beliefs and rituals, which are most barbaric, you know. Terrible! And it still goes on. Our people keep reverting, they need firm direction, that's the trouble.

But you must go to bed. I see many of your people coming through our village, once or twice a week at least, and I know how tired they get, always having to rush.'

I thanked him for the beer and wandered back to our camp through the little village with only six visible houses, one Catholic church, one Protestant and soon one Non-conformist. Which would be the fullest of a Sunday, I wondered, or did it really matter? I had once been to a small local church service in Northern Zambia, not far from the Zaire border. It had been a most beautiful and uplifting experience. All the way through the service there had been harmonious singing by the whole congregation, sung with gusto and joy, a perpetual, acquiescent chant that sounded somehow like a call from Africa's past.

Night, when it came, was the purest of African darkness, the deepest of deep black, broken only by our fire. From the forest all about us came a whole spectrum of noises; chirps, squeals, growls and cheeps. And, of course, the usual clickety-click crescendo from the crickets and the sporadic roar of a thousand, ten thousand, frogs. They would be silent for a long time, then one would give a tentative croak. This would break a barrier and all the rest would suddenly join in. Then they would stop, just as suddenly as the end of a tape, until the next outbreak. Worst of all, though, was the call of the hyrax, a small, ratty, tree-bound creature. He screams time and time again, each time increasing in volume until it sounds like a whole legion of women being mauled just behind your tent. Lying in the dark night, fearful thoughts of leopard prowl your mind.

In the morning we were woken by the clang, clang of the village bell calling the people to church. The bell was an old wheel hub hanging in our camp, being bashed by a small boy. We gave some presents to the village boys before we left and were waved on our way.

Moving deeper into Zaire, the forest on either side of the road became denser, less broken, until it was a continuous, pressing presence. Villages, hardly distinguishable from one another, spread all along the way, almost without break. There were small plots of cultivated land a little way into the forest, but otherwise the road was their domain. The villagers fished and washed in the rivers, grew pawpaw and pineapples by the roadside. All the palms along its way had gourds attached like leeches to the buds high up on top; sap leaked into them from gashes cut there. Periodically, men shinned up the trunks, using a strip of bark around their backs and around the tree, to collect the gourds. They made a delicious palm wine from the sap; it was a refreshing drink, a bit like lemonade and, when fermented, very potent.

All the time as we drove along, village children rushed to the edge of the road at our approach, wild with excitement, waving and shouting, their faces contorted in frantic throes of animation, some in terror, some in joy, some in make-believe anger. They gibbered and danced, waved machetes, and ran away as we passed. From the truck it was disconcerting to see this continuous flow of disembodied, twisted faces. Yes, I thought to myself, these spirited people must have put up a jolly fight in the days of the 'Congo Free State'. Also, wherever we passed, people stood and waved; everywhere, women and babies, young men and old, stood and waved with the freedom and innocence of children. I wanted to stop and be with them. Sometimes we did and they were amazed at it. Vehicles are a good way to travel in some respects, but I always feel a little cut off. The people you pass do not really see you as another person to whom they can relate: they see only the vehicle as a single entity. When we climbed out, though, things were different. The children no longer jibed and shouted; they became shy and normal again, but the elders, though friendly, rarely invited us to stay. We were too far from them in our super alien shell. Its presence was an intimidation and an unknown. It did strange things like boil water for tea. They peered inside at the sumptuous comfort, at a piece of the Western world, with wary, awe-struck faces. And we went on our way having seen but not felt.

Wherever we stopped away from a village, it was never long before small boys, naked and lithe, appeared from the bush. They came and stood around us in a circle, watching our every move with wide, curious eyes. They were spirited and full of games, these children, and could easily be enticed to fun. Once they felt confident they would show great feats of skill, throwing their spears and leaping off bridges into crystal-clear rivers. They swam like natural water beings, flowing with the current in and out of the rocks below the surface. Then for no reason they would become shy and grin with a set of perfect white teeth, behaving coyly, like well-mannered children. Anything discarded from the truck, an old tin can or a bottletop, they grabbed for and squabbled over, and no doubt used in some ingenious way. They were master craftsmen at making their own toys. I have seen intricate trucks made from wire and tins with suspension much better than the real thing, drivers, steering wheels and flags. On one occasion I saw a remarkable aeroplane made from balsa wood. The detail was astonishing – the struts, the wheels, the shape of the wings, everything. The boy stood by the road, selling it for a shameful pittance.

One day we came across a big river, like the Ubangi a tributary of the Zaire. Here was a small market and a river port, a concentration of humanity, a place that was part of the more active outside world. A barge had just arrived piled high with nothing but crates of beer. Rivers are the highways of Zaire, and beer is their daily freight. Some men were trying to unload but complete confusion reigned. Trucks blocked the road or backed down to the water's edge to collect the crates and take them off to smaller places. Pirogues were being so heavily loaded from the barge that water lapped over their sides; still, swaying from side to side, they ferried the crates ashore. Strong men, naked to the waist and glistening with sweat, worked hard carrying two crates at a time, chucking them up to a truck where one man stacked them in a frenzy. After an hour or so the trucks pulled out of the way and we could drive onto an old diesel ferry. We boarded amid sudden shouting: it seemed that all the many passengers thought it their duty to give direction and encouragement. Our wheels spun on the greasy ramp, then gripped, and we shot forward, scattering our advisers with yelps to the ferry's rusty sides.

On we drove to the other side, the forest and landscape changing but little. The villages were always there, with women pounding the grain. Old men as always sat in wicker chairs and the children still waved and yelled as we passed. They had a sort of half-life, these people of the road. Half of their lives was in the eaves of the forest, where they grew and scavenged and cut down, and half of their lives came from the road – their village radios, their pots and pans, a packet of cigarettes, their modern, cast-off clothing. Of animals we saw nothing, except maybe a monkey or a snake crossing the road, but we heard their cries at night.

On the seventh day we came to a hill, and climbed up to a plateau. From there, between some bushes, I had my first sight of the great Zaire river far off below; I could see its swell and tremendous strength as it carved like a flood through the forest world. We twisted and turned down towards it, the river disappearing for a while and then re-appearing again, and then we were on its banks in the old Portuguese settlement of Lisala. Here there was decay; a place built up and then abandoned. Elegant colonial houses with wide verandahs and wooden-shuttered windows, and rusty old factories stood dejected and crumbling on hills above the river. Of course, people still lived here but they used it as little more than a village. The factory worked, but only sometimes, and that sometimes was long ago. Lisala was unimportant now, dwarfed by the magnificent river that passed by its empty port, an unheeding, welling mass slipping by silently but surprisingly fast.

We camped for two days in Lisala, next to one of the factories. In the evenings we would wander down to the river, a drowsy old monster, dotted here and there with floating islands of plants that had pink river roses on them and little birds and their nests. The sleek pirogues looked like pieces of flotsam as they glided over its glassy surface, the fishermen paddling slow, powerful strokes in perfect unison.

On our first evening we saw one sink. The man jumped out and baled with his hand, then quickly he was in again, paddling for the shore. He didn't quite make it and swam the last few yards, pushing his waterlogged boat in front.

We made for a very small beach, really just a clearing in the reeds, to swim and wash our clothes. As we sat there afterwards, with our feet in the water, lots of tiny silver fish nibbled and tickled our toes. Small boys came down with fishing rods made from bamboo, hooking the tiny fish till they had enough for a meal. Women brought down their children to be washed; each little chubby thing, barely a few months old, would be covered from head to toe in thick white soap suds, then ducked under the water and up it would come, gurgling and wailing its heart out.

Slowly the sun sank but still we sat on, in a trance of calmness and peace. An old man paddled past close by in a long, heavy pirogue, his grandson also paddling in the bow. The old man wore a straw hat that looked nearly as old as he did. He greeted us politely without breaking his strong strokes. What had this old man seen, what type of Zaire did *he* know as a boy, I asked myself. A girl nearby borrowed my soap. She caught my eye as she tried to break off a large piece for later use. Blushing terribly, she handed it back.

The sun had disappeared by now, behind the trees, after washing the clouds pink and gold. The river moved on the same as always, on its mindless journey to Kinshasa and the sea. We broke our trance and wandered back up the hill to our camp.

When we left Lisala we were given a policeman to take with us who wanted a lift to Bomba. His machine-gun lay on the seat. It was a short journey, only one day. Halfway there, three startling figures appeared from thick forest, their skin charcoaled to an intense pitch-black. They had on grass skirts, leather thongs and carried spears. Their eyes and teeth gleamed pure white and alive, like streaks of lightning in a dark, stormy night. They were off for a dance, our policeman said. As we neared Bomba, he became more and more animated and excited because he was returning home, pointing out plantations of coffee and palm oil with pride. These were Zairese industry, working for a better future, so the slogan said.

81

5

Bomba

In Bomba I parted from Carsten and Nils. They went on their hurrying way through Zaire to Uganda and beyond. We made a rendezvous to meet in Kampala, but I knew I would not catch up with them and so would probably never see them again.

Bomba, like Lisala, is an old Portuguese town, but here the Portuguese remain so the town and port are alive. There were two families of them living in modest houses on the river front near the port, remnants of the seafarers who had been trading with Zaire for many centuries. They owned a big sugar cane factory that employed most of the town. Bomba was small, one street of houses and a hotel, kept smart and clean, functional but also peaceful, surrounded by a suburb of villages.

There was a lovely new boat in port, preening itself on three decks of steel, fresh white and green; its older, sadder cousins moored alongside blushed rustily. It was only a small boat, just an engine and quarters, though it had barges strapped all about it.

The captain was a Belgian with a handsome face and beautifully pressed white trousers, no doubt done by the careful and loving hand of his wife, who was also there. The whole of the top deck and half of the second formed their home; I saw air conditioners on the top deck and a clean and sparkling chef's hat popping in and out of port-holed doors. The captain loved his job. He was all about the boat giving orders and talking to his crew, keeping an eye on a gang of labourers loading coffee into one of the barges. Ancient,

rickety trucks piled high with sacks, vehicles escaped from a museum, pulled up to the bank that ran down to a gangplank going across to the barge. Each man took a sack on to his head, and, singing and shouting, muscles bulging and straining like tempered steel, ran down the bank, across the gangplank with a bounding step, and dumped the 60-kilo load with a thump into the hold. At the end of the day they would be paid 50 zaires per sack or a choice of some new clothes the captain had brought from Kinshasa. They then stripped off and, like happy boys, splashed around in the river, washing the day of toil away. All the real small boys were occupied meanwhile, as always, fishing. They stood on the bank or on half-sunken boats or down in the reeds with their rods, in gaggles or alone, using skewered grasshoppers as bait. When they felt a touch from the finger-sized fish, they whisked the line out of the water, hoping with their speed and skill to foul the fish on the hook which was far too big for its mouth to take.

I wanted to take the passenger river boat upstream to a town called Kisangani, about 400 kilometres away. It was not due for about seven, maybe eight, days so I went to find a hotel. On the outskirts of the town, near the market, I found two long low buildings facing each other across an alleyway. At one end of the alleyway was a well and a thatch screen to wash behind. This was the local hotel. Everybody sat outside their rooms on the skinny verandahs, opposite each other. There were charcoal fires and washing lines in between, and women pounding

83

grain. I was led to my place, outside my spartan little room. The men came and talked with me and invited me to their rooms as to a club. The women thought me funny, all on my own. One of them, a bossy girl called Maria with a coy smile, latched herself on to me. She did all the things for me that a man should not do: cleaned my room, washed my clothes and cooked me some meals. Whenever I did these things I was looked at in an odd way, and the children came and stared and made me feel a fool.

'Come and sit down,' Maria would say. 'This is not a man's work. You need a woman to look after you.'

At night we sat in the homely way, lit with the steady glow of charcoal fires, not doing much, maybe having a beer, until quite late. There were murmurs and laughs and young men came and sat with me and asked me many questions, trying to work out why I was here and what the point in it was. Pleasure was never enough: you did not come to Bomba for pleasure when you could go to Kinshasa, or even stay in the West. They would tell me about their hopes, always to get away, to study, to learn English and go to Kinshasa. They thought education very important; everything they did was geared towards that. They wanted to be part of the more modern life. Only old men wanted to stay the same.

The Bombans were very jolly people. They dressed in flamboyant colours, could take a drink or two, and did, in the town's many bars – long seedy halls, walls decorated with naïve art, or thatched huts with tables and chairs outside. The bars played loud music, the lively, swinging tones of the famous Zairese bands. It was the sort of music that compelled you to get up and dance. Indeed everybody loved to dance and did, with elegance and poise, men and women together, hands clasped behind the other's back, moving in slow, shifting steps, hips swinging with perfect time. Everybody danced. It was deep within their bones. Even people walking along the street about some ordinary job, with a bundle on their head, would automatically change step when they passed a music bar, and dance as they went. Children, women, old men, all the same. Even nowhere near a bar, still they would sometimes walk, a-flippity-flop, arms swinging to the natural beat somewhere inside.

But mainly the bars were for drinking beer, a loved and serious ritual. Men, with their weekly money or money made as officials on the side, would set themselves up for the day as early as eight or nine o'clock in the morning. A table covered with open bottles of beer: the challenge, the prestige, with all those bottles being seen.

'Come here, my friend, come and take a beer and we shall talk about the important things in life.'

'Ah, you girl, come here. Sit down. Not too close to my friend, he you cannot trust. Come and sit here, close to me and I'll look after you.'

They become bigger and bigger as the day goes on. Everybody is their friend, by order. Later they slouch lower in their chairs, faces glowing with perspiration, eyes becoming bloodshot and blurred.

'Come 'ere, where'sh tha' girl? My friend musht 'ave taken her . . . the simple life, your village, your woman, thash all you need. None of these damn cities full of damn thieves. No. No! Don't take the bottles, leave 'em all there.'

Eventually they stagger away, supported by their chosen girl.

Beer was expensive in Zaire and the people were mostly poor, but it was consumed in large quantities everywhere. A labourer's money would pay for a bottle a day but they would spend a week or two's wages at a time. It was their luxury and their pleasure. Other things would look after themselves. Their families were quite self-sufficient. They gave them some money, if they had any left, but mainly the wives made the extra in the markets, selling this and that. But the men who were like this were 'bad' men, Maurice would say. Maurice was not the same.

Maurice had a house near the hotel. He used to come and talk to me: he was trying to learn English. After a couple of days I was invited to stay with him, so we packed my bag and carried it round the corner. His house was a little bungalow of mud with windows and doors carved out and a tin roof. He had

85

made it very nice and respectable inside. There were three rooms, made by a low wall and hanging sheets, and mats on the floor. A table stood in the centre with ashtrays and a pretty cloth, chairs placed about. A long bureau against the wall bore his prized possessions, books and pieces of crockery and his old, tatty radio. On the walls were posters, advertisements from magazines, a football team photo and his collection of pinned-up moths. Maurice's best treasure, though, was his wife, a small, shy girl, delightful and charming, called Teresa, who knew how to work hard and keep a house. She loved him very much. They had no children but always there was a collection of small and medium-sized things in and out of the house, cousins, nephews, whatever, who lived in the same front yard that ran onto the street. Their house adjoined another, and another on to that. On the other side of the yard in a block were many tiny rooms in which a selection of women lived. They had babies and children, but not often a husband. Maurice was the man about the yard.

Maurice was young, wore spectacles and flowery shirts, and was of a very solid build. He came from Kisangani. Set up in business there, he had come to Bomba to buy some fish to ship back home and sell for a profit. Unfortunately, before the purchase had taken place he had run out of money, so he had found himself a wife and moved into her relations' house near the market. Now he was wheeling and dealing in a small, local way, trying to make enough capital to further his business aims. He was having some difficulty, though; mainly, I think, because Maurice never worked at anything *too* hard. And money just seemed to slip through his fingers because he liked to buy nice things for himself and his wife. Meanwhile he was learning English, and with that he had another venture up his sleeve.

'Yes, I shall learn English,' he told me, 'and then I shall be in a much better situation to do business. Many people now speak English in Zaire. It's a proper language in which to conduct trade, don't you think?'

'But surely Swahili or French are widely spoken? Aren't they good languages with which to conduct trade?' I asked.

'Oh yes, they're OK. But English is the most international language in the world. You know, you can make a great impression if you speak English. Everybody of importance speaks English.'

'What sort of business will you do?'

'Ah, what sort of business shall I do? I'm not quite sure just yet, but there are many opportunities if you keep your eyes open. There are many ways of making money but the best thing to do is not to rush into anything too hastily. No, it's best to wait, stay at home with your family, and watch carefully for any really good opportunities that might come by, and then suddenly pounce and snap them up when you're sure. Then you can take your competition by surprise. That's the way to do business. To wait and watch, not go rushing around chasing dead ends.'

I settled down very comfortably with Maurice and his wife. I slept in one room, they in the other, and we sat around in the third. Teresa dried and pounded manioc all day in between her chores and sold quite a lot, charcoal too. Her profits provided them with their one meal a day in the evening. Normally this was manioc, made into a pat, like dough, and eaten with the manioc leaves ground into a rich, sticky sauce, a bit like spinach. It was very good, especially when you were hungry. Sometimes they would add some strong-tasting dried fish. They looked after me like a king. Maurice, I think, enjoyed making a great fuss to see that I was all right. Every evening Teresa would set out our dinner on the table with spoons, napkins and the hurricane lamp. We ate in silence as she busied herself outside and ate her meal with the children in the yard. If I had not been there I'm sure they would have eaten together, but not with such decorum as was afforded to me. There was always so much for her to do: drawing water, preparing food, washing and generally trying to keep house on only a small amount. She would heat some water in the cooking pot after the meal so that Maurice and I could have a hot wash. The radio was played continuously, very loud and screeching like a child, a terrible sound.

Behind the house Maurice was digging a new toilet, or water

closet as he called it, quoting the text book from which he learnt his English, dated from colonial times. At this he worked very hard, digging a pit, perfectly straight, about four metres deep. Around it he built a solid hut of wood and thatch. He was a good craftsman and rightly proud of this piece of work. There was electric power in parts of Bomba and Maurice, with a complexity of wires, had managed to hitch himself on to it. The wires hung over trees and posts, coming from some indefinable place leading to a strip light he had hung in the tree outside the bungalow. Every evening there would be a protracted effort to get the thing to work, accomplished with seriousness and concentration until it sprang into life. Then Maurice would stand back and admire his handiwork. The light was the only one in the stret, so it drew a lot of prestige. Unfortunately, being the only one, it also drew every moth, fly or insect in the neighbourhood. They buzzed around it in a huge, solid cloud. As we sat outside on chairs placed purposefully beneath the light, the insects would crawl down our backs, catch in our hair and get stuck in our eyes. The evening would become a trial of endurance, a continuous battle, rather marring our sundown peace. But for Maurice it was worth it, even though the light itself was a blinding white. He suffered all with determined pride and became a man well known and respected.

'What a lovely evening,' he would say, as we sat there, waving a squadron of midges from our eyes. 'It's considerably cooler tonight. Will you have a beer?'

'Yes, I'd love one, thank you.' Slap, slap.

'I'm afraid the beer here is not as cheap as it is in Kisangani, it has to be transported so far.' Scratch, scratch, wave. 'But it's excellent all the ... Quick, quick! Look at that one, it's a beauty,' he'd suddenly let out, and launch himself into the overhead aerial battle to snatch a vast moth from its midst and squeeze it dead between his fingers.

'I've been looking for this one for months. I used to have one like it in my collection but my wife knocked it into a cooking pot by mistake. And this one is much more beautiful than the last.' Slap, slap, wave.

As their house was by the market, friends and relations would drop in all the time, coming to sit with us and the insects. At first they would be very formal, greeting me, '*Mbote, sangonini – sangote,*' and making polite remarks. But once the rituals were over they would ask me all their questions and tell me of their lives.

Maurice would introduce one of these people thus: 'Peter, this is the uncle of my wife's sister's second husband; her sister's first husband died of a broken heart because she fell in love with the second. He is a very good man who is married to a woman with only one leg. But still they have made many babies. You see the big scar on his arm? He got that fishing. He is a good fisherman but very lazy.'

And the object of our discussion would grin broadly and then tell me the long tale of how he had caught the biggest fish ever seen in Bomba, and how, after many hours, he had landed it – but it had bitten him and jumped out of the boat and got away.

Most of the people in Bomba, like Maurice, were very poor. They had just enough money to feed themselves, and that was about all; the children were often malnourished, with big distended bellies. They had land about them that was green and fertile but they did not work at it with much energy. With their mud huts, their few possessions collected over a lifetime and their large, extended families, they felt no need or enthusiasm to push too hard for more. The basics they could always have with a little extra work. There was no famine here and their families could help them in need. Their lives remained comparatively simple, so their happiness came from simple things, little extra luxuries. To them an occasional piece of meat, a packet of American cigarettes or a pretty printed dress were worth a lot, could fill them with warmth and pride. But seriously ambitious they really were not. Fun and happiness mattered, pride and decency of life. So they worked for what was necessary, but did not let work get in the way of the other, more important things. Of problems there were many. Any man I spoke to had something that to him was bad. Maybe he owed some tax and had been threatened with jail, or his brother needed an operation for which he could not pay, or students needed books that were too expensive, before they could rise to the next grade. These were things talked about, but also things that could quickly be put to the back of the mind.

6

An Excursion in a Pirogue

I wanted to take a pirogue on the Zaire river for a few days. I tried asking some of the fishermen on the banks if they could take me, and the answers were always vague, so I asked Maurice if he knew of anyone who could help.

'Of course,' he said. 'That will be simple.'

But of course it was not. The only men with boats were the fishermen, and they needed to fish, not go gallivanting. Quite apart from that, they did not like the idea of taking their boats far from home. Paddling about the Zaire is no easy jaunt; it is very hard work because of the fierce currents. This was one problem, but not the main one. Somewhere along the line the local witch doctor had decided to play his part. As the sign outside his house proclaimed, he was called 'Monsieur Devereaux, Docteur en Médecine Traditionnelle. Dev, as he was commonly known, was a smallish man with a bright, mischievous face. He spoke French well and was a bit of a rogue, but an engaging one.

He appeared one day in Maurice's house with his leopard-skin and rattles with which he warded off passing evil and without which he wouldn't venture forth. He was not a complete charlatan, though: he came from a family of witch doctors and he knew his lore. He knew about herbs and potions, brews and beetles, but he also knew about men's minds. He could convince simple folk that they would be cured, and equally he could convince them that they would not. Their belief was so strong that either dictum could have an effect. But mainly, of course, he used his trade to very profitable ends.

Dev now saw an opportunity to visit some villages by boat that were normally outside his sphere. With me in tow, a European, to add to his prestige and power, he could spook up some new customers. At first I did not realize his game, but Maurice, I think, knew from the first. He did not trust the man but could do nothing at all: one did not mess about with a witch doctor, so we spent two days making the 'programme', as it was called. Contracts were drawn up and signed amid intrigue and complications. We sat in Maurice's parlour and discussed the thing. Different people were brought in to debate and give opinions. We examined, questioned and made conditions.

Maurice would say to me, aside: 'Peter, Peter, you cannot go with this man on the river. You don't know him, how can you trust him? You know, out there, there is nobody but the natives. People might capture you, take your money and throw you in the river. Oh, no, no, no. I must come with you to protect you. How can I, who am responsible for you – because you know if anything happens to you the police will put me in jail for a very long time – how can I sit here and let you go in the hands of this witch doctor who everybody knows is a bad man?'

Maurice was terrified of the river and the bush. It took me a long time to persuade him that I was not going to certain death and that he really did not need to accompany me. A relay of fishermen were brought in and I would ask them their price.

'Fifty dollars,' they would say shortly.

'No, no, five dollars I will pay,' and we would bargain and eventually agree.

But each time Maurice would suddenly jump up again and dismiss the man saying, 'He can't take you, no, no. He is a thief and a fool.'

And so we would start again. The programme was forever changing but to them the result was not so important. It was the talk that mattered, and eventually we all became tired of it and so were set to go.

The morning of departure dawned but the good doctor did not appear. We went to his house and found him deep in ritual, surrounded in his dark, mysterious room by the many weird, and dead, artefacts of his trade: snakeskins, the ashes of a burnt frog, the dried stomach of an okapi, a rare antelope, seeds and sticks, bones and evil-smelling potions. He said he was preparing something for our protection on the journey. Eventually we set off: Dev, a fisherman, a small man who was a relation of Maurice, sent as his representative, and myself. The fisherman was a good man, steadfast as a rock, who eyed Dev with deep suspicion. We walked far out of town until we came to someone's house, where bottles of beer and maize spirit were produced and drunk. Time passed and there seemed a general reluctance to leave. Eventually I persuaded the party to move on. The boat was long and heavy, only leaking here and there. We paddled off, powered mainly by the fisherman in the stern. Dev sat in the middle, looking unsafe and unsure of the river. He clasped his leopard-skin and chanted Christian hymns, odd, I thought, for a witch doctor who proclaimed himself a Muslim. When I asked him about this mixture he told me he found the blend very satisfactory to his well-being of mind.

The Zaire is immensely wide. It takes a long time to paddle across, the shores are distant things. And then, when you do reach the 'other side', you discover the land is just a set of islands. They are thick with jungle, these islands, their water's edge flounced with floating plants of green, glossy leaves; here and there beautiful river flowers bloom and bees buzz in and out. Rounding one of them, strong water swirls and slashes at the boat as it is caught by a current and swept into a lagoon of secluded river that stretches away like a lake to the thin strip of green hemming in this peaceful place, dividing with a stroke the sky from the broken reflection of blue and black and rippling white cloud. The boat slides through, dividing the oily surface. Silence hangs intense, disturbed only by the rhythmic strokes of the straining paddle; twisting, it flips out, scattering sun-filled droplets in an arc.

On one of these islands somewhere in the maze, a small area

had been cleared for a one-family village. The big wood and thatched house stood high on stilts near the bank. From the boat, as we approached, it looked like a perfect and idyllic set with a curtain of luxurious green behind, a drape of opaque blue hanging overhead, all faithfully mirrored upside down in the still water. We pulled up at the bank where two other boats were moored, shattering the reflection. A small family wearing tatty modern clothes greeted us shyly and sat us down by a smouldering fire that sent a trickle of smoke, like a crack, into the sky. They gave us some food and stood aside, as though we had a perfect right to intrude upon their home. They were very quiet and diffident, these people. Maybe a witch doctor and a white man were too much for them. But they soon livened up when they saw my camera, rushing indoors to fetch a home-made tin guitar and a radio. They combed their hair and put on flowery shirts and sat in a family group, in a charming pose, holding their babies and the guitar, on the steps up to their home. When we left they waved for a long time from the bank.

The next island village we stopped at was much larger. Most of the land was cleared with only a few big trees and banks of bush left. There were maybe a hundred people, all of the same family clan, as noisy when we arrived as if they were holding a regatta. Dev set to work on them at once. I watched while they came and told him their problems and he gave them his address, telling them that they must visit soon. Many of them in fact lived in Bomba, but came back here to their village when the fishing was right. Dev picked amongst the fish lying on the bank, selecting the biggest and the best, saying he would like them as payment in advance. I was brought a bunch of bananas and led off to be shown around. Many of the houses were on stilts, in anticipation of the seasonal flood. I met the elders and watched the women at work; they were all jolly and not shy at all. They smiled at me a lot. At one end of the village there was an ingenious house, a large framework of many rectangular boxes, places to sleep, each one completely curtained off with sheets and sacks. There were six levels of them. The mosquitoes here were terrible for those used to a town life, so this dormitory was where they slept.

A sudden storm came across the sky while we were there, sweeping away the blue like a wave. It started to pour very hard and everyone rushed into the church, a building without walls but with a thatch on top. We sat on pews that were single poles going across. The rain was fresh and cool, exploding little puffs of dusty earth; smells of vegetation became vivid and exhilarating, the thatch a musty scent. The river hissed and bubbled like a stewing pot. Trickles came through the thatch, puddles formed, and we all shifted round to end up in the one dry spot. The storm passed as quickly as it came, lumbering its way to the outer edge of the sky. The eaves and leaves twinkled with the last fat drops and the air was light and new once again. Children splashed in the puddles and the women continued their work. All the men gathered together to see us on our way. The doctor took a few more souls and I another bunch of bananas.

The paddle back to Bomba was long and very hard; we were by now quite far downstream. Still, the only man who did any paddling of worth was the fisherman. The doctor and I were not asked to help and Maurice's representative tried hard but was too weak. The fisherman stroked the water with concentration and without a break. Sometimes we barely seemed to move; we were nothing in the river's grasp, a piece of straw, a bit of wood. With all his strength the fisherman worked in silence for about three hours until we made Bomba, and he could paddle home alone. The veins stood out on his temples, he could barely talk, but, like a machine, he could go on. I thought perhaps we would not see him again, but sure enough next morning there he was, ready to do it again.

This time Dev did not come, so we were freed from his presence and weight. The fisherman, Maurice's representative and myself went to a small forest market about two hours away somewhere on the opposite bank. On the way we stopped at an island 'belonging' to an old man and his wife. They had the same thatched house on stilts in a clearing of bush as I had seen before, but all around their house was a lagoon of shallow water planted with rice which swayed with the waves we made with our arrival, and so the house seemed curiously unanchored. The man was very small and so was his wife. He had thick eyebrows and a flat, healthy-looking face and his body, naked to the waist, was like a knot of rope, sinuous and strong. He looked much more natural, more part of his environment, than the people of the day before. He was a nomadic fisherman who lived and moved where the fish did, depending on the time of year and the rains. He showed me his nets and a huge fish he had just caught. He would be taking this one to Bomba, where he could get a good price and so be able to buy some maize or manioc. He did not unbend much in his manner but all the same was very polite. When we left they stood looking after us, expressionless.

The forest market consisted of a few thatch lean-tos and an open-walled house. One stall was selling modern items, mirrors, cast-off clothes and many bottles of what looked like vitamin pills but were unmarked. Women sold maize and manioc, and there was a large selection of dead animals, especially monkeys of all shapes and sizes, burnt, fresh or dried, that had been trapped or maybe exchanged with the pygmies for some maize. The dried-up ones were a pitiful sight, small blackened things curled up on the ground like babies asleep. There was an okapi doe as well that looked long dead, the coat crawling with maggots. A big black-and-white Barbary monkey was chucked on a roaring fire to loosen and take off its coat. When I squatted down to photograph this, all the women and children round about quickly rushed in front of the camera, completely blocking out the fire. It was a wonderful, spontaneous pose, the women holding their babies high. They all had such vivid faces, maple syrup brown and smooth, and their babies were healthy, squirming bundles, rosy and whole.

In the afternoon all the men collected under a thatch and started the serious business of drinking bottles of maize spirit. It was a very clean and clear spirit, and very strong, passed round with speed. Soon we were all very happy. They were local fishermen, these people, full of fun and contentment. They wore rags and no shoes, their hands were heavily calloused, they had seen little and knew only about their own

lives, but we were equals. They made me photograph them
and laughed at those who were scared.

'Come on, you old fool. What do you think he's going to do
with that little box, capture you inside?'

The paddle back was a merry one. All the fishermen from
the market tumbled into the pirogues parked by the bank and
came with us, singing all together and jumping from boat to
boat. They swayed from side to side alarmingly, but drunk or
not were as sure as if they had been on land. We raced into the
sunset that spilt across the water, and strove against the
current, hugging the overgrown banks on the long haul home
where there would be another market tomorrow and they
would sell their week's catch, and celebrate once again.

7

The River Boat

That night the river boat, the *Onatra*, arrived on its way from Kinshasa to Kisangani, a journey of about 1500 kilometres. In the morning Maurice and his family and friends took me down to the port to buy my ticket and see me on my way. There was a continuous stream of people with bags and boxes between the town and the *Onatra*; everybody seemed to be leaving. When we arrived, at first I could hardly make it out from the pier and sunken barges and the mess of other boats. Then I realized that it *was* the mess of other boats. They were all strapped together with a modern-looking engine boat towering above the rest, a complex of white steel streaked with rivulets of rust. The whole conglomeration already seethed with movement and noise.

Down near the gangplank, which was just being put in place, a frantic, pressing crowd waited to get on. Soldiers with automatics tried to keep them back. They had everything imaginable with them, this crowd: animals, bleating and crying, bedsteads, buckets and bundles of wares. When the gangplank was at last ready there was a mad rush and crush. People poured and spilled, over the railings, up and under the stairs. They were caught in bottlenecks and trodden on, things were lost. They fought to get free, like wild animals. I, too, had to find a place in one of the third-class cabins. Caught up in the crowd, I was squashed in a serious way and suddenly I was fighting too in order to breathe again. Maurice and his wife came on board more leisurely, saw me securely settled, as we thought, and said goodbye.

The *Onatra* was long in going. The sun reached its zenith and began to sink. I was congratulating myself as on some considerable feat when a man appeared in the cabin doorway. It seemed things were not so simple. He took me off the boat and walked me silently to the other side of town, where I was ushered into a room to confront his boss, a big fat policeman sitting behind a large, cluttered desk. Of course, he explained genially, I had done everything wrong. I did not have the correct stamps in my passport. I wandered around as if I was a mercenary or a spy. Perhaps I had guns in my bag? Generally I was a nuisance and behaved in a disrespectful way. I had to be investigated. But he did not really mean it. He only wanted a bribe, and this time, I may say, he did not get one.

I made it back to the *Onatra* again, just in time; it tooted and hooted and slowly pulled away with people still trying to get on and off: as the gap gradually widened they leapt and caught hold of their friends. At the last moment, when the gap seemed too wide, a man with two goats appeared, pushing himself through the waving, cheering crowd. He was determined to give it a try. The unfortunate goats, held by a rope around their necks, had their terrible bleat suddenly cut short as they were swung across the gap and were caught by willing arms on board. With the crowd shouting encouragement, the man took a great run and leapt, grabbed the railings and was hoisted over by eager hands. We were on our way. The quay, with its icing of colourful swaying bodies, slowly shrank and became part of the town, the town part of the bank, and the bank, eventually, an unbroken green line. There was only the river and the boat.

I say this was a boat but mainly it was a market, its wares bringing whispers of Kinshasa, that much-talked-about, distant capital. During the five-day journey I gradually made a round tour, starting at the very back of the last boat, the engine boat of white, rusty steel, sitting in the one and only *cabine de luxe*. This engine boat was the main boat and the only place with a veneer of calm and cleanliness. The cabin belonged to an Englishman, a writer, with his wife and his pipe, and an American girl as well. The 'cabine' was not very 'de luxe',

99

though it did have a half-hearted air conditioner. We'd sit there and discuss and I'd share their waiter-served meal.

'What, meatballs again?' they would exclaim. 'We've had the same every day, for a month on end. What happens to the fish the fishermen bring on board?'

The waiter was a bit grumpy – what could he do? – so they placated him with, 'But it's always very good, anyway.'

Strolling out of their double doors on to the verandah at the very back of the boat, I had a wonderful view of the slowly receding river, streaked with our frothing propeller lines. In the evening the sun set directly over the water. It was always spectacular – this extravaganza of changing sets, staged at the end of each day. How many photographs of sunsets did I now have? Villages passed as though on a screen. Sometimes there were very straggly ones, a kilometre or so in length, basking on their brown banks like crocodiles. It seemed to me that the river folk were not too badly off. They had fish from the river, monkeys and birds from the forest, small crops of maize and manioc grown with ease, and abundant fruit. That was not too bad.

Making myself at home in one spot, then another, I toured the smart second floor, rounding the verandah on to the wide, first-class promenade. The passengers here, all Africans with a little wealth, pulled out their chairs on to the wooden slatted deck, listening to loud Zairese music on modern ghettoblasters. The women were sumptuous in many-patterned dresses. They sat on stools, but somehow looked a bit forlorn. There was nothing for them to do.

Leaning over the railings here, I could see many pirogues tied on, being pulled along at the boat's side. They belonged to the local fishermen who paddled out to us to exchange fish with goods from the market. Watching the performance of them trying to dock while we were still on the move was a pastime which entertained all. It was a very tricky process of waiting upstream and then paddling frantically in to catch at the boat's fleeting side. There would be mad scramblings and shouts, cheers and yells from the watching tiers of faces. Pirogues would sink, people would be fished out, confusion, ropes dropped or let go, and boats that failed drifting off behind, their occupants, men and women with babies spaced between the racks of fish, standing up hands on hips with sad, blank faces that quickly shrank to blobs. They would have to wait for the return journey. It was an opportunity missed.

Having watched this performance for a while, I'd wander to the end of the first-class deck to see my friend the crocodile. He was only a young one, about a metre long. Day in, day out, he lay in the gutter in the corner, a rejected, dejected thing. He never moved. The only sign of life was the slight contraction of his skin as he breathed, and a wicked gleam in his eye. Scurrying nearby was another croc, but this one was really a baby, scarcely a hand's length. One day he disappeared and I wondered whose shower he might be in.

The first deck, below, housed the engine and the crew's quarters, with their families camped all about. The noise was deafening. Torrents of water gushed perpetually from pipes and holes in the walls and on the decks. This facility, though, was greatly appreciated by the women as ideal for washing their children, clothes, pots and pans. I had to walk very carefully, not to slip up on oil or soapsuds, or trip over a baby left out to dry.

Alongside this smart engine boat was a terrible old barge, seemingly held together by rust, some families living round a big fire on its bare top. One day this barge disappeared, I knew not where, and another river steamer came to join the *Onatra* litter. There happened to be some pirogues tied up when it arrived and those that could not be cut loose in time before it docked were crushed. The lucky owners of those cut loose had to jump in the river to swim after their boats and were left far behind. Our new addition did not stay long. He was only refuelling.

I moved down to the front of the flat-nosed engine boat; this was where real life started, behind a curtain of water falling down from showers somewhere above. I dodged my way through and up some steps into the next big boat tied in front. This was the main passenger boat, a third-class ghetto block of unremitting dank steel, mazes of smelly corridors and tiny tin

101

cabins. Everything was dirty with the grime of years. Every inch was occupied. Faces lined the ways and crowded the cabins. The lower decks, below the water line, were mysterious, dark places. There were sweaty little bars full of drinkers and beer crates, storerooms, other rooms unknown, and string-vested people. I'd climb down the lethally steep stairs and ask for a bottle of beer.

'That'll be one zaire fifty, and two for the bottle, please. Bring the bottle back and I shall give you the two back.'

'No, no. Don't let him buy it,' a drunk on a crate would cry. 'Come here and I shall buy you a bottle and you can be my friend.'

I managed to escape, taking my bottle with me, up again on to the first deck, easing my way through passages stuffed with stalls. Beautifully woven baskets, blankets and beads, little boxes of incense, posters and t-shirts – the stall-keepers always had them laid out attractively in the cramped space. Their cabins behind them bulged with the dried fish they took in payment from the fishermen.

Up some more stairs, I'd find myself by the kitchens, glorious, Gothic places of steam and shouts, murk and mould, dark dingy corners and huge bubbling pots on coal fires stirred by powerful mammas with wooden spoons, presiding here like queens. Once a day at four o'clock a gong announced that dinner was up. Then everybody would rush there with plates, pots and bowls, crowding the doorway in an impenetrable mass. The regal mammas would dole out huge quantities of beans, meat and rice, there was never a shortage and never any change of menu. The rice was nicely laced with weevils, the beans were very good, but the meat, which was monkey, was too strong for me.

Opposite these fiery but friendly caverns, on the corner of the gangway running down the side of the boat, I had my cabin, a small steel box with one small porthole. There were two bunk beds in it and many bananas, pineapples and pots. When I climbed into my bunk, the top one, the whole contraption would sag, leaning far out from the wall. I slept soundly, though. I shared the room with a small religious man, his very large wife, his sister-in-law and her baby. On the skinny gangway outside were long wooden benches where I sat down to drink my beer, watching the sky and the unchanging, faceless forest stooping to drink from the river, or at least what I could see of them through the multi-coloured clothes hung up on the railings to dry. The whole boat looked like a washing line. People would throng up and down the gangway, squeezing past my knees, and stop off for a chat.

'How do you like our boat, mister? Is it not very good? Tell me why you are here, where are you going? Ah, a tourist, that is a very good thing.'

One boy, the boat boy, was my friend. 'I come from the Congo, ye-es. There life is very good. The markets are full of white women. I follow them around because I am very trustful, you know. I can help them out . . . Ah, this boat. This is my home. I know *everyone* here. Got any problem, come and ask for me. I know the captain very well. The boat is my home, yes. My mother, my father, my friend. Look at this boy here, come here, my friend. No one likes him because he is a thief, but I understand him well. Hey! Don't do that, stop you rascal!' and they would disappear round the bend, chasing and laughing happily, knocking people out of the way.

Older men, officials changing posts, would want to know all about me, asking questions in a condescending way because they were wary of me. But they were only trying to be nice and would soon become more friendly. We'd all hang over the side to watch the pirogues come in. Once I spotted a very small one trailing after the rest; in it was a solitary and very small boy. He paddled towards us. The bow wave nearly sank him, but he paddled on, defiant, dwarfed by our passing hulk. He so wanted to be a man and come on board. The crowd cheered him on. '*Courage, petit, courage,*' a man called from nearby. But it was too much; in his efforts the child dropped his oar, and had to give up, defeated for this time.

Sometimes we'd pass a village from which many small boys swam out as we approached. They'd swim almost directly in our line and then, to my surprise, these little fishy beings, whilst being washed alongside, would grab on to the tethered pirogues and scramble on board. Quickly they'd rush through the boat, on to the roof at the front, and jump with waving arms over the side, disappearing under the passing waters and appearing again as though they were made of cork. Again they'd catch on to the pirogues and repeat the performance. They did not swim as land people do, but in a unique, confident way, flopping and flapping, almost crawling across the river's surface as if there was some solidity there with which to propel themselves. When we were too far from their homes they'd wave us goodbye and swim off. On the boat the passengers had a name for them: 'the little ones with no fear'.

As well as the daily meal laid on by the mammas, most people on the boat had some of their own food, and in the passageways on this second floor they sat outside their cabins, cooking on charcoal fires, lowering buckets over the side on strings when they needed water. At the end of this deck were many small, rusty cubicles with a toilet and shower. It seemed a special feature of the *Onatra* that the showers were permanently running, so if you needed to relieve yourself, you had to have a shower as well.

At the side of this passenger boat was another ghetto block as tall and as wide, of burnt red steel. In between the two was a chasm to the river trapped far below and all the debris of a thousand people was deposited there. On the railings a small monkey was chained. He'd watch his brethren being eaten in the kitchens nearby, but he was safe as he was someone's pet. I climbed over the railings and jumped across the chasm to the other boat, arriving in a bar of trestle tables all tightly pressed together, packed round with people and bottles of beer. Very loud music played here almost all day and night.

'Hey, you, Mr White Man,' someone would call to me. 'What are you doing here? Only one white man all on his own with all us black men, ha, ha! Come, come and join us. Come and dance with this beautiful girl. Have a beer and talk to us.' And they'd laugh and joke and squeeze over, making a place for me on the bench.

On the first deck below there was no class. The cabins were filled with beer at one end and livestock at the other; unhappy goats and pigs whose grunting and squealing competed with the din above. A rich, farmy smell pervaded far and wide. In the middle of this deck was a large open area where women lived among a sprawl of fish stalls. This was the stock exchange. But, rather than go down there, I climbed the railings again, upwards, on to the roof which was in fact the highest point in the mêlée of boats, sloping down gently at the sides. There were only one or two other people up here. It was a quiet spot, away from the commotion and the crowds. Moving carefully to the front I could watch the river and its life coming towards me. It passed very slowly. Other river boats passed occasionally, pushing a string of barges. They were long and very low, these river trains, seeming barely to move when going upsteam, and when they turned they became powerless, swivelling fast in the river's grip. They looked small and insignificant in the vast reaches of river and sky.

Once or twice a day we stopped for an hour or two at a small town. The shore was always lined with a colourful crowd of waiting people. But they didn't wait long. As we drew near, an armada of pirogues came out to greet us and we were invaded by the town. The pirogues were piled with high-smelling fish. A dance of brown arms stretched out from the lower decks to take them by the gills and notes of money fluttered down to be collected like leaves by the fisher people. Looking down from the roof, our boat seemed to be beseiged by a muddle of twisting forms boarding from every angle, spouting fruit, fish and all. The railings became a ladder as people stepped over the washing women on to the decks, wet and oily. There were arguments and shouts, laughs and smells that wafted upwards. It was good to see it from up here, not to be caught below. When we pulled away again it was like tearing one thing in two: the boat was sewn to the shore with a tapestry of angled forms. Some were left on the wrong side, so pirogues came and gave us back our own, and bodies jumped overboard.

We left the broken piers and the old, blackened factories of the town behind. I could not stay on the roof for long, though; the sun made the metal too hot, so I left it to the piteous, drying monkeys, blackened and obscene, like mummified foetuses, all strapped up in a line, and made my way down to the last boat of all, a barge tied to the front. Green and white tarpaulins covered it, tied at every angle with poles and ropes. Puddles sat in the dips; odd corners, brown and frayed, flapped in the wind. It looked like an Arab encampment. A smart red truck stuck out from somewhere in the middle, a proud thing adorned with the washing of all. Beneath the awnings the market continued. The stalls were woven together; there was no clear space. Piles of combs and sponges, shiny plastic shoes and little pots of paste and cream; modern clothes and expensive patterned pillows. Tea was brewed and iron pots of paste were stirred by strong-armed women. There were beds and rolls, secret corners and heaps of yellowing maize. Right up at the front was a high bank of stacked sacks and boxes, used to recline on. In front of this was squeezed a skinny pathway where there was nothing to be heard except the wash as it rolled off the flat-nosed front, and nothing to see but the river lying ahead. I'd sit there dangling my legs in the spray and debate how soon to make the trek back to that other quiet spot in the stern. People came to slaughter their chickens and goats here, where the water could be reached with ease. So pretty soon I'd set off again and plunge back into the whirl.

Most evenings the river boat became a very jolly place indeed, a carnival. The population seemed to double at least, as more and more fishermen came on board to exchange their fish. They only had a short time before they would be taken too far from home, so they bargained with energy and haste, and squeezed as much enjoyment into an hour or two as they could. Towers of fish-racks were balanced on heads, fish-racks hemmed in the stalls. There were large fish, a metre long, with ferocious teeth, razor chips in gaping mouths. There were crocodiles in the alleyways that looked half dead, and large turtles, which were very good to eat. People hawked pine-apples and pawpaws. One poor man sold peanuts in a basket. Overhead a network of wires was strung with light bulbs, white and red. There were record players at every corner and dancing and, of course, there was lots of beer being drunk down in the bars where 'loose' women were on display. As the evening wore on the piles of fish increased, the crowds got stuck in bottlenecks and I had to find another way through.

'One rack of fish? No, no, two for this shirt. It is of a special design. Do you want me to starve?'

'. . . and then she said to me, "What will my father say when he learns who you are?" '

'Now, why does he have to leave all his fish in my cabin? What does he think I am? Whenever I ask him he always says, "Oh, just for a short time," but it's been two weeks now.'

I had made a few friends with whom I might stop for a chat. My friend in the most congested gangway, sandwiched between two boats, sold shirts hung on the wall. Opposite was a disco bar, so he danced all the time, in and out of the people struggling to pass. He was always lively, and always there.

'Come and sit down on this box, Englishman. Look at all my fish. I have to work *so* hard, day and night,' he said with a grin on his face. 'Don't you feel sorry for me? All I have to do is dance.'

Further up the same corridor I had a nodding acquaintance among the heavy brigade. They were street people from the ghettos of Kinshasa and knew how to look after themselves. They played poker in the gangway, not letting anyone pass. They sold clothes and tapes and other things you might want besides.

'Hey, come here, man. You want to change some money? I can give you a good rate. No? Well, sit down anyway. You know I want to learn English. Do you have any books I can have? You come from London, yeah, well, tell me something about it. Is it really like they say? I should like to go and see Big Ben. That's right, isn't it? Big Ben's the name? Yeah.'

The evening party continued late into the night. It lulled me to sleep and woke me up again around five or six o'clock in the morning. By seven the boat would be truly astir as hundreds of people woke headlong into the day, washing themselves and their pots and pans. The gong would go for coffee and doughnuts in the kitchen and the new day was here.

Life went on like this for five days. On the fifth, one of the

107

boat's engines broke down, so we were reduced to a walking speed. Eventually, though, we arrived in Kisangani, a veritable metropolis in this part of Zaire, but really only a smallish and very quiet town. At the port I had another charming encounter with a customs official. We came to a friendly agreement. I would pay him some money – as a fine, of course – and he would kindly waive the law that, he pointed out, demanded he took all my money and sent it to the central bank, because of course my currency form was out of order, due to the official who liked rum so much on the border where I had come in.

I camped at a Greek hotel in Kisangani for another five days, waiting for an opportunity to continue on my way.

8

The Utari Rain Forest and Onwards to the East

The road from Kisangani to the eastern side of Zaire is about 600 kilometres long. It passes through the Utari rain forest, a region of classical primeval beauty inhabited by pygmies. It then rises up out of the low Zaire basin to meet the Ruwenzori mountains, the 'mountains of the moon' that level out to the great East African plateau. The road is the main road across the north of Zaire but it is in an appalling condition, often impassable. Many heavy trucks ply the route, transporting coffee, beer and other goods, but not many other vehicles make the attempt. The truck drivers' job is to get from one side to the other. Any problems along the way are just part of the journey. Sometimes it can take them a month, or two, but they never give up. Surprisingly, the trucks are not simple affairs; they have trailers and can weigh up to 25 tonnes like the one I found a place to travel in.

The owner and driver was Steve, a Greek who had been born in Zaire. He was transporting beer and we set off late one night after he had had a few last drinks. We trundled out of the silent town like a ship set to explore. All 22 wheels squeaked and scrunched over the last good roads, the brakes hissed and burped, and the cabin was filled with a terrible roar from the engine, which was built inside it and upon which I perched. Almost at once we were engulfed in darkness, the forest closing in on either side, and Steve's battle began. He had to fight his truck every inch of the way on completely broken roads. He smoked non-stop, and drove with the easy concentration and skill of a cowboy who knows his horse. For five nights and four days we drove, stopping only to sleep for an hour or two on the ground under the stars. We ate very little – small meals cooked on a gas stove and some bananas from a village. We did not care when problems occurred, we just went on. Sometimes the road was like a river bed, sometimes it was of soft mud with deep ditches either side, descending very steeply in one continuous slide into thickly jungled valleys. These valleys were terrible things. Once rolling, the truck picked up a tremendous speed: braking would only make us skid and jack-knife. At the bottom, shaky wooden bridges crossed streams. Sometimes we did slide, with 25 tonnes at our back, and sometimes we hit these bridges at a frightening speed. But Steve was a master at his trade. He played with his levers like a conductor, making fast judgements with his years of experience. He kept us in one piece and I soon grew to realize his skill when I saw the trucks that didn't make it. Some were on their sides; some were buried on the roadside; some were in ravines; and some were just decaying, mangled steel. On steeper hills as many as twenty trucks might be stuck, each one pulling the other, and all sliding into the deep ditches of soft mud at the side.

Sometimes when we stopped at villages the people would know Steve well. They would bring him a chair and he'd set himself up outside with a bottle of beer, if there was any to be had, and stretch out his long dusty legs. The village girls would flirt round him and he'd grab one by the waist and pull her onto his lap.

'Come here, my beauty,' he'd say, 'what's your name? How old are you? You look young. Where's that elder sister of yours, then?'

'I can give you a job, Peter, if you like,' he told me. 'It's not a bad life. Once a month you make this trip and you can live like a king. There are lots of benefits, too,' he added, pinching the girl's behind.

'I've lived all my life in Zaire. I've only been to Europe once. Zaire has treated me well. They're good people in Zaire. You'd like it here.'

It was an interesting ride. I found the long pontoons the most unnerving part. Built by the Belgians in the colonial period many years before, they were now decidedly rusty, cracked and old. They spanned wide rivers and 25 tonnes was a lot to hold. I sat in anticipation as we crossed, at an agonizingly slow speed, crawling less than a metre at a time. The whole structure groaned and shivered. I fixed my eyes on the patch of green at the other end. The river surged by below. Wooden planks flipped and split. We rumbled to the end, and I breathed anew. We had made it this time. Some day someone won't, and then they will build a new one.

Some say the Utari rain forest is the original 'Garden of Eden', the birthplace of mankind. A place of age-old magnificence and beauty, it impresses, awes, captivates, then strikes you deep down with a reverence for trees. Their girth is great and smooth, they rise, branchless, straight up like pillars of living, wooded steel, keeping the sky and earth apart. At the top they bear elegant crowns of full and fussy foliage touching tip to tip, eclipsing the land below. Somehow they have a power, a mystery. They are the lords of Mother Nature's earth. Below them, lesser trees and bushes strive in the dusky light for lives of their own. Here, I thought, would be monkeys, leopards, insects, and deer, stealthy and wary, playing in their great garden the survival game. Small glades of sunlight show where a tree has fallen. There are clear little streams and there is the road, solid and arrow-straight here, proudly defying the natural world. As we streamed along it, I would see people up ahead slip into paths at our approach to be swallowed up like magic in the forest, disappearing like wild and timid beings. When we passed there was no sign of where they had gone. It was as if they had not been at all.

There were no villages by the road in this, the primary forest, but later on they began to appear. They were of mixed peoples: some were the taller Bantus, wearing cast-off modern clothes, and some were smaller, stocky and strong, wearing rags of modern clothes or natural, grassy skirts. We stopped at Epulu for a while. This was a *station de capture* for animals and a sort of 'pygmy centre': in the forest nearby there lived many groups of them. I longed to visit them but felt the here and now were not quite right. There were one or two wandering about in the small roadside villages, selling arrows.

One morning shortly after Epulu we woke at dawn. In the night there had been a great thunderstorm; we had huddled and slept under the truck. The morning was a rare one, the sky was clear, the sun just appearing. Everything was wet from the rain and alive with sun-filled drops. Every leaf, every tree and bush, was delicate with a sheen of reflected light, fragile like frost. The air was nectar. You could almost see the oxygen oozing from the trees. The first low sunrays caught the straight trunks of bare bark, gleaming with dew, standing out of the dawn-grey forest, shining like shafts of divine light. The sky was a tapestry, a harmony of colours; starting red, to orange, yellow, fading to gem-blue. As we passed villages of steaming thatch, sleepy people emerged from doors and stood blinking, yawning and stretching, sucking in the sharp, effervescent air. They looked up, unmoved, at the apparition of a 25-tonne truck rumbling out of the milk of mist draped like a blanket, with the forest sticking through. We were happy in our truck, filled with a new vigour and enthusiasm by this crisp and solid forest of dew, and damp, breathing green, of trees high up, dying and being born again.

After three days we rose out of the grand forests to a higher altitude. The vegetation changed, became more open. The air was cooler, too, with the scent of a different place. We passed Mambasa, an administration centre with a street of solid, stone houses. There were patches of cultivated land and forests of smaller, spindly trees. Komanda was the end of the trip. We arrived, as we had left, in the middle of the night. The main road went south, Steve was driving north, and I looked for somewhere to sleep.

9

Pygmies

I slept peacefully for what remained of that night in an open rondaval in the middle of Komanda. In the morning I saw far off some peaks, or were they clouds? I was told that the Ruwenzori mountains were there, but that what I was seeing was a refraction of their image: from here they were too far to be seen in reality. The vision was impressed upon my mind.

Although I knew little about the pygmies, I had decided before I came to Zaire or even to Africa, that I very much wanted to meet them. I had been intrigued by this most ancient of African peoples who still live now in much the same way as did all the peoples of the earth at the dawn of mankind, as hunter-gatherers. They are the living fossils of our forefathers and even now they reject development and change in preference for their traditional lives. I wanted to meet a people who truly do this, and perhaps get a glimmer of insight into what it is about this ancient, natural people that they can so completely resist the trappings of the developed world where few others can.

Many of the pygmies of Zaire live in the Utari rain forest: others are scattered around the northern forests and tributaries of the Zaire river. Those who live near to the main roads, such as a group I had encountered near Bangui before crossing into Zaire, are frequently visited by the overland truckloads of tourists who, sadly, often travel across Africa as through a great game park. As a result the pygmies I had met near Bangui were not very forthcoming to Europeans and looked upon them as fools.

Here in the far east of Zaire, in the eaves of the great equatorial forests, there were some pygmies living near a mountain called Mount Hoyo. I was quite close and felt I now had the freedom and time to go to these pygmies without intruding too much. First, though, I must go to an old tourist lodge, about halfway between Komanda and Mount Hoyo, to use as a base.

I hitched a lift on a truck about fifteen kilometres down the Beni road, the road going due south. The driver dropped me at a junction where a rough track met the rough road; the lodge was another fifteen kilometres up the track. Not far along this I met a boy of about sixteen pushing an old bicycle and struggling to balance its load, a full beer crate and a bag of maize; the bike was bending under the weight. Almost as soon as I met him he got a puncture, his fifth so far, he told me. He had no tools so I waited by his bike whilst he disappeared into the bush to find some. He went at a run and re-appeared an hour later, having gleaned them from nearby villages. Quickly he fixed the puncture and then disappeared again to return the tools. Another hour later he was back again, still at a run and sweating freely. He said we must hurry now to be at the lodge before nightfall: it was a long and very arduous walk and it was all uphill, he pushing his decrepit bike and me carrying my pack and food supplies. As we walked we talked. His name was Paul. He was second cook up at the lodge but also accepted this job which took three days of hard work to supply one crate of beer. He was a delightful, calm boy, intelligent and independent, viewing life with a relaxed resignation. He laughed a lot and was quiet a lot, and was obviously very conscientious about his job. He told me about the intrigues in the lodge, about the good men and the bad men, as he called them.

'Ah, that *chef*, my boss. He works me like a slave, he is a ba-ad man, very bad, he does no work and cooks terribly, so terribly, and he steals rice from the kitchen. But he will be sacked one day and then I shall be chief cook – I cook very well. My friend Chaloma – he's chief night watchman – saw him stealing some beer from the bar only last week. He says he'll tell Monsieur Jacques. He's Belgian and he owns the lodge. He's coming to stay next week, that's why I have been sent to buy some beer. Chaloma will only tell if the *chef* doesn't pay him some compensation for his son. He works in the kitchen too, and the *chef* hit him so hard one night when he was drunk he had to go all the way to the hospital in Beni because he kept seeing things blurred. He's a good man, Chaloma. He'll get the money because the *chef* is very scared of Monsieur Jacques. And he's even more scared that his wife will leave him if he loses his job.'

No one came to the lodge much nowadays because further up the road there was a bad bridge which the overland trucks dare not pass and the tourists did not like to walk too far. In some ways Paul was very worldly wise – he certainly understood a good deal about the mentality of Westerners – but in other ways he was a villager whose world lay about him in his immediate surroundings. He would ask me about Kisangani and Beni.

'They are like London, no, or maybe a bit bigger?'

When I told him no, they were smaller, he looked a bit crestfallen. Then he would say, 'And what is the capital of London?'

All the things I had with me, like my tiny radio, my camera and my tent, he immediately fell in love with. Most of all he wanted my radio, as did everyone I met, but Paul could not get it out of his mind, it almost tormented him. I did not give it to him, but later on I gave it to someone else who could not be parted from it, so great was his love.

We walked and walked through a rising landscape of matted jungly forest and small open areas of villages, cultivated patches and pawpaw trees. The sun was hot and penetrating – we were very near to the equator here – but at this height the air in the shade of the trees was fresh and cool. The last part of the journey was up a steep hill in a grand forest of thick vines and bulbous, gnarled trees. Night fell upon us in all its deep African blackness. I stumbled on in a stupor of exhaustion, up winding tracks, through tall reedy grass and then we were at the lodge. It was dead, dark and deserted but for Paul's friend

Chaloma, who we discovered hunkered over a small fire in a little shack; and there Paul cooked a chicken we had bought from a village on the way up. Chaloma told me I could sleep in the hut in the campsite, an overgrown garden of flowers and bushes. I slept deeply on its floor.

In the morning I was woken by a soft but determined tapping on the door. When I came out to see who it was, I found a small posse of pygmies sitting round a fire, waiting for me. Word had got round that I was here and they had come to see if I wanted to buy any small trinkets – arrows, necklaces of monkey teeth and dried seeds.

They were small people but not as small as I had expected, light-skinned and light-boned. Their faces had a delicate, foxy quality, with their coy, slightly mischievous smiles. My heart sank a bit, as I had hoped to avoid being taken for this category of tourist, and their hearts sank a bit as I politely turned down their offers. They did not seem unduly upset, though, and happily accepted some coffee which they passed round amongst themselves. Then they hopped up and lightly jogged back into the forest and were gone. I felt they thought it of little consequence whether I bought something or not. In this first encounter I was aware of an air of security and confidence in these small wiry people, just in the way they talked and walked about. They were strikingly different from the ordinary Bantu villagers who seem somehow to live despite their environment rather than with it. The pygmies were in their home – the forest.

I was captivated by this meeting. I wanted to go into the forest after them so I set to organizing a trip. At once I met with difficulties but Paul was a great help. He had become my friend, my helper, my mentor, my interpreter. He could not take me himself because of his duties but he brought along a man who would be my guide. His name was Manos Boybyos, a quiet, unassuming local man with a kind and relaxed face. I liked him at once. He was a small man, almost a pygmy himself, and seemed to be a forest African, at home and easy in his surroundings. He walked barefoot and he could speak the language the pygmies spoke here. He also spoke some French.

We set off early next morning into the forest. The trees here were not the giants I had seen before but smaller, seeming to grow outwards more than upwards. They had tremendous girths that were split and twisted. There were mosses and mats of leaves and many straight, spindly trees. Thick vines drooped and strangled here and there. Surprisingly colourful flowers and succulent new green shoots grew in the twilight on the ground and the sky twinkled with shifting spots of light as the canopy was blown about. In many ways it was not so different from what I always call the English jungle, the thick ancient copses; but here, of course, there were also many types of palm, and all the different sounds of strange insects.

Fortunately, at some time or another, a proper path had been cut and although it was now clogged with new bushes and brambles, it went in a straight line, unlike most forest paths that twist and turn so much you can walk for hours and not get very far. Manos walked at a fast pace, almost a jog, as the pygmies do. I often lost sight of him for long periods, but always I could find him stopped somewhere further up the path to show me something of interest. In many places the bush on either side of the path had been trampled down, and the churned-up path had small elephant prints in it. He said they were made by pygmy elephants who often pass through this part of the forest on their way to the savannah. They stop on the path, he said, to frolic and play.

After about four hours on this difficult path of hook-nail branches, mud and clouds of midges, the trees suddenly stopped and we were descending fast in tall elephant grass; it was thick and yellow and met over our heads. The path was only a slight parting, then only a broken stem or two; I could just see parts of Manos as he tunnelled and wove his way through. The air was different, we were about to be somewhere, I felt, not just engulfed in endless forest as I had been for the last few months. Suddenly I was out of the grass, standing at the top of a great plain, an immaculate greensward of swirling grass, rising and falling clear and fresh, running far down to a distant valley. Beyond the valley the land rose again in patchworked green and dark, grass and forest. It splayed out

117

to either side, like arms, straight on to the horizon where it hugged a big, hazy mountain which sat, like a buddha, looming, presiding over this new, discovered land, peering back at me. It was Mount Hoyo.

The scene struck me in the stomach like a blow. It was overpowering and exciting to suddenly be in all this space. I could see so far, over the untangled land ahead, such a contrast to the closed-in world of the Zaire basin. I wanted to put out my arms and clasp it to me.

Nearby in an alcove of grass was a bush market, a few little lean-tos and lots of low bamboo tables displaying various forest foods. There were different kinds of bush rats, hyrax and monkeys, manioc roots, maize and sacks of maize powder. One stall, the one surrounded by people, sold things that could not be had from the land: packets of refined sugar, candles and scented soap, mirrors and sweets, shoe laces and other useful things. Children stood around, wide-eyed, wishing they had a few coins to buy those sweets; women haggled over the price of soap and men spent saved-up money on cigarettes and tea. After the first glance up when I walked on the scene the people accepted my presence. I was only another person to be taken with the day. I found it a change from most places, where a European is rarely left alone. When a light rain started, space was made for me under a lean-to next to a fire and I sat there amid the quiet hubbub, watching the children play in the rain and the old women smoke at the fire. They rolled cigarettes of bangi (marijuana) in big dry leaves and puffed till wreaths of smoke drifted about their hair. Manos had gone in another direction and shortly returned, bringing with him a tall, important-looking man wearing a Muslim cap. He was introduced to me as Abdul and he asked me, politely, why I was here. He made no comment but somehow I sensed that he could take me to the pygmies, if he decided in my favour.

He led us from the market when the rain had stopped. Leaving was like stepping into a picture; I saw myself a diminishing figure walking down into the beautiful plain, an insignificant dot under the vast African sky. The country was

wide open and the grass much taller than I had thought. The
mountain, the valley and the plains were all vivid in the
slanting rays of the afternoon sun. Walking down with us were
some women balancing round gourds and baskets on their
heads, on their way home. The distance was much greater
than it had looked and topping a rise I suddenly found we were
entering a spinney where the path became a mud shoot, the
leaves and branches dripping water on to the sodden ground.

The women with loads on their heads and the inevitable babies on their backs walked down without founder or fault; I followed on my arse.

On the other side of the forest the land quickly flattened out again, dotted with mud huts and small plantations of maize and manioc. One by one our host of followers dropped off as they reached their homes, and we made for a big two-storeyed mud house with a sloping roof and an outdoor stairway to the first floor. Smoke trickled up from a fire in the yard. From a distance it looked like a Swiss chalet, seen against the still-distant mountain, bathed in sunlight. The Muslim man, Abdul, who up to now had been quiet, startled me by setting off at a run towards the house, yelling and shouting, waving his arms. Before we caught up with him we were met head on by a running band of maybe twenty pygmies, yelling and gesticulating. We were engulfed. '*Jambo, jambo, bonjour, bonjour.*' They all tried to shake my hand, dancing about telling me their names and touching me with delicate caresses that felt like a shower of autumn leaves, swirling round and round. Abdul was still calling, rousing all the pygmies, telling them that I had come. I wondered fleetingly whether he was making an unnecessary fuss in order just to impress, but all suspicions left me. I had never had such a reception. Everyone was laughing and smiling in a way that looked disarmingly genuine. I seemed to be expected and most welcome. I only had to look at their faces, one moment coy and pensive, the next cracking into wide open smiles as innocent and beautiful as uncurling forest flowers.

The pygmies love to be merry and to dance and sing, and my arrival seemed sufficient reason for a dance, so I was told in no uncertain terms that they were going to dance, and that I must pay. I did not want them to dance for money, to put on a staged show, but they were so excited I felt they would dance in any case. As it turned out, the money was not very important and in some ways quite right: I should make them an offering, anyway, as a guest always does. It did not seem to affect the atmosphere. We sat down in a circle to discuss the price, a long and drawn-out ritual. Everyone joined in, shouting 'oohs' and

120

'aahs' when one of us was being too hard. We all enjoyed it and after a suitable time I was told, anyway, to pay what I thought right.

The pygmy camp was behind Abdul's house in a clearing in the tall grass. There were about ten huts, looking almost as if they were piles of hay. They were made by planting long sticks in the ground and bending them over to form a dome. When a good frame was completed, grass and leaves were spread on the top in a thick matting that keeps out all but the heaviest rain. In each hut a small fire was smouldering, little wisps of smoke escaping here and there through the grass.

On the ground were some locally made pots and pans which, along with a few oddments of clothing – a pair of boxer

shorts, a cotton wrap-around – were the only modern things I saw. There were sticks and stones littered about and the odd bone, but not much else. Normally the pygmies live exclusively in the forest, moving from one place to the other in their search for animals, plants and fungi, building their makeshift homes wherever they settle for a while. Now and again they come to live for a short time amongst the local settlements in order to exchange their meat for village food.

As I walked into the camp clearing, inquisitive faces of the very young and very old, those who had not joined in the reception party, peered out of black, round doorways with wide-open eyes that followed me closely as I went by. Everywhere else pygmies were preparing themselves for the dance. Young girls were painting their faces in simple red and black lines with stain from some forest plant. They twisted small branches with long leaves round their heads so that the leaves all stood up, forming little coronets. They looked enchanting.

The men made themselves short skirts from the same leaves, then they sat about smoking bangi in big bamboo water-pipes, shrouding themselves in pungent clouds. Children splattered the red and black stain across their bodies and faces at random, dashing to and fro between their elders. Everyone was getting more and more excited as they smoked and prepared themselves. Some were already jumping about, unable to contain themselves any longer.

Out in front of the house, in the yard, some chairs were placed for Abdul, Manos and me. Two big round drums made from wood with antelope skin stretched tightly across were put next to us. When everybody was ready the women came skipping in a line round the side of the house closely followed by a mob of boys and girls jumping up and down. This was 'the dance of the women', a slow, controlled dance of graceful hopping and gyrating on one foot. Gradually the long line went around the yard, stopping now and again in a half-circle, waving their heads and their haloes of leaves in circles. They sang in perfect time with the drumming of a man who was introduced to me as the leader of the gang, and boys joined in with a languid, calling song. Their faces and bodies glowed, they were relaxed and unselfconscious as they sang and waved their arms back and forth in unison. This was no staged show. I was forgotten.

From the other side of the house came a roar as the men surged forth, wild and strong. Theirs was a different dancing. They brought with them a powerful force of movement and energy, sometimes deliberate, sometimes breaking into fast, excited action. They, too, danced in single file, hopping and tripping, behind the women, who dropped to their knees, swinging their head-dresses round and around. The tempo of the drums increased. The men danced fiercely, swinging their arms and heads in jittery motions with the beat. The singing became louder but still maintained its harmony and sense of calm. It was led by the women, who moved the more demurely as the men became more insistent. Linking arms, the men turned about and stuck out their leafy, skirted behinds, shaking them so that they rustled and swayed like bushes in the wind. I seemed to be watching a dance of the forest as much as a dance of the people. Pounding their feet and churning up a mist of dust, the men now formed a circle round the swaying, singing women. With knees bent and bodies held low, they burst into a fast and furious striding motion, tightly pressed together and moving like the pistons of a steam train, grinding and pushing round and round. The audience of women and children cried their applause and joy at this frantic excitement. The men kept going round till the sweat poured off their bodies and they could no longer hold the position. Then they straightened up, and continued to circle the women with heads bowed, taking short, lilting steps, and the drums drew back. Slowly, the drum beats, the tempo and the tension then rose up again, until once more the men broke into the same fast motion circling and circling faster and faster till their ecstatic climax, and they broke off, whooping and shouting. In this dance, which lasted maybe half an hour in all, so compelling and so exciting was it that nearly everyone took part, joining in and dropping out as they wished. Understandably, it was called 'the marriage dance' but my eyes were so beset with the many images of the individual dancers that the narrative was lost on me. Abdul told me it was not just random dancing but portrayed various aspects of marriage and married life.

For the next dance, 'the hunt of the antelope', the women stood aside, swinging their hips together to the beat, clapping hands and singing, leaving the stage to the men.

Crouched low, with arms outstretched above his head for antlers, one man crept warily into the yard looking suspiciously around at the audience, swaying like trees in the wind. His face was covered by a black cloth with eye-slits, giving him anonymity and menace. He did not see the two hunters slowly stalking him, circling around behind under cover of the audience who made up for bushes and trees. He rooted about the ground, looking for something to eat, now and again stopping, stock still, his nose raised, scenting for lurking danger, hidden predators. Long, eerie mating calls came from the hunters, confusing him more and more. He went back to his grubbing in the earth but then, as the hunters continued their stalk, his head shot up again, sniffing the air and quivering like a taut bowstring. Tension and anticipation rose to such a pitch that the audience had to yell warnings and encouragement, to relieve things a bit. Still the hunters bided their time, waiting for an opportunity to loose their arrows. The antelope was fraught with nerves, he sensed the danger but could not find its source. The drums beat a steady, perilous beat, boom-boom-boom. He was near the point of bolting, when suddenly out jumped the hunters and loosed off their shots. The phantom arrows struck true, but this was no ordinary antelope, he would not die so easily. With a loud yell, he charged the two men, he flung them aside, and ploughed on into the forest of people with wild abandon, crashing his way through the undergrowth of tables, babies and chairs. Finding a large blanket lying on the ground, he crept under it for cover, whimpering and gesticulating his terror and pain. The hunters ran about searching for him, and at last pin-pointed him to his lair. Like a game of blind man's buff, they slowly advanced upon him. Whenever he stuck out his streaming face, and barked and snorted his warning, they stood stock-still. The audience collapsed with laughter at his pitiful state, slapping their thighs, pointing to his frightened face and laughing at his desperate antics; rolling on his back, the antelope shook his legs and arms. Slowly the hunters got closer and closer until, with a sudden leap and cry of blood lust, they dived under the blanket. After a lot of struggling and shouting, the whole blanket got up and ran offstage with the prey hidden inside. The audience could contain itself no longer: yipping with joy at the success of the hunt, they broke into impromptu dancing and stamping.

The three men who had performed this dance were the most prominent members of the pygmy group.Through the bangi they were smoking and the spirit of the dance and the music, they had such vitality and involvement that they seemed almost in a trance. The next dance was 'the dance of the baboons'. On all fours, two of these men came back, their bodies glistening with sweat, twisting and contorting to the music. Both wore animal-skin hats, one made from black-and-white Barbary monkey fur and one of leopard-skin. Their eyes were red and popping, and flickered from side to side as if they had a life of their own. On their haunches, they circled the open space, arms stretched out in front, shaking and searching. They snarled at the audience from a wary distance and then suddenly, with a roll of the drums, they burst at them with anger and speed. Everyone fled as they approached and threatened. Every antic and movement of the men was so identical to that of a baboon that only people who have lived with and studied them for a lifetime could mimic such a likeness. Now and again, they would drop their cornered-animal aggression to become coy and inquisitive. They sidled up to objects on the ground with an uncertain and broken sideways shuffle. They picked things up and, tucking them under their arms, made off to a safe distance to finger and study them, their heads cocked to one side. When the owner of the hat or whatever it was, approached to try and retrieve it, the baboon would snarl and jump, flaying his arms, gibbering and screeching. When the crowd of spectators pressed too close, they would burst into another fury of aggression, scattering everyone; once they leapt after a terror-stricken village girl who, with a wild and white face, ran headlong into the tall grass nearby and stayed hidden there. The two men became a very real and wild menace in themselves. No longer were they play-acting, they were taken over by some overpowering force. Their faces had lost the safe, human look. They were no longer faces you felt you could reason with and say, 'That's enough, let's stop now.' Looking round at the audience of villagers, I knew this was no figment of my imagination. They wore transfixed and captivated masks of fear and awe at the uncontrollable and unpredictable.

In the yard there was a tall ramrod tree, like a telegraph pole with a few branches at the top. One of the baboons leapt on to it and, jerking and twisting to the frantic beat of the drums, shinned his way up with the easy dexterity and assurance of his species. When he arrived at the top, he hooked his feet over a branch and, suddenly letting go, hung upside down, thrashing his arms madly and convulsing his body as though he had a fit. His beetroot face poured with sweat and froth splayed from his mouth as he uttered guttural growls and yelps. His eyes were like two hot orbs, glowing a bloody red. At last, spent, he descended to the ground in two large leaps and, with a heaving and glowing body, disappeared into the tall grass with the other baboon.

For a while there was a stunned silence. Just as people were breaking from their trance of concentration, with a high-pitched scream the baboons came crashing back through a bush to fling themselves at the spectators in an orgy of abandoned fury, and chased them out of control, far and wide. Only little clusters of people were left in the yard, some dumb, some tentatively giggling. The baboons did not reappear and slowly the others came back. They looked about suspiciously and when it seemed certain that they were no longer in danger of being chased, they began to laugh and joke about their own and each other's fear – after all, it was only make-believe.

By now it was almost dark; only a few ribbons of daylight were left in the sky. The men went over to an open extension of the house where there was a big fire burning on the muddy floor. I joined them and we sat around the fire in the company of chickens, goats and dogs, watching the women outside. They stood in a row, singing beautiful and far-off-sounding songs, gently swaying their bodies from side to side, their clear forest voices the only certain thing in the broken light.

It had been a very moving experience to watch the dancing, to see people who had such involvement yet such abandon. All the time their seraphic faces had seemed unfocused, as if they were concentrating on some other presence not visible to me. I think that presence was simply their forest. They dressed in it, they danced in it, they lived off it, they were part of it, so how could they celebrate but in union with it? It was not just around them but within them, in the same way that a fox has the woods, the rivers and the fields in his make-up and his instinct, not merely under his paws. When they danced, their force, their energy and serenity came from this union and not from themselves alone.

We sat late that night round the fire in the house, using the big logs sticking out of it for seats. Abdul did not stay with us. He was very polite and friendly and brought us lots of food, some of which he refused to be paid for, saying it was a gift, and some for which he expected payment. I had noticed that he was referred to as '*le patron*' by the pygmies. Manos told me that he looked after them. I thought this stange at first – the pygmies did not give me the impression that they needed any 'looking after' – but later I learnt that this was part of a relationship of convenience. The pygmies got from Abdul maize, manioc and tobacco in exchange for the fresh meat they caught in the forest. But it was not merely a business relationship, I thought. Abdul seemed to have an almost paternal feeling towards the pygmies. He seemed to care for them as something special. They, in their turn, had respect for him, not the normal respect for someone who is wiser, but based, I think, on the fact that they trusted and liked him. He did seem to be a man with a good deal of humility, even though he behaved as their protector. The pygmies seemed to accept this role of the protected, at least sometimes. Not because they needed it, but because they did not want to upset the balanced relationship they had: they understood that for it to work they must give rein to the brittle ego many of the village people have. It seemed a happy arrangement, both sides getting what they wanted: the pygmies a base and security when in the local village sphere, and Abdul a monopoly on fresh meat in the area, neither side losing dignity. The pygmies were confident enough in their belief in themselves to be able to act submissively. They know and everybody else knows that they are not really so, that they can and do disappear back into the forest whenever they wish, independent of the rest of the world.

I found I was beginning to respect the pygmies, a people who remain untouched by the materialism of development and also by the more insidious trappings of Westernization, and all the confused resentments that come in its wake, such as a belief that they are inferior to anyone with wristwatches and jeans. I have never met a people so free of inhibition and who laugh with such ease. I have never met a people whose smile alone tells you so much about their freedom and happiness with themselves and their way of life. In some ways they are like children. Their frank eyes, their unconcern with things that are not immediately important, their timid, uncertain trust and shyness of strangers, their lightness of spirit, their playfulness and enjoyment of life. It would be a mistake, though, to suppose that they are like children in all ways. Maybe they are innocent of selfishness and greed in themselves, but they are not innocent of it in others. They are not faultless but they are balanced. Their wisdom and knowledge of forest lore have come down to them through endless generations and have taught them everything they need to know about good and evil and survival and so, it appears, given them the ability to stand back and reject development and change where others are unable to. They know what they have got in this life of theirs, and they can see the sort of life the local villagers have, who have accepted development and change, or at least not consciously rejected them. They can see the frustrations, the yearning always for something better, lives lived with fewer morals and less dignity. Some small hints of development and change have inevitably seeped into their lives but as yet only into their lives, not their minds.

The pygmies were free and at ease to come and go in their patron's house. Because of the language problem there was not much conversation between us, other than asking each other simple questions through Manos, but this did not matter. They tried to teach me how to be as adept as them when cooking on an awkward fire. When I burnt my fingers on a hot pot or a cob of maize they laughed until the tears ran down their faces. By a few hints, a few words and our shared laughter, we became as close and friendly as if we could speak the same language. They taught me something of their language, not their language of words but their language of laughter, and their joy of life.

There was a mongrel pup with us by the fire and I was particularly struck by their attitude towards it. He was a friendly, hungry puppy who was transfixed by the smell of cooking food. He would edge his way gingerly towards it but just when he was within snatching distance, one of the pygmies would give him a hearty kick in the ribs that would send him yelping back into a dark corner until the smells drew him out again. If it is ever possible to kick a dog with affection the pygmies managed it. I had seen the way they would stroke and pat it, with that warm, purring look on their faces. Kicking the pup was like slapping a child when he was being bad. Dogs have a bad lot in Africa on the whole, because Africans do not have the same understanding of cruelty as we do in the West. They often treat animals abysmally, as if they are inanimate objects. The pygmies seemed different in their attitude. They treated the dog as a creature with feelings, to be treated roughly but not without understanding and compassion.

Now and again a silence would descend upon the pygmies. Watching them sitting hunched up on their logs, gazing into the fire with large, wide eyes, there seemed to be a look of sadness and despondency about them. It is easy to fall prey to this compelling look, and to feel pity. But I feel that with the pygmies, as with many other very natural people, it is not a sad look. Rather it is a normal and natural look of acceptance and stillness that comes on the face of someone who lives close to nature and the harshness of its realities, when he is relaxed and not thinking of anything in particular. The pygmies are content and need no pity.

Long after I slept that night, the pygmies sat up watching the fire and murmuring among themselves. When, sometime in the pitch-blackness of pre-dawn, I left my bed in the chicken coop above the goats and with the rats to answer a call of nature, I saw a red glow coming from a crack in a wall. When I peered through I saw I was looking into a small, closed room with seven or eight sombre pygmy men closely huddled round a big fire. Their faces were alive with flickering light and their eyes transfixed, reflecting the bloody flames. The fire leapt up as someone threw on dry twigs, illuminating a blackened and leathery rack hanging above the blaze with a skinned and red, gory monkey spread-eagled on it, sizzling and dripping juices into the flames. The acrid smell of burnt hair hung in the air

130

like a terrible incense. Looking at the men with my sleepy, half-conscious eyes, their oval faces starting out of the darkness like ghouls, I saw a scene far detached from reality. I saw a ghastly ritual taking place, the tortured, writhing body of a child being roasted alive. I saw contorted faces in the throes of a trance-like ecstacy. I saw a wild and barbaric people. These are the fantasies and dreams built into our brains by a childhood in societies where fact and fiction are brought together for everyday use in a life far removed from nature, and where fact is often interpreted through a gauze of fiction. The pygmies were merely having a meal.

The next day broke cold and wet; full-bellied clouds hung over the valley like an eiderdown. I spent all morning sitting around the fire with my pygmy friends, chatting, laughing and being silent, much the same as the night before. The young men told me they would be going on a hunt for antelope in the afternoon if it stopped raining in time, and asked if I wanted to come along. Of course I eagerly agreed. Soon enough the clouds rolled back over Mount Hoyo, revealing a clear blue sky. There were about ten of us in the hunting party. Setting off into the tall, reed-like grass down in the valley with backs to the afternoon sun, they loped along in single file, bows and arrows clasped longways to dangle at their sides like the spears of an impi of warriors. Many of them had brown, soggy stumps of home-made cigarettes drooping out of their mouths, and small, smouldering embers from the fire tucked behind their ears. Now and again someone in the line would stop to blow on the coal until little showers of fire shot into the air; then he would re-light his bangi and move on. They told me that sometimes the bangi makes them more aware, so that they can hunt better. As we meandered along what were to me unnoticeable tracks in and out of gullies, through small plantations of maize and manioc, and across clear, rippling streams with high mossy banks, they joked and laughed like people who are doing something they know intimately and are masters of.

When we got to the thick, tangly forest on the broken valley floor, a place of secret glades and banks of monkey-puzzle bush, the pygmies skipped in headlong, following secretive animal tracks and seeming to make as much noise as they liked. After a while the line of men split up, some taking one track, some another. The jokes and mumbles of the other group became fainter as they got further away and were muffled by the forest. Soon they were lost. Now and again the leader of my group, a sleek, sinuous man, stopped dead in his tracks like a startled antelope, stiffly scenting the air. He stood with one leg relaxed, head cocked to the side and the hand with his bow and arrows in it cupped to his ear to catch any sound. Then, putting his hands over his mouth and nose, he gave a long, warbling cry, the cry of an antelope calling for a mate. From not far away came back another mating call from the other pygmies, like an echo; they seemed to be circling ahead of us. Soon we left the animal tracks we were following and, crawling on our stomachs and knees, wriggled our way through the maze of bushes, creepers and twisted trees, going deeper and deeper, until I became disorientated and lost. The pygmies were as light as elves. By now they had stopped talking altogether. They were as silent as the wind as they slipped and picked through the undergrowth on a route that was not there. Now and again they stopped in small clearings to inspect the silvery trees and the carpet of leathery leaves and sodden moss for signs. We came to a wide, flat-bottomed gully that gouged its way through the forest and gave refuge to coarse, impenetrable thorn bushes. Some of the pygmies worked their way down into it and started to follow it along, disappearing into the waves of gorse and bramble to pop up the other side like magic.

On the far bank the other group suddenly appeared. We spread out along the rim, forming a cordon around the group beating it through. For a long time we watched the gully, expecting at any moment the elusive antelope to come crashing out, when the tense, alert pygmies would loose their poisoned arrows, and follow the track of the wounded animal until the poison did its work. But our luck was not in, or maybe it was my not-so-silent presence. There was no antelope and shortly the pygmies gave up, and opted to go back.

They did not seem upset by the failure of the hunt; it had not taken them too far from home, and they still had some meat and manioc there anyway.

As soon as it was decided to go back, the pygmies' serious demeanour left them. Once again they were loose-limbed and jovial, telling me stories in mime of hunting elephants and leopards as they jogged along. I had noticed again the difference in the pygmies once they stepped into their forest. Gone was the shyness and quiet acceptance of lesser beings that was noticeable back amongst the Bantu villagers. Here they dropped all that pretence, like a robe. They were forthright and confident, they could do what they may. They did not even need to be polite to me or please me. I was in their forest and they were in their forest, and no one was superior except maybe they. As a result they seemed to be even more free of spirit and more gay than I had seen before, but with a difference. They were not as trivial as they can make themselves out to be, or as childish. A harshness, a more steely side to them showed itself. Once they had started hunting they had at once become unsmiling, as if they must not fool around when dealing with something that is important and dear to the harmony of the forest; they must treat it with respect. When we arrived at a small river edging its way round a bank of shingle, outside the forest, they washed the tree green off their bodies before idling back home.

That night Manos prepared a big meal of rice and mushrooms with a delicious peanut sauce. We shared it with the pygmies of the hunt, and a rapt audience of women and children. While it was cooking, sweet potatoes were pushed under the grey ash and coals to bake, and the last of my cigarettes were hungrily smoked. I felt immensely at peace and happy with these people. They accepted me so easily, didn't demand or give too much. Again we sat late into the night.

The next day I left. I turned round again and again on my long walk out of the plain, trying to imprint it on to my mind. The pygmies had not been at the camp when I left; they were busy helping their patron to build a church. When I passed by they all came running up to me to shake my hand and wish me well, and ask if I had any parting gifts. For a long time I could see their pale palms waving to me above the tall grass and hear their voices calling after me, *'Jambo, jambo, bonjour.'*

10

To the Bank

A few days later I was back in Komanda, the small town from
which I had glimpsed that apparition of the Ruwenzori mountains. I decided I would go and climb them. For now, though, I
had virtually no money left so I had to head for Beni, that other
metropolis about 130 kilometres due south, to go to the bank.
This, I thought, would be easy, as the road was the main and
only one from north to south.

I had a leisurely and luxurious breakfast, expecting a truck
to turn up at any time. I sat and waited, and waited. I spent my
last spare zaires on some cigarettes. I watched the town eat its
midday meal, go for its siesta. I was left with only the
immovable market women sitting in front of their dusty
wares. The sun sank and still I waited. At last a very old
pick-up truck clattered into town, so heavily laden with dried
fish that its wheels were barely visible under the body, and it
stank. On top were perched a knot of people in a solid lump,
like a camel's hump. The driver, pulling up with wheezing
brakes, was a Ugandan. With an expansive gesture, he said that
because I was English and because Uganda used to be an
English colony, we were brothers, so he accepted my last
money as a poor fare. I scrambled on board and wedged myself
into the hump. We set off into the sunset and the darkening
bush. I was on my way at last.

About two kilometres out of town, some very 'ill' sounds
came from under the bonnet. We stopped. Heads disappeared
into the engine. Much discussing was done until it was

135

announced that we were just going to have to wait while the driver went off to get 'a spare part'. He walked back down the road. The rest of us built a fire next to the unfortunate truck and cooked some maize and a fish from the load as the night became complete. Much later I enquired what the driver had gone to get. What was this spare part?

'Oh, a new truck,' his boy said.

He had gone back to his home town, many kilometres away.

I walked back to Komanda where I found some other trucks stopped at a bush café. They seemed reluctant to take passengers and I was not the only one looking for a place. Eventually I found a willing driver and climbed on top. As we sped along, the cool night air rushed past me and I felt exhilarated with that wonderful feeling you get from riding a truck: high up above the world, you are free, no strings attached, off into the unknown on a sturdy chariot. As the night got colder, though, and the bumps and jumps had truly penetrated to the marrow of my bones, I huddled down and watched the night of murky shapes flying by, outlined against the blue-black sky, the beam of our headlights the only thing alive. As the night wore on, the smell of vegetations once known came to me, a certain musky dryness and dust-caked earth that conjured up east Africa. My stomach fluttered with adrenaline. We arrived in Beni as the sun came up and was struggling to clear away the last wisps of fog. I was numbed with cold and covered from head to toe with palm oil from a leaky drum.

Having found a small hotel and cleaned up a bit, I set off to the bank, arriving as the doors were opened. The banks in Zaire are known well for their lack of haste and this bank was certainly not a place of speed and affray. My traveller's cheques and some cash were taken by a clerk and he set to. It was a good bank, this, the people very conscientious about their work. The problem my demand made was quite great, but they went at it with determination. There were duplicate and triplicate papers to be checked, filed and discussed. There were currency laws and regulations, permissions and all, to fit into the equation, to try and make it work. There was one-finger typing, and signatures, and stamps with no ink.

And on top of this, the nuisance of other customers. Lunch-time came. The doors were locked. A cup of tea appeared for me through the cash window. I sat down outside in the back yard with my controller, the original clerk, and had a hasty meal of meat and rice. Then it was back to work. The afternoon started to pass. Just a few more signatures, check the rates. The ordeal was coming to an end. It was over. Everybody was happy. The team had done well. The procedure had been followed correctly, no corners cut. I shook hands all round and made an appointment to meet my clerk for a beer later on.

In the evening we went to the main hotel in town and sat on the verandah with all the other smart, rich people. Everyone was half-drunk, whether they were ladies in elegant dresses or business men with suits and pockets full of cash. Across the road, as on a stage, we watched a motorcyclist, driving at a comical speed, run down a pedestrian. There was dead silence for a second and then, as one, everybody on the verandah shouted, 'Aaah! Oh, no!' and rushed out into the road. The victims were engulfed in wafts of beer and scent. Fortunately there was a very smart ambulance about; earlier on it had turned up at the hotel and disgorged a party of women and men. Now they were all in the bar, so the medics only had to cross the street. They were quick and efficient and in no time at all the ambulance was disappearing with lights flashing and siren wailing. The merry-makers returned to the bar full of excitement and drank with a new enthusiasm.

My clerk's brother turned up on his motorbike, so all three of us got on to go and find something to eat. The bike was very small, but then so were they. We had to bang and shout to wake the restaurant up, to be served eggs and ham. The eggs were bad and made me ill all the next day. After the meal, my two friends accepted a cigarette which they refused to light but puffed at in a debonair way, passing it between them like schoolboys. In the unlit restaurant amongst the upturned chairs with the dead African night outside, they made a touching scene, this bank clerk and his brother of business.

11

The Mountains of the Moon

Now I had been to the bank I was free to climb the Ruwenzoris. The morning I left Beni there was a torrential downpour. I got a lift in a pick-up truck. The roads were running as rivers and the clouds were black and angry in the sky. We came to the top of a pass and there below us was a new land. The sun found some chinks in the clouds and illuminated rivers and lakes of silver in a country that was red and broken, plain and valley moulded together, rugged with various greens. Far off in the distance was a mountain range of cloud stretching the horizon high into the sky. I knew that hidden beneath this encasement of cloud was the solid rock of the Ruwenzoris, those mountains so shy of the human eye which Ptolemy of ancient Egypt had named 'the mountains of the moon'. I was dropped off at a village somewhere beneath the bank of cloud and had to walk a long way to the base camp from where I could prepare my campaign.

The base camp was at the foot of the mountains in an area of thick greenery with neat flower gardens and a cold clear stream where I washed every stitch of clothing I possessed. A steady trickle of people come to climb the Ruwenzoris but at that time I was the only person in the camp, though there were others in the mountains. I checked in with the camp officials, organized my route, paid for a guide and porter and put all my valuables in the camp safe. There was a small guest house where I stayed for one night and was fed a huge bowl of rice and chicken by a man who told me I was too thin.

My plan was to leave early next day but of course I did not. My guide and porter were brought along by the camp officials whilst I was having a last, large breakfast of fried eggs. I had no idea what lay ahead and found it difficult to decide what I might need. Trying to find out details was not so very easy. The officials spoke little French and always liked to please.

'Do I need to bring a water bottle with me, or is water available en route?'

'Yes,' they would say.

Eventually, though, I sorted something out. I slung a shopping bag over my shoulder with what I thought the basic essentials in it: sleeping bag, jumper, jacket (Oxfam's best), two pairs of socks, a handkerchief, torch, matches and cigarettes. And off we set – downhill! – to the market, to buy food. It seemed a long walk there and I was already quite puffed when we arrived. We bought a big bag of milled manioc, salted fish and rice; that, together with my few supplies from Beni, would be enough for our four-day trip.

At first we passed through low-lying foothills, green runs and rivulets of rock and earth. They were patched with little plantations of coffee, bananas and manioc, lying at angles, and flat, small mud houses with blue ribbons of smoke tucked amongst them. Occasionally the sun broke through the layers of fast-flying cloud and shafts of light marked the hills with pools of gold, traversing like divine disco lights. Looking upwards, I could see why Ptolemy named these mountains 'the mountains of the moon'. Many layers of cloud billowed at their top, like smoke. Snow-clad peaks or grey granite sides poked out now and again for fleeting moments, but quickly the curtain was always closed, leaving only hints as to their magnificence, leaving most to the imagination. They were elusive, somehow ominous, milky white and mysterious as the moon. I began to realize that this climb was not going to be an easy jaunt.

After a while we came to a mud hut in a little plantation on an idyllic terrace looking over the long view to the smudge of forests of that different Zaire on the horizon. It belonged to my porter, Molengo, so we stopped while he got himself prepared

139

for the journey. His wife cooked us some delicious bananas and beans which we ate on little stools, admiring the scene. Molengo was an old man, but as tough as leather. He changed out of his smart clothes and put on a pair of shorts and three ripped shirts that added up to less than one. He wore no shoes. In a big brown hessian sack he put pots and pans and all our supplies. Tying it up with bark stripped to slithers, he fixed a long one to go round his forehead to hold it on his back. It looked a formidable load, but up he got and set off at a great pace, leaving Edward, my guide, and myself to catch up. Edward was young, about seventeen, and had only been up the mountains once before. He spoke good French, his main qualification to be a guide, whereas Molengo didn't.

The path rose steeply, winding through the little planta-tions. Small wisps of cloud occasionally reached down to touch us. As we plodded on the world opened up behind us. Now and again the sun shone and the air was clear.

After an hour or two, when the foothills had become mountainside, we came upon a big wooden house, the official guides' post. I flopped down, my muscles tired, but inside I felt as strong as an ox; the vitality of the mountains had infused my veins. Molengo put still more food in his sack. He carried his load and that of Edward, but I carried my own: that was part of the deal. While we were sitting there a Dutch couple in puffy red jackets and sturdy climbing boots appeared on their way down from the top. From their state I got my first intimation of what was to come. They looked completely wrecked. So exhausted they could not speak at first, they collapsed in a heap. From head to foot they were soaking wet, and covered with mud. After some minutes they spoke to me.

'It's impossible to climb, there is so much water and mud now. Coming down was terrible, going up will be much worse.'

I wasn't equipped for really bad conditions but when Edward and Molengo made to leave I joined them, not heeding too much the enlightening remarks of these people. Immediately we entered a different terrain. There was thick jungle on either side, long bamboos and grasses closed overhead. It was steamy and humid, drizzling now and again as we entered cloud. The path became slippery with mud. Around a corner suddenly there appeared another Dutchman going at such a pace he seemed to be running from something. Steam was pouring off him as if he was on fire, his face was brick-red and he dripped water. We greeted each other briefly but he really could not speak and hurtled past me, glazed and intent.

The path deteriorated badly almost at once, becoming long mud slides in places. There seemed no way up them, hemmed in as they were, except on all fours, using fingers and toes for tread. Molengo, amazingly, loped up them like a young gazelle; Edward was no more adept than I. By now the world from which we had come was lost behind interlocking valleys, and beneath a blanket of cloud. The land as far ahead as I could see was very rough, and broken into deep gorges and gullies of thick forest. The path twisted and turned round rocks and trees, up and down the valleys; the ranks of tangled hills seemed to go on and on. We edged our way round some cliffs and walked straight into a colony of soldier ants. A large area was matted with them; the only way through was to run and then spend the next ten minutes picking the vicious beasts off. We seemed lost in an alien, hostile land. The ever-present mountains, high above, occasionally glanced at us from their secret place and beckoned us on. I was taken within their grip. I had to go on, and climb, and meet them before I would be given release.

By now we were in a profound forest of tall trees and brambly undergrowth. I caught glimpses of troops of small, chirping monkeys, who passed in a flurry overhead. And there were some of the big black-and-white Barbary monkeys. When I saw my first one, just catching sight of his back, I thought irrationally that it was a gorilla, as there are gorillas in eastern Zaire, but quite far south of here. Occasionally, these Barbaries put on a wonderful display of acrobatics as we passed. I found it hard to believe that they were not showing off, but they were only demonstrating their territory to strangers. From high up on a tall tree they flung themselves off and came crashing down like demons through the layers of branches, snapping them as they fell, plummeting with arms outstretched to a much lower branch that did not break. It seemed to be completely reckless, done only for pleasure and a thrill. They worked themselves up into a frenzy, picking ever taller trees for their displays.

After a couple of hours we came out onto a high ledge overlooking another ragged valley with a rushing stream at its bottom. On the far side a skinny and treacherous path was cut into the sheer hillside and along it I spotted a group of elderly European climbers being shepherded by their guides. I watched for a while as a rather large lady was pushed from one side and pulled from the other over an obstinate boulder blocking the way. When I met them at the stream they told me they had come 'from the third hut'. Later, when I had climbed some more, my respect for that lady deepened; I could have done with pullers and pushers myself.

All afternoon we kept a steady pace, climbing as much as walking. Edward got pretty exhausted and lagged behind. He was a polite boy but completely detached, not, you might say, happy in his work. The old man was boss. He plodded on steadily, like a carthorse, drawing us after him, the sweat on his brow and a bulging vein on his temple the only signs of the strain of his load.

After what seemed an indefinite time, when dusk was falling and I was having to force my weary legs every inch of the way, we came to a clearing among big trees where there was a wooden house. At one time it must have been very picturesque, but now it was run down and neglected. This was the first hut. A sign on the door announced that we were now at 2,500 metres. Edward and Molengo made for a small outhouse and began building a fire with any dry bits of wood they could find. The inside of the main hut was bare except for a wood-burning stove and a couple of beds. As in the outhouse, the floor boards had been pulled up in places and no doubt used as firewood: most of the windows were broken, so the wind rushed in. It was already getting very cold so I dumped my bag down and joined my companions by their already blazing fire. We huddled round it and hung our wet shoes and clothes over it to dry. Outside it started to rain heavily. The night became pitch-black. All that could be seen were our tired faces illuminated by the fire glow. Molengo produced from his sack a big black iron pot and a vast wooden spoon like a paddle. He boiled some water, then put heaps of manioc flour into it. Taking the scorching pot between his bare, calloused feet, he stirred it mightily with the spoon, twisting it round with both his hands. Very skilfully he made a large, round ball of dough, about the size of a football, which barely fitted the pot, manipulating it round and round with the pleasure of a craftsman. Squatting there with the big spoon clasped tightly, red from the fire, he looked like a guru performing some ritual in his dank, wooded hideaway. When this was finished he heated up some dried fish and made a watery, yellow sauce. All three of us tucked in ravenously. I copied their method of eating, taking a lump of doughy manioc and, with my thumb, made a large indentation in the middle of it. Then, with this makeshift spoon, I scooped up some sauce and popped the whole thing into my mouth. The fish had a strong, slightly putrid taste but was good with the manioc, which is tasteless; I was so hungry I gulped down a lot. We finished the meal with very sugary tea and sat by the fire being warmed by its heat. We did not talk much, comments on the day just gone and the days to come. I listened to the pouring rain as it drummed and streamed off the roof and clattered in the forest. I decided I would sleep the night in the main hut with the comfort of a bed. It was a mistake. I should have stayed with my companions by the fire as the night was bitterly cold and, despite sleeping with all my clothes on in my sleeping bag, I kept waking.

The next day broke bright and fresh. The rain had stopped, but only just. We ate last night's remains heated up in the iron pot and set off. I felt optimistic again, not so worried about being poorly equipped. The interminable valleys and hills of the day before had now ceased, and we started to climb in earnest. Almost all day we climbed through a forest of bizarre, twisted trees, short, with intricately tangled, exposed roots. The path rose as steeply as a staircase up ridge after ridge, an

143

endless tunnel of greasy roots with deep holes of wet, sucking mud in between. Progress became a task of climbing as if up one continuous tree. Very occasionally, when the gnarled black trees fell sharply away down the side of a ridge, I caught glimpses of sheer mountainsides opposite and cloud-filled valleys below.

At one time we came upon a clearing on a level bit of path where there were many doll-sized huts made from grass and twigs. In each I could see small offerings of food. Molengo told me this was a sacred place of the mountain gods: if I wanted to please them, which I must to be allowed to continue my journey, I must make an offering of money. Unfortunately I had none with me but some cigarettes would do, he said. He put them in a little plastic bag from one of the huts, together with some money that was already there. Nearby stood a timbal made from wooden sticks of different sizes. He squatted down and played a simple, tinkling tune with a wooden drumstick. It sounded beautiful in this remote place. It broke the silence, and did seem to be announcing our presence to the gods. Once a year, Molengo told me, all the guides and porters climbed up here and, with the money, gave a feast to the gods.

At midday we reached a spot where we could sit down properly and rest, a small, clear hillock at the top of one of the long ridges standing out from the falling forests like a bald head. There was a magnificent view. I felt as though I had climbed through some sort of barrier, into a land of unreality, quiet and eerie. Below us were sheer, forested cliffs falling to distant, lonely valleys; above us were clouds and the clustered, hidden peaks. Once the clouds parted, giving me sight of a hard, cruel crest shiny with ice. As if aware of my stares, though, the vision was quickly veiled. For a brief interval the sun broke through and shone down on our island in this sea of rock, tree and cloud. We soaked up its feeble rays and ate some spiced sausages I had bought in Beni. The silence and stillness were profound, only occasionally disturbed by a gust of wind and the cry of a few black crows circling high on currents of air. The time passed quickly in this refuge, but we had to continue.

I was lulled into a sort of trance, my mind focused on the next set of roots. I followed Molengo, trying to find my way through without slipping or falling. The high banks on either side were covered with thick moss creeping up the trees and down into the dips. Every imaginable shade of green was there, formed into beautiful, delicate stars and crystals, glinting with moisture. Whenever I trod on it, the soggy, spongy surface gave way and my leg went in up to the knee or thigh. I felt like a vandal. All the trees were draped with dripping green lichen, hanging from their branches like old men's beards. From ahead Edward gave a sudden shout. *'Un serpent, un serpent!'* I hurried to his side to see his snake but it was a worm about a metre long, and very fat. It fitted well into this strange, fairy-tale place.

All through the afternoon hours the world was hidden from us as we slogged on, hauling ourselves up and up. It seemed as if it would never end, but at last we came to the second hut on another of those clear hillocks; on its door the laconic message: '3,500 metres'. There was a group of French alpinists inside, down from the top peak which could only be reached by experts with ropes. They were full of exhilaration and stories about sub-zero temperatures and blizzards. They had every sort of equipment imaginable, with about twenty porters, and were busy preparing a big meal on the stove. Leaving them to it, I went outside again to look at the long view to the plain and the micro-life that could now just be seen huddled against the horizon. It was a clear and powerful evening, the sun just setting in a blaze of red and purple behind the big mountain opposite. The distant peaks, for once startlingly visible, dripped blood in its light. Looking down over the ridges, the forests and ravines, over small wispy clouds and tall tree-tops, I felt all-powerful, as if climbing the mountain had increased my stature. The world was laid out before me and I had only to stretch out my hand and I could grasp a piece of it.

'Get some more wood for the fire and make sure it's dry.'

Back to reality. I broke off my reverie and squelched my way through bog and mire to carry out my orders. Inside the hut, which was as dilapidated as the first, only with more floorboards missing, there was Gallic activity. I found myself a bed, stripped off my soaking clothes and hung them over the wood burner. Already it was freezing and a light drizzle was falling. Molengo and Edward had gone to another small hut with all the other porters, so I stayed and ate with the French.

I took another look outside as the last of the daylight disappeared and was again filled with awe at the majestic scene. I no longer felt so euphoric, though, as the vast mountains covered themselves in weighty cloud and the darkness of night, and distant thunder rolled around them. Instead I felt small and at their mercy.

The night was a wild one of thrashing rain and wind; I was so cold I got little sleep. Next morning broke clear again, but still very cold. I found my two stalwarts in the outhouse, shivering and looking miserable. Molengo announced that he had malaria and could go no further. In a feeble voice Edward chipped in that he was not feeling so great himself. Angry and frustrated, I told them they were just cold and that if they did not come with me I would not pay them. This heavy threat evoked solemn faces and a lot of muttering. Looking closer at Molengo, though, I saw that he did look pretty ill. He probably did have a touch of malaria, which is endemic in many of the local Africans and comes on regularly as a mild fever, especially after exertion. So he was to stay behind, but I was determined to continue and poor Edward would have to come with me, as he would almost certainly lose his job if, arriving back at the base camp, they discovered he had let me go on my own: he was supposed to be my guide. I didn't think he was properly ill, just unused to the rigours of climbing mountains. I decided I would try to reach the third hut and come back down to the second in one day: I didn't feel like carrying Molengo's load, which I'd have to if we were to stay the night in the third hut. I realized, too, that I really was too badly equipped for the cold up there, having only a thin cotton jacket, gym shoes and an inadequate sleeping bag. We left Molengo looking very pleased with himself, busily making a little nest by the fire to await our return.

Soon the upset of the morning was forgotten as once more we tackled the same type of endless snarled path as the day before. After the night's rain everything was streaming with water, and before long we were wet through. Most of the time we were in cloud, and dead silence encased us, broken only by the grunt of our efforts. Now and again I had to wait for

Edward to catch up. I felt sorry for him because he looked quite miserable, but I was selfish in my determination, and not sure that he wasn't just lazy.

On and on we climbed the steep staircase path, using our arms as much as our legs, like a couple of monkeys on an assault course. The air was tense and fragile with the cold stillness. My left knee, with which I have periodic problems, started to play up, hurting so much I could not bend it, so we stopped to strap it up with a bandage the French had given me, and I cut a long bamboo stick as an extra leg. We only passed one clearing all morning where it was possible to sit down and rest, but there was no clean water to drink.

At last the woods came to an end at the edge of a boggy gully with a crystal-clear stream running through it to a cliff. This marked the beginning of a new and strange land. Gone was the tortured time-tunnel. Misty clouds swirled before us. Standing out of them, like ghosts, were monstrous, overgrown plants, some like huge toadstools two metres high, some like giant groundsel and lobelia grown to nightmare proportions. They looked as if they belonged to a prehistoric filmset. I almost expected a fearsome prehistoric bird to swoop in on us. There were soft, fairy bushes with startling white flowers sticking up like candles; short, rubbery trees, spongy and feeble to the touch; the débris of decaying vegetation and carpets of spiky fern: all fragmenting and dissolving in the mist.

We sat down by the stream and ate sausages. I gave Edward some aspirin, which made him feel better, but it was so cold we had to keep moving. We set off again through the thin clouds across open, moor-like mountainside, weaving our way among the statuesque plants. It was now that I first started to notice the effect of altitude and as we went higher it got worse. My head was swimming, my limbs felt as if they were not part of my body, but made of lead. Each step needed hard thinking and each one took more effort. I felt as though I was moon-walking. I was breathing very fast yet with deliberation. After every ten or so steps I had to stop and sit down. Slowly, slowly we drifted upwards, two wraiths now in a wildnerness. Was it minutes or hours we had been there? The mountainside led up to a series of ridges and valleys, thickly clogged with wind-blown ferns and gorse bushes. We followed a path going up and down into gullies and over banks. Each seemed bigger and more formidable than the one before. Then I noticed we were in open country. The path seemed the only thing under the now thick clouds. There were no mountains, no cliffs or valleys, just the rocky path and us, alone.

Eventually, after a few hours of this, we found some rocks to sit on, on a ridge. A numb silence pressed in upon us. We could not speak, could not impose words on it. I knew that if we wanted to get back to the second hut before nightfall, which we had to, we should turn back now. Somehow I did not mind; the third hut must be very close by now and I felt a sense of release. I had arrived in the secret domain of the peaks and now I was free of the power that had compelled me up here. I could not see the peaks but I could feel them. They seemed to acknowledge my presence, my homage. I could descend in peace. I told Edward we must return now, much to his delight.

For the first hour or two we flew along like newly released birds. We ran and jumped with new-found energy, each step becoming lighter as we dropped, I hopping and skipping with my stick and straight leg as best I could. We twisted and turned down through the wild and watching landscape, up and over the gullies, in and out of the strange silent trees and rubbery plants, splashing through bog and mire as if escaping from some grim giant, until we crossed the crystal stream once more into the deep, dank forest. I felt like Jack who had found his beanstalk that would take him back to his own land.

Going down through the slippery tangle of roots was much more difficult than going up; one slip could result in real injury. Hours passed unmarked. I had nothing else in my mind but the treacherous series of hurdles, dips and catwalks ahead of me. The faster and more adept I became, using my limbs like a juggler, the more things became a blur, of trees and mud and moss, down and down, until I had to stop a minute to regain my sense of reality. By the time the sun had sunk below the horizon I began to despair of there ever being an end. I was more exhausted than I could remember. I almost believed the forest had stretched, that it was playing with us and would not let us out. But at last, there was the second hut, sitting on its hillock below us. We found Molengo by a big fire, cooking a meal. He looked up with a grin but said nothing and continued his work; he had obviously recovered from his 'illness'.

Sitting by the fire that night I felt invigorated and content. My muscles and bones relaxed in the heat and my mind picked over the hard day, savouring the good times and feeling snug and smug when thinking of the bad ones that were now in the past. The night was very cold again but this time I slept well. We started back down at dawn, through the thick woods, resting again at midday on the clear hillock where I had watched the circling crows, over the harsh ridges and valleys; under the grand trees where the Barbaries had been and where the small monkeys still were chirping. We stopped again at the first hut, made a quick meal and then set off, running a good deal of the time when my knee allowed, sliding down the long, mud shoots, through the bamboo and reed jungles, past the place of the soldier ants and finally round the mountainside to face the remembered world.

At Molengo's house we stopped once more to eat another meal of bananas and beans as the sun sank, and Molengo once again changed his clothes. Then the three of us, our spirits revived by the meal and the beautiful evening and the nearness of the end, continued to the base camp. This last walk was the hardest. The mountains had been conquered so there was nothing to draw me on, no overpowering force to combat my exhaustion except maybe the promise of rest and the knowledge of having touched something at the heart of Africa. Edward was cheerful for perhaps the first time and when we came to his parents' house he said goodbye and left Molengo and me to trudge on to the base camp.

12

A Fishing Village and Departure

My stay in Zaire was coming to a close; I had an appointment
in Kenya to keep a couple of weeks hence. Before leaving,
though, I wanted to visit a fishing village called Kiavinyonge,
about which I had been told. It was on Lake Amin, once
known as Lake Edward, on the border with Uganda, so I could
quite easily fit it in en route. Getting there proved quite
difficult, however. Somehow I managed to spend a whole day
hitching on the wrong road and walking a very long way in the
wrong direction, but eventually I got a series of lifts that
brought me to it.

Kiavinyonge is surrounded by the Virunga National Park, a
park with all the East African beauty, a wide open swathe in
yellowing grass with the occasional umbrella acacia tree
solitary beneath the spread of clear sky. Waterbuck and buffalo
idle in its painted space like cricketers in the field. The village
lies under a wall of hazy mountain on the sandy banks of the
Semolick delta, a tail to the lake like the tail of a minnow.
There are literally thousands of hippos in the lake, snorting,
yawning and wallowing away their lives. At night-time they
invade Kiavinyonge and the lake shores to graze until the
dawn; no one ventures too far out of doors for fear of bumping
into their dark, bloated forms. Antelope, duiker, waterbuck
and gazelle also live close to the village, clearly unafraid of the
proximity of man: here there seems to be a harmony between
the animals and the villagers. One evening I saw some buffalo
come out of the bush to drink, not a hundred metres away.

Some villagers carrying wood did not see them until too late, and were immediately half-charged, but it was not a real attack.

At first I had difficulty in being accepted. Kiavinyonge, too, was visited from time to time by truckloads of tourists who stayed for an hour or so, photographing all they saw. The villagers made no effort with tourists who only came as to a zoo; neither, it seemed, respected the other. As a result, I was continually mobbed by children who shouted and jeered wherever I went; the women stood and laughed and the men ignored me. Fortunately, the place I was staying in was a good retreat. It was a large compound with a tall grass wall all around and long mud buildings of many tiny rooms. In these a mixture of people stayed: wives with no husbands, men come to buy some fish, and the man from the room next door because he was on holiday and liked the place. In the evenings people sat outside their rooms, cooked meals of rice and fish and talked easily. The women would come over to see what I was about, some men exchanged courtesies and gradually I relaxed and was soon accepted by them and consequently by the village. Then people smiled at me and invited me into their homes. One man, a park guard in a very smart uniform, took me to meet his wife. He lived in a small mud hut with only a table and two chairs inside. His wife served us food in silence, only mumbling monosyllables to his enthusiastic questions. She was very cross with him, in a silent way, because he drank all his money and gave her very little with which to keep their many children. No doubt she made ends meet like most of the women, by smoking fish and selling them. Snubbed by his wife, the man spent a long time trying to make his radio work to show me his worth, but he could never get the batteries in right.

A beer transporter, a jolly man, round like a barrel, and his friendly clerk, lived in a small room 90 per cent full of beer. He took me to see his girlfriend; we sat and drank beer in a neat little parlour with a lacy tablecloth, but again the woman was silent and blank-faced. Only when I was walking in the village alone, where there were gaggles of women at work and merry, would they talk to me and invite me to sit down. Then they were full of life, friendly and playful.

'Have some of this fish,' they would say. 'It is good and very strong.' They would watch my face as I ate, waiting for me to show surprise at the taste. They would be so pleased that I ate the fish that they were the ones who laughed with surprise. I was now a normal person. Babies would be placed in my arms and small boys made to shake my hand.

'Ah,' they would say, 'look at him squatting on the ground. Why are his trousers ripped, why is his hair so long?'

I became a part of them through their open criticism. They could treat me as a brother or son.

'Why are you not married?' they would continue. 'Then your wife could mend your clothes and tell you to cut your hair. My daughter is very beautiful, don't you think, that one over there. Why don't you take her?' They would laugh as the girl blushed. The women liked to talk a lot, just talk for the sake of being gay and making communication. They did not like loners or unhappy people.

The village was made up of rows of round and square thatched huts with whitewashed walls; outside were the cooking pots, the lines of clothes and barrels upon which fish were smoked. Each evening when the fishermen returned,

there was a fish market on the beach. The boats, piled high in the stern, were pulled up in a line stretching for half a kilometre or so, their bows pointing to the sky. They were painted in bright colours and customized with slogans and naïve pictures of aeroplanes and birds. Trucks came from far and wide to buy the fish in bulk, and the whole village congregated there. People crowded around shouting prices and handling the brown, bony fish. There were fish everywhere: on people's heads, in baskets, under arms, strapped to bicycles, in wheelbarrows, in carefully counted piles. Small boys, the sons of the fishermen, untangled yellow nets. The whole beach and the grassy bank behind were thronged with people, most busy but some just idling in the evening air, sitting in groups or strolling to meet friends. The sun would set behind the mountains, the sky would turn from gold to red, and all the vivid colours would stand out in the dusk.

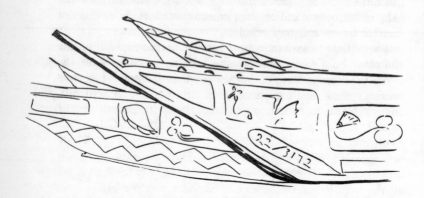

In the twilight I would sit on a boat at the end of the beach, watching the evening play of the birds. Swallows darted about on sharply pointed wings, feasting on insects floating in the warm air, then stood at the water's edge, ducking and preening. Kingfishers hovered then knifed into the still water to spear an unwary fish, shattering momentarily the mountains and sky. Sometimes big fish eagles, all white and black and fierce, would swoop down to the surface and clasp in their grappling claws the floating body of a discarded fish. There were also many duck, gliding onto the water and paddling amongst the hippo nostrils and grey, protruding backs; and hundreds of ugly marabou on backward-bending legs, looking like so many disgruntled old men with their hands behind their backs. They would stand by the lake like mourning statues or perch on rooftops, but mostly they'd lurk about the families cooking their meals, towering above the children. Occasionally, people would get fed up with their beady-eyed presence and shoo them away. Then they would run and hop, their great wings all a-fluster, and take to the air like reluctant jumbo jets. When the hippos began to emerge, silent lumps of granite-grey flesh, to start on their night of foraging, I would leave my perch and go home.

When I left Kiavinyonge I got a lift in the same pick-up truck that had brought me in; now it was stacked high with fish, many people riding on top of them. I knew several of them this time and we were a jolly bunch as we drove away. It was very hard to stay on top; at some corners people and bags slid off.

We were poled across the Semolick in a barge. The four boatmen took us a long way upstream, working very slowly and methodically; when we crossed, the swift current caught us and we were swept down to the landing place. Sitting next to me on the truck was a man who spoke excellent English. He was wearing full skiing gear, from shiny red plastic jumpsuit and jacket to a bobble hat. A surprising sight here. We talked all the way. When we came to a military post we had to give the soldiers some money. There was no reason for this, and no pretence that there should be.

'This is the way,' my friend told me. 'It is the system here in Zaire. Everybody takes money and bribes. It is the only way to survive. These soldiers would not be able to feed their families if they did not take money from others. There is no money in Zaire, except in Kinshasa. All the money goes there. Food is expensive and wages are very bad so all the people do this: the school teacher only teaches half his day, the other half he will do another business; the police make laws as they wish, and take money for any service they do. It is an accepted thing. There is nothing else to do. It has a sort of harmony in its own way: maybe you lose out here, but you gain there. We do not like it, but we cannot change it. All the young people would like to change this country. But we have not the power.' He was voicing what I had come to realize on my journey across Zaire but had shrunk from expressing, not wanting to invite these very criticisms. My friend smiled and nudged me cheerfully.

'But of this we should speak no more. What is the point in it? Accept for now and be merry is what I say.'

And so we drove on through the Virunga Park. We saw a family of wild pigs, red from the earth, trotting in a line: Pa, Ma and four little ones, all with tails in the air like tufted banners. They quickly headed for the tall grass and disappeared.

At the park entrance I left the pick-up as it was going the other way, to Beni. It was evening and the road was deserted, so I walked in the direction of the border, only a few kilometres away. I was happy and content. I had enjoyed and been impressed by Zaire. There were so many different faces to it, some of which I had seen, but many I had not. The people were as kind and genuine as I had hoped they might be; even the corruption I no longer condemned, because I understood. I knew I should want to return.

The road wound steadily upwards. I rose to the top of a pass and over. Zaire was behind and in front was a new country, laid out before me in chequered plots of land, blue with yard-fire smoke and browning in the evening haze on low undulating hills. I walked down into the deceptively calm scene, and walked directly into a country in the throes of turmoil and strife, for the people of Uganda were not accepting and being merry: they were having a coup.

As I could cross the border at any time, I decided to return to the Zairese border village to wait a bit for things to cool down. One morning, still undecided whether to cross that day or not, I wandered in and out of the immigration post, as I had been in the habit of doing for some days, to sit and talk with the many truck drivers also stuck because of the coup. But today, as I wandered through, a man I had not seen before called me over. He was dressed in a fresh white suit and sunglasses, and he had an arrogant, bad-tempered face. He was the *chef de poste*, the local dictator.

Being in a happy mood, and not in the mood to show the customary fear and subservience this sort of man expected, I did not answer his abrupt questions immediately but gave him 'Bonjour'. This forced him to 'Bonjour' me briefly, which was obviously not his intention. He continued to be rude and asked me unnecessary questions which I answered lightly. This was a mistake. Angry at losing face to a Westerner in front of the people standing around, he demanded my passport. When I had fetched it, he took one look at it, snorted with satisfaction and marched into his office, saying, '*C'est faux*, you've forged the visa.'

Well, it was obvious I had not but he was going to use and abuse his power to show me and the others who was boss. Loudly, to be heard, he told me to go and get my belongings. When I hesitated, angry myself now, he and another man went for me, which sent me on my way. When I returned, my bag and everything in it was pulled apart, searched and tossed in a heap in the middle of the road. Then my passport was quickly stamped, shoved into my hand and the next thing I knew I was ejected from Zaire.

At the Ugandan border village there was chaos. Drunken, dangerous-looking soldiers, armed to the teeth, lay everywhere like litter, and scared-looking policemen cowered in the bars. A convoy of about 60 trucks was parked, waiting for permission to cross the country, so I latched myself on to them and was put up very comfortably in one of the trailers by a tough young Somali driver called Abdul. Eventually I crossed Uganda with him, stopping off very frequently along the way for Abdul to visit his many 'wives'.

I spent a month in Kenya seeing game parks, swimming in the sea and resting in the lap of luxury before I decided to move on once more.

157

PART THREE

SOMALIA

13

Into Somalia: Kismayu

I was drawn to Somalia for three reasons. One, because I knew so little about the country. Two, because I had been impressed by the few Somalis I had met so far; they seemed a race apart. And three, because one morning I was standing at the main Nairobi bus stop with my bag and some money in my pocket, undecided whether I should go south to the Bantu once more, or north to make new discoveries and be amongst Muslims again. I missed the bus south, so took the one to the north.

Somalia, known in Pharonic times as the land of Punt whence came frankincense, spreads further than its present frontiers imply. As Ibn Battuta, the great fourteenth-century traveller wrote, 'The Somalis, an ethnic race completely independent of foreign rule, live in a country extending throughout the length of the Horn of Africa.' And so they do still, but now they spill far over the official borders imposed upon them in the nineteenth-century 'scramble for Africa'. From a small area in north-east Kenya, they spread up into the Ogaden which, in the fourteenth century, was annexed by the kingdom of Abyssinia (Ethiopia) and on up the Horn of Africa to the tiny republic of Djibouti at the tail end of the Red Sea. The cities on the Somali coast such as Mogadishu, Merca and Brava in the south, and Seylac (Zeila) and Berbera in the north, were once part of the extensive Arab-controlled trans-Indian Ocean trading network, part of the chain which took in Malindi, Mombasa and Zanzibar further south. Arab immigrants settled in these cities and gradually the Somalis were assimilated into Islam. In the sixteenth century the trade network and hence the prosperity of these cities was destroyed: the Portuguese had discovered a new trade route to India via the Cape of Good Hope. In the scramble for Africa, Somalia was divided between the British, who took the northern part opposite South Yemen in 1884, and the Italians who took the southern part alongside the Indian Ocean in 1889. The French took Djibouti rather later. Independence was granted to a united Somalia in 1960 and nine years later a military coup brought the current president to power. Since independence, Somalia has waged war on and off with Ethiopia over sovereignty of the Ogaden desert, though their claims on northern Kenya territory are now of a much lower key.

Most of the country is a harsh scrub and waterless waste. There are no famous parks and lakes here, no tall mountains or palm-fringed beaches. It is a land of people, their camels and their towns. My trip through it, therefore, became more of a relationship with them than a journey.

The bus from Nairobi, after five or six hours of hard motoring, took me across a slow, sandy river and left me in a town called Garissa in the east of Kenya. I felt immediately that I had already crossed a border of some sort. Here the people and the very atmosphere were different. The few people I saw wore long, flowing robes. They were tall and aloof with soft, curly hair. The town was almost deserted, silent and lifeless in the afternoon heat; it was not until the evening that it came to life. Then it unfurled like a flower, as all the people came out to stroll and do business, and I was caught at once by their looks and manner. They took no notice of me, only throwing glances at my incongruity as a passing thought. When I spoke to them, though, they responded warmly.

I stayed in Garissa only one night and next morning went to the petrol station, where I had been told I could find a lift to the Somali border. I got there very early and sat waiting on my own. Two or three hours later small groups of Somali women and their baskets and bundles, with babies peeking out of wraps on their backs, started to congregate across the road. Men with tattered suitcases came and sat near me, and we all waited. All morning vehicles came and went, but none that was leaving town. Eventually a Landrover turned up. Barely had it stopped before there was a mad scramble to get in the back.

A young man called over to me, 'You're going to Somalia, quickly, come here. You must get in.'

I plunged into the shouting scramble. My new friend hauled me up and deposited me unceremoniously on top of some women. My hat was squashed and my bag slipped down amongst the struggling bodies and disappeared. We sat for some time in awkward angles, waiting for the driver to re-appear. When he did, he told us that he was not now going to the border after all. We untangled ourselves and climbed out again. But he soon changed his mind, so we piled in once more, shuffling about until we settled, like a pie. Suddenly the engine revved and off we shot. At the last moment several bystanders flung themselves on to the sides of the car and clung there precariously. We went at a great pace, but into the town not out of it, and about an hour later were back sitting outside the petrol station again, having visited seemingly everybody and his brother-in-law. Many sacks of mira, a popular stimulant, had been collected and were squeezed under us so that now we perched high above the ground, something like a howdah. Two armed and sleepy soldiers got into the cab with the driver, our protection against shifta, the bandits and smugglers who keep the military in this area in a state of idle alert.

During the whole of the 200-kilometre journey to the border I saw only two places of habitation. One was a desolate, tented military outpost and the other a small sandy village with a sign in the middle of it saying 'Equator'. The country grew uninterrupted, head-high gorse and thorn bush that in most places looked impenetrable. It pressed in sullenly on either side of the road, as if trying to suffocate a breathing space. Now and again we passed some nomads with their impervious, sandy-gold camels, strolling casually, totally at home in this searing, inhospitable land of sand and bush. Small, half-naked boys shooed goats out of our way and as we drove by stood

163

silently watching us. Our passing did not touch the nomads; it only left them shrouded in our dust for a while. There were frequent groups of duiker along the route; as we drove past, they dived for cover. Once we came upon two slim gerenuk standing in the road with their backs to us. They seemed not to hear us approaching until we were nearly upon them, then they leapt into the air with little shrieks and streamed into the bush, twisting and turning this way and that in confusion, their eyes wild with terror, their long necks swaying back and forth like pieces of rope in time with their lurching bodies.

My travelling companions in the back of the Landrover livened up as we neared the border. Among the assortment of draped and sashed men and women were two students, smartly dressed in tight, modern trousers and patterned shirts. They spoke English and were returning from Nairobi to Mogadishu. Their names were Mohamed and Ahamed. Mohamed was very fair-skinned, almost white, and Ahamed was a deep, charcoal blue-black. Both had wide, wild halos of frizzy hair. They questioned me about where I was going.

Ahamed said, 'My name is Hassan Ahamed Mohamed. I am Hassan, my father is Ahamed and my grandfather was Mohamed. But I am called after my father. Ahamed. Tell me, Mr Peter, why do you not fly to Mogadishu? It only takes an hour instead of three days. That is how everyone else goes.'

When I explained my reasons to him, he said, 'Ah, so you are a tourist. I welcome you very much to go to Mogadishu. You will like it so much. The weather is perfect and the people are very friendly. They are not like these people in Kenya, who do not know how to live decently.'

Ahamed studied in Nairobi because he had a rich uncle there and because it was more fun, he said, but he was very proud of his own country and loyally thought it far superior to Kenya. Mohamed was quieter; he told me he didn't like Kenya because there were too many thieves, whereas in Somalia: 'You will be quite safe,' he said.

There was one very Italian-looking man, the progeny of some Somali-Italian marriage, no doubt, sitting on top of the cab. He did not speak English but had a very friendly smile and wanted to make sure I was seated securely. He had a huge suitcase that he clasped close to him the whole way.

The Kenyan frontier, when we arrived towards evening, was a typical border post of ramshackle huts surrounded by a dusty, abandoned-looking village; a place forgotten on the perimeter of life. The customary long wait was eventually broken by the arrival of a pick-up truck loaded with sacks. An immigration man came over and started to search our bags. We unpacked them and he fingered through the contents, saying, 'This is a nice radio. How much will you sell it to me for?' Or, 'This biro, you would like to give it to me as a small present, no?'

Meanwhile men staggered amongst our innocent articles, unloading sacks from the pick-up truck which had just arrived from the direction of Somalia. The sacks were clearly marked: 'Milk powder. A gift to the people of the Republic of Somalia from the people of the United States of America', and they were being stacked in an office equally clearly marked 'Kenya Immigration Post'. The Italian-looking man had long, surreptitious discussions with the immigration offical over the contents of his case. Exporting quantities of silk underwear, expensive tights and scent was obviously taxable, but also negotiable.

By the time we were through, the sun was only a glow left on the horizon. There was a curfew on the roads after sunset but we managed to persuade Ali, our driver, to take us on to the Somali border post a few kilometres away. Unfortunately on the way we passed a military vehicle, which immediately gave chase. After a hectic, bumpy pelter, Ali gave up trying to pretend he had not noticed, and stopped. A heated argument at once broke out between the impatient-looking soldier and Ali who put on a show of: 'Yes, I'm terribly, terribly sorry. But you know what life is. I'm sure we can come to some arrangement.'

We all piled out and two or three people started to walk on up the road saying contemptuously, 'We shall walk, we have not got time to waste in this way.' They had no time any more for petty Kenyan officialdom because they were nearly in *their* country. Naturally, this annoyed the Kenyan soldier even more.

'I'm just doing my duty. I should take you to the captain and he will fine you,' he said, eyeing the sacks of mira.

At these words everyone decided to take a different tack and looked suitably resigned. Before long we were on our way again, leaving the soldier standing at the side of the road with a big bunch of mira that had appeared in his hand almost magically. Just before we reached the border the Landrover stopped again. The same two or three people got out and started to lug the sacks of mira into the bush, hiding them with sand and leaves. Mohamed explained that mira was now illegal in Somalia but that the soldiers still virtually lived off it. You had to hide it in the bush before you could find an officer of a high enough rank to make arrangements with, or else every Tom, Dick and Harry soldier who happened along would demand a cut, leaving nothing to sell.

The border village was in a grove of trees. We were given permission to stay the night by the immigration chief, a dangerous-looking man who sat outside his office in a chair, surrounded by his lackeys. He oozed confidence like a tyrant. Everywhere was dark, only broken here and there by the warm glow of lamps in the shops and cafés. The village was alive with nomadic-looking men with aquiline noses and stern faces. Many women still sat on the dusty ground in silent circles, selling camels' milk. There was an exciting undercurrent here so different from nearby Kenya, an air of unknown qualities hiding in the darkness and behind those dignified faces.

I spent the night with Mohamed and Ahamed at a bush hotel. Next day we showed our respect to the appropriate officials, and were once again on our way, in a Matato this time, a Toyota pick-up converted with a cage on the back for maximum capacity. We were headed for Kismayu, some 220 kilometres away, along a road with a fearful reputation of being impassable during the rainy season and infested at any time of year by the military and shifta with automatic rifles.

The drive was long and through the same country of sand

and gorse bush, featureless except for the wrecks of trucks set into the concrete mud. One of our party was a furtive little man trying to smuggle a small sack of mira. Each time we stopped at a police post he was taken aside and lengthy discussions took place. There was no formality. All the occupants of the truck joined in, arguing with the soldier, the man and each other about the rights and wrongs of the case. Each time the man returned, he looked more miserable and his sack lighter. Eventually he called a halt in the middle of nowhere and got out, saying he had had enough and would walk by another path rather than give any more to those thieving soldiers.

We arrived in Kismayu at dawn. The air was hot, thick and salty and the streets were deserted. I did not see the nearby sea but its presence hung over us, dominating the town. We found a hotel and slept.

The next day was my first real day in Somalia and I was glad to have Mohamed and Ahamed with me; I needed an introduction to this different place of different people. There seemed to be a certain code to life here, but before I understood it I felt alien and helpless. The people looked unapproachable, and their customs incomprehensible.

Much of this first day was spent in eating. This was a good thing for me; I always think a people's eating routine gives useful insight. First thing in the morning the three of us went in search of breakfast. We walked down wide, spartan streets of sand. A strong wind blew, whisking up the sand, stinging our faces. Groups of dusty boys ran about playing, a few robed and hooded men hurried along, hugging the walls, and donkeys strolled or stood stock-still looking dejected with their backs to the wind, flicking their ears and frisking their tails. Ahamed led the way through an unmarked doorway into a large, dark room containing long trestle tables with plastic baskets of bananas on them. At the back was a stone, clattering kitchen that looked like a cave with open fires, blackened by smoke and grime. Two dirty, aproned waiters flew about flinging plates, cups and jugs at the tables. A few men sat in inconspicuous corners, and behind a tall wooden pulpit by the

167

door an old man sat conducting the waiters and counting money. We sat down. *'Caano Lo! Canjeero! Lahore! Bearr!'* Not having the slightest idea what I was being offered, I agreed to eat the same as my friends. Plates of chopped meat in oil and onions, a pile of pancakes, bread and sweet tea were brought, and I watched in fascination as Mohamed and Ahamed rolled up their sleeves and proceeded to knead the pancakes and bread to a pulp, adding the meat and a banana as they mashed, and then, for good measure, pouring their tea on top. Without further ado they scooped up great handfuls and stuffed their mouths with such rapidity that they had finished while I was still deciding how to tackle mine. We washed and dried our hands on pieces of newspaper when at last I had finished and found ourselves back outside with a toothpick in our hands at such a speed that were it not for the heavy sag in my stomach I could begin to doubt I had been in there at all. Mohamed had paid for the meal against my objections.

'What is the point in us all paying separately, like you do in the West?' he asked, laughing. 'The money is unimportant. I like to pay for my brothers when I have money and when I don't, they can pay for me.'

This universal attitude to money in Muslim Africa was enlightening. Whoever has money spends it freely, sharing it among friends almost as if it were communal. You can even ask your friend to give you money and he will not expect to be repaid. But when he asks you for some another time, whether less or more, within reason, you must give it to him.

Black Ahamed, as Mohamed called him, had some relations in Kismayu who owned a small shop on one of the main streets, selling everyday things like orange juice, cigarettes, sugar and tea. Ahamed and I went there later in the morning and sat on stools sipping tea served by a shy, pretty girl. Ahamed talked to his handsome and handsomely dressed relatives, tall men who came in and greeted us both very politely and formally, but he never gave a second glance to the girl, who, he told me, was his sister by the same mother. She went off to prepare a meal for us. When it was ready we went through to a whitewashed courtyard and into a small house.

Inside it was clean, with smooth white walls and straw mats on a sand floor. Taking our shoes off at the door, we sat in the quiet, mosque-like atmosphere and waited while the girl brought us water to wash our hands, and glasses of tea. The food when it came was a delicious stew of steaming chicken, vegetables and nuts beautifully presented on a large steel dish surrounded by a lace of rice. Ahamed fanned it for a while with a straw fan and when it was cool enough to eat, picked at it with great delicacy and restraint, rolling the food into neat balls in his hand before popping them into his mouth. Here in the home the meal seemed more of a ritual than merely satisfying the appetite as in the restaurant that morning. Ahamed quickly finished, having eaten little, and so yet again I was caught out and had to finish what remained. Whenever I showed signs of flagging he got very agitated.

'You've eaten so little. Don't you like it? . . . Good, good. Eat then, eat. Here, try this bit of chicken,' turning the dish so that my little excavation was replaced by another wall of rice and vegetables. One must see one's guests well fed. Don't believe them if they say they've had enough; they're just being polite, naturally.

When eventually I had finished and was well bloated, the girl came back to clear away. She blushed deeply when I thanked her and praised the food, and Ahamed looked embarrassed too. She poured water over our hands to clean them and brought more tea, passing it to us like an offering, curtseying with bowed head and saying, 'Thank you, thank you,' as we took our glasses from her outstretched hands. Then she backed away and disappeared quietly.

Although I partially understood the complex role played by women in Muslim societies – they are often not nearly as subservient as may seem – I did not really understand Ahamed's total indifference to this girl, who was his real sister and whom he had not seen for a year or more, so I asked him the reasons.

He did not seem surprised at my puzzlement. 'You know, we in Africa have very big families. Our uncles can be as important to us as our fathers, and our cousins, nephews and nieces as close as our brothers and sisters. This girl is my sister, but I have not lived with her for a long time. I live with my uncle who is like a father to me. All my relations are my family, but for now I know my uncle and his family well. My sister is the same as a niece or a cousin: we do not know each other well, so our relationship is only that of two members of a big club. She cooks us a meal and we eat it. This is because we still love each other even though we now have little to do with each other. It is only with the true mother that one is always very close. She has a special relationship with her sons which never changes. It is a good system. Always we know that any member of our family will do what he can to help us, and we shall do the same for him.'

Rarely did a shop or business belong to an individual; they were all part of a large family concern. Maybe one son will run the shop, another work for the government and their brother-in-law may be studying or abroad. Perhaps the father or an uncle dabbles in wholesale or transport business. A couple of nephews work the markets and streets with suitcases of watches and clothes. The wives weave baskets and the daughters and nieces keep themselves beautiful and pure to marry a man from another equally expansive family, thereby increasing the web of influence and self-help. In this sort of set-up there is always room for another dependant, who in due season will be able to add to the dynasty.

Mohamed, who joined us after our meal, and Ahamed took me down to the sea in the afternoon, so different from the luxurious palm-fringed shores of Kenya. Here scrubby sand dunes and desert ran slap into a short sharp beach scattered with seaweed and seagulls. It stretched away in an unexciting uniformity of shadeless heat along the entire coast of Somalia, reputedly the longest coastline of any African country. In front of the town the beach was littered with rubbish and the rotting shells of boats, deserted except for a few boys kicking footballs around and one or two nomadic-looking men strolling, robes blowing between their legs and outlining their form like soft sculpture. They looked oddly out of place against that vast stretch of water.

The wind was blowing hot and hard, and a light sea drizzle fogged the air; when the sun came out later it beat down with a relentless force. The beach had about as much charm as the wind-fluffed marabou, stiffly stepping amongst the piles of wind-driven débris, picking and squabbling like vultures. The far north end of the beach was dominated by a crumbling pier and three huge naval boats left over from the Second World War, dead and rusting on wooden supports. At this end of the beach there were a few boats anchored offshore. One of them was a small cargo boat that looked as old as the naval wrecks, painted in sombre greens, reds and blues, all weathered and flaking. Men were busy shifting sacks into a smaller boat bouncing alongside in the choppy water. When it was full, it chugged heavily through wreaths of sticky seaweed to the beach to be unloaded by another team of wiry men, naked except for a piece of cloth wrapped round their hips and tucked between their legs. They waded out chest-deep and staggered back grimacing, bulging sacks across shoulders and heads. On the beach a group of donkeys and carts waited patiently, tended by small boys. When the carts were full of sacks the boys tapped the donkeys with sticks and they strained and pulled to dislodge the heavy carts from the soft sand. Once free they trotted nimbly down the beach, the boys bouncing on their backs.

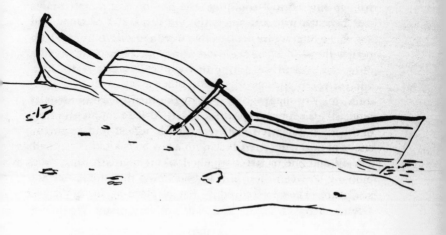

For me the real lure of the shore was an enormous Arab dhow being built in the traditional way, by hand and entirely of wood. Its lines were smooth and beautiful and it towered above the beach like Noah's ark. Invited to come aboard, I climbed up to the deck and stood there, excitement coursing through my veins. I could feel the life-force of a craftsman's boat beneath me, and smell the earthen scent of wood and stain. The huge, solid deck beams were a platform from which to view the world. The sculptured prow jutted into the sky like a finger confidently pointing the way. This was a real ship, a ship for the high seas.

The three men building it lived in a small encampment at its side. 'It's taken us six years to build,' they said with pride, 'but now it is nearly finished and ready to sail the seas for as long as a hundred years.'

Walking back, I asked Ahamed why there was no sign of fishing. Here was the third biggest town in Somalia with a whole ocean next door and no fishing.

'Some people fish,' he said, 'but not very many. We do not

172

like fish. When we are hungry we must eat some meat. And anyway it is a hard life to be a fisherman, always on the sea away from land. And after all that, you only get a mouthful of bones when you eat it. It's not worth it.'

The town of Kismayu had the same air of cowering under the elements as the beach. The houses were built of jagged, coral-like rock, squat, hugging the earth. By day the fierce wind and harsh glare made the streets inhospitable, places to be ventured into only at need. In the evening, though, Kismayu was a different place, transformed into a town of intricate colour and motion like a coral reef that is dead and grey at low tide but a place of dancing light and life when submerged in water. People left their cooped-up homes and poured into streets that were now cool and pleasant in the lucent dusk. I almost had to push my way along. All the houses that had been shuttered and dumb by day now had their doors wide open to display small shops and stalls. The pavements were lined with tables and chairs where huddles of men sat and sipped tea out of glasses. On every doorstep and street corner people gathered. Single, sedate men walked up and down, greeting a friend and going on, greeting a friend and going on. Young men in modern clothes; old men in tradition-al robes with well-carved sticks; well-fed boys and scraggy urchins; scruffy working men; rich manicured men and state-ly dames with entourages of giggling girls: all mingled in the evening promenade. Donkeys and carts jogged along, a path through the crowd appearing miraculously ahead of them, like the parting of the seas for Moses. Vegetable-green taxis inched and urged their way through, beeping and bumping. Most people had no particular reason to be there. They came for the pleasure of strolling, seeing and being seen. You could walk around this meeting of shared humanity for hours, stopping here and there for a glass of tea, sipping the party atmosphere.

Somali women have startling beauty. It is as if they have been moulded out of the most delicious ebony-brown honey by someone who has only one idea of a classic, completely natural beauty. They have strong chiselled cheek bones and noses, soft, full-lipped mouths and dark eyes that shine with

173

coy determination. They move with liquid poise, always they hold their backs straight and their heads high. They wear long flowing dresses and drapes of thin silky material, mostly transparent, consciously displaying gleaming white bras and petticoats put on for special occasions to appear fashionable and rich. They are womanly and alluring in a way that Muslim women should not be, but the wonderful blend of Bantu and Muslim wears down the harsher edges of Islam, adding zest and freedom to women normally concealed in shapeless black, and rigid codes.

The men are handsome too, upright and collected, with strong-shaped faces. They also have a smooth, shining quality, and many of them wear the traditional ma'awwis, colourful, chequered calf-length material wrapped round the waist, loose, comfortable and easy, and cotton shirts. Dignity is of vital importance to their way. Observant, noticing, they carry themselves serenely, the stiff-limbed gait belying their agility. They are people who respect other people's affairs: to force themselves upon strangers would be demeaning. It is easy for a stranger to mistake their controlled faces as unfriendly, but once you speak to them, and become their concern, they lose that hard, sculptured look and melt into warm, honest smiles.

I noticed that some men would frown at me with puzzled, uncertain looks, but once they discovered that I was English, they would press cigarettes and tea upon me, almost apologetically. The street urchins have the same dignity and courtesy, even a haughtiness, as do their respected elders. When an argument breaks out between two young men the cause is soon lost: it is their dignity and self-respect that they jostle over, like two proud cocks, strutting and denouncing the other. Their machismo, though, rarely leads to a fight, a degrading and humiliating affair. No, normally at just the right moment they are pulled apart by the willing crowd, still shouting at each other, still putting on a great show of struggling to get free and fight.

Next day Ahamed announced: 'Today we shall go and see the Hotel Touristique. It is very beautiful.'

174

It was out of town a bit, along the coast, on a barren, windswept cliff. Perhaps once it had been a hive of handsome tourists, of fun and games, but now it was decidedly run-down. It was still a proud place, though. The manager greeted us warmly. Very pleased to see me, he said. Full of pride and bearing, he led the way to the restaurant, a huge room with an immaculate, glossy floor and row upon row of empty tables adorned with virgin white cloths and the usual plastic baskets of bananas. Away in a corner sat a lonely couple being fed by a relay of smart waiters, who squeaked across the floor to the kitchens. A few suited and subdued men sat under gnarled, widespreading trees by the dry, cracked swimming pool outside, sipping tea with their decorated girlfriends. Ahamed and I wandered for a while along the mossy footpaths between the shuttered rondavals that were innocent of guests. Ahamed walked stonily and stiff, with his hands behind his back, as if up a church aisle. He talked in museum whispers, proud to be in this place of class and symbolic wealth. We sat beneath a tree and had some tea served by a girl who sloped around with a wonderful air of languid sexuality and pretended boredom. Before we left Ahamed talked to her and took her address.

'She's just a friend of my sister's,' he said, guiltily.

The following day I left Kismayu. Mohamed and Ahamed came to see me off. There was only one bus a day to Mogadishu, so inevitably it was packed. Under Ahamed's directions, however, I managed to secure a seat by climbing through a window whilst a scrabbling crowd bottlenecked at the door. This bus journey was just the sort I enjoy: not too long, not *too* uncomfortable and there was plenty of interest to look at inside and outside the bus. At first, on any journey like this, fellow passengers are uniformly anonymous. As you motor along, though, individual characters and groups start to emerge; little stories about them, real or imagined, evolve.

On the bench at the back of the bus sat a gaggle of ladies, deep in purdah. They held small black masks over their faces, when they remembered, and veils and shawls of bright colours fell about them; their small, pudgy hands were prettily decorated with indigo stains. They were expensive-looking ladies, heavily bejewelled, and chaperoned by a smart, self-possessed young man. Why were they travelling by bus, and whose wives were they, I asked myself. Surely not his? They seemed to be enjoying the trip like a day out, giggling and laughing and generally causing a buzz. Whenever we stopped at a village, as we frequently did, out would be sent the smart young man to buy bottles of coke, brochets and bananas. They hung out of the window, laughing and shouting orders to him.

'No, no. Don't buy from him, he's far too dirty. Get three brochets from him, with lots of chilli, and two cokes from over there. And don't pay more than three shillings.'

Eager hands grabbed the goods through the window and they munched and gobbled like children on a picnic.

Across the aisle from me was an odd young man accompanied by two women: he brought me food at one of the stops and then announced that he had no money left. There was something furtive about this group. They whispered and giggled and smiled like conspirators and the women nudged the young man repeatedly, pressing him to give them a cigarette. They smoked with the concentration and poise of boys behind bushes, and then asked for another. I had never seen a Muslim woman smoking before, except the prostitutes in hotel bars. Were they eloping, or was he recruiting some women for 'business' in the capital? Or were they doing both?

At one point we came across a blind beggar sitting at the side of the road. The bus screeched to a halt and the ticket collector went up and down among the passengers, collecting money. He hopped out and gave it all to the beggar without a word, then jumped back on to the already rolling bus.

We passed many military checkpoints along the way, each time waiting maybe a half an hour while all the bags and bundles were passed down from the roof and searched. Towards my bag, though, the soldiers showed complete lack of interest, shouting up to leave it where it was. Everybody else was frisked from head to toe, except the women, of course. My furtive young friend told me they were looking for guns.

The road between Kismayu and Mogadishu was about 300

kilometres long and passed through an often surprisingly green landscape. On one side the sea could occasionally be glimpsed, a peeking v-shape of deep blue between sand dunes. Some of these dunes had been planted with a light furze of bush in an attempt to stop them moving, and resembled balding heads implanted with a grid of hair. On the other side, the long Webi Shebeli twisted and ran up to the bus and away again, on its journey down the coast to Kismayu and the sea. The Webi Shebeli has its source far away in the heart of Ethiopia. In this part of Somalia it gave life to a wealth of vegetation. Flooded fields of green, swaying rice looked sumptuous after the days and weeks of dry, cracked land; startling white egrets, knee-deep in the runs of sky-blue water, picked and pecked at the soft brown earth. Ragged and tattered banana plantations, green and yellowing, messed the otherwise neat landscape. Of people there were many, tilling the earth with bent backs and fast, flickering hands. Small boys with goats seemed to live on the road, and oxen pulling carts piled high with straw, lurching along the avenues of spindly trees between the fields, flashed by as we passed. This was the garden of Somalia, a place of softer light and different people. I was tempted to stop and explore the villages behind the dunes on spits of coast, or in the small valleys, but I was in the bus and the bus was bound for Mogadishu. It was another of those lands I must come back to another time.

14

Mogadishu

Arriving for the first time in a big town in the dark of night, at the height of the evening rush, is always exciting, but it can be confusing too, even intimidating to a tired and fuddled mind as mine was when I eventually arrived in Mogadishu. I could get impressions only, of lights swirling, noises beckoning and blasting, and the swag and swing of pressed humanity. Unusual scents came and went, leaving a sense of an empty stomach stretched with wonder and nerves. Luckily my odd friend on the bus took me in hand. We walked through areas I knew I would soon be accustomed to, and found a hotel, where he left me with a sweet goodbye.

In the clear morning air Mogadishu seemed somehow richer and more affluent than I had expected, a far cry from that country of refugees and famine I had heard of; that country of fruitless desert and economic catastrophe, being nursed back to health in the lap of American benevolence after the expulsion of the Russians following their switch of allegiance in the late 1970s to Somalia's traditional enemy, Ethiopia. The town centre was a mixture of Italianate design and old Arabic architecture, quite pleasing to the eye. Multi-storeyed hotels backed on to worn, stone buildings: a museum with huge wooden doors and two little cannon guarding it; a vast cathedral and a large mosque; footpaths through gardens and wide tree-lined streets. The modern bank seemed to be the focus of the city centre. Mirrored doors swung continually to

178

take in or put out men with rich, cultivated faces and well-tailored suits. The pavements moved with a mixture of expensive, colourful ladies, businessmen with briefcases, bureaucrats and an assortment of touts, sellers, loafers and beggars. The centre was not really so smart, though, if you looked closer. Dust and scraps blew about, some streets were little more than excavations of earth, and the gardens were not so very green. But this was unimportant. The eye was busy with the pleasing look of wealth, the cars making a stir and a commotion in the streets: Renault and Toyota models, barely on the market, jostling at the lights with Mercedes and Landrovers. Porsches and Rangerovers were also to be seen. An eye-catching blue sign saying 'UNHCR' was noticeable on the doors of the majority of cars. Wherever I looked it jumped at me, far outnumbering those proclaiming 'taxi'. This was the insignia for the 'United Nations High Commission for Refugees' – big business in Somalia.

Other parts of town were, of course, not so wealthy-looking, though I saw no bad ghettoes. People looked reasonably healthy and clean but their houses were shifty affairs up broken alleyways, low, dingy and overcrowded. It was not a very big town, Mogadishu: there was just the centre and the port and long main streets, fanning out to a scattering of richer and poorer suburbs, down which ground a continuous flow of overloaded buses and trucks.

Having arrived in an African city, my usual aim is to get out again as fast as possible, but for a variety of reasons this often takes quite a long time. So in the meantime I get accustomed to and often end up quite liking that city's particular brand of life. Nicely balanced between the southern Bantu style and the Islamic north, Mogadishu was a slow, day-by-day city where most of life happened on the street. It was easy to join in and pass the time in much the same way as the majority of the inhabitants passed their life. Everybody had his part to play, whether he was a beggar, a businessman, a government employee or a tourist. On every street in town there were rich and poor rubbing shoulders in the markets and at the stalls. A poor man, but a respected Muslim, had as much prestige or more as a richer man who was not so devout. In the mosques the very rich and very poor humbled themselves side by side, bowing to Allah. The poor were the concern of the rich and the rich the concern of the poor. As a friend once told me, 'If at any time you have no money, you only have to find a mosque, go in and ask, and you will be given.'

The main activity of Mogadishu is business. Business in every shape and size because Somalis are born businessmen. If it is possible to make a profit transporting a commodity a few kilometres from one side of town to the other, they will do it, and milk it for every penny it is worth. They start at a young age. In any part of town, at any time day, swarms of children, some barely more than five, can be found clasping packets of cigarettes. They will sell the cigarettes, one by one, until they have enough profit to buy a carton. With patient determination, they will work the streets all day, every day, until one day they are the proud owner of a small collapsible street-corner stall selling not just cigarettes but combs and mirrors, ointments and scents. And one day perhaps they will end up in the big time, exporting goats to Saudi Arabia and importing whole container-loads of cigarettes.

These people account for a good many of Mogadishu's population. Ask almost any man and he will tell you he is a 'businessman'. Some parts of town are more lucrative than others, and the general favourite is the area surrounding the central market place. In the mornings, but mainly in the evenings, the streets are crammed with businessmen. At the bottom of the scale are the boys and young men who wander in and out of the crowds, displaying their goods on their hands and heads. They drift about, working at the carefree, evening-happy people, now and again finding someone willing enough to finger their wares, perhaps buying a little something and perhaps not. Slowly they eke out a profit and will promote themselves to the lines of men crouching in front of plastic sheets on the pavements and down the centre of the road, displaying piles of plastic shoes or stacks of chequered ma'aw-wis, red and yellow socks, white Muslim caps sitting on each other in bendy towers, and multi-coloured heaps of dirty, discarded Western clothes.

Occasionally there is a hue and cry as a disgruntled police-man who has not been paid his due appears at the end of a street. In a moment the businessmen are gone. The sheets are whisked up in a single, practised movement, the goods safely inside; suitcases of smart shirts and plastic watches are snapped shut and their owners hurry off down the street as if about to catch a train, mingling with the crowds of other passengers who have no baggage. If a policeman does catch one of them unawares, his shirts and combs are strewn on the ground and he is knocked, butted and denounced to all as a criminal while he stands with a submissive, naughty boy air. But one day some of these men will rise to the ranks of secure and legal shop owners, men of property whose stores edge the streets and the alleyways that delve into the medina. The old town is badly run down now, with many of the mosques demolished, but it still crawls with life in the bumpy ways and the leaning coral houses that almost touch overhead. Many of the shops are only cupboard size. They overflow on to the streets in waterfalls of purple and red silk shawls and streams of intricate lace. Glittering slippers stitched with gold march their way out amid bundles of pure white bras. Some are music shops, stacked with tapes of wailing native music, competing with the piercing tones of Michael Jackson. Chemists also play a big part in any higher-street life; it is as if rumours of a chemist-free Africa have spawned a whole new breed. In Mogadishu they even have some medicine on the shelves

Following the current of people cascading round the businessmen, planted in their midst like rocks, I arrived at the big market square where men sit in the arcades to carve walking sticks or sell scrolls and books of the Koran. On one side are long stone halls filled with the food of the city. Crisp, wet vegetables cover stone slabs – cabbages, carrots, freshly dug, and watermelons sliced in half. Oranges, mangoes and bananas are weighed and chucked in bags. Internal organs of animals, gory and dripping blood, swing from strings, followed closely by a buzz of flies. Healthy-looking fish in tombs of ice give off a smell reminiscent of a pleasant day at the seaside; but the working men and women, in stained clothes, gibbering and juggling behind their earthy goods, want customers not spectators, and their attentions forced me out into the open square, into odious heat and unwelcome glare. Out here is all the food the sun cannot harm. Patient work-worn women sit in rows in front of sacks of milk powder and maize, wheat grain and rice, sacks of sugar and salt. They sit under that sun all day, even through the siesta, in front of these sacks that are marked so clearly 'Aid for Refugees from the People of Germany', or from Sweden, Australia or the United Nations, and selling their contents to little boys and girls sent along by their families to fill a pot with maize for the evening meal. A friend said to me once, 'It is good that we now have all this Aid food. It is so much cheaper than the local produce. But the farmers are the ones who suffer. How can they compete with such prices? They now grow only as much as they think they can sell or use themselves.'

Also in the square are huge piles of pineapples, watermelons and bananas. Men stand guard over them as they steadily rot.

Boys push around wooden carts piled high with deliciously baked bread made from wonderfully superior and abundant 'wheat for the refugees as a gift from . . .'

The hotel I was staying in was situated in the heart of this business area. For the first few days I found it very hard to find, as it was not on any street but tucked away down a little alleyway which had itself been converted into a restaurant where sweaty men sat on boxes eating large quantities of rice and greasy meat. In front of the hotel every evening, the storytellers would tell their tales, old men with a rapt, silent audience squatting or standing in a circle round them. They

183

would tell tales of Mohamed and Allah, throwing their arms in the air, and chanting verses of the Koran, acting out certain parts. I would spend most of every day out in the town, wandering about, sitting in cafés and trying to organize my further travel plans. Most afternoons I would return for a siesta, then watch the storytellers from my window until it was time to sample the evening.

The hotel manager, Hassan, was a neat, well educated man, and very good-natured. Each night when I came in he would detain me downstairs while he closed up the small hotel café or sat behind his counter. He would talk to me as if it were a game, trying to draw unguarded answers to his clever questions. Whenever I said anything that sounded particularly foolish, he would slap me on the shoulder and say 'Oh, Peter, you are so funny.'

The nightwatchman was a bald, leathery little man with a huge, lethal-looking stick and a mischievous, friendly smile. These two were perpetually at jovial odds and used me as a yardstick. Hassan would point at the nightwatchman as he prepared his bed on the floor.

'Look at him, he sleeps curled up on the floor every night of his life, like a dog, and then spends the rest of the time chanting his Koran. Isn't he a joke?'

Of course they were trying to get a rise out of me, to test my understanding. I would have to agree with Hassan.

'Yes, what a waste of time,' I would say. And then the wiry little man would jump up, brandishing his stick, dig me in the ribs and attack Hassan, bending his arm and scuffling amongst the tables.

In my wanderings I had met a man called Hamud from the north of Somalia who used to come and see me at the hotel. He had come down here because he hoped to find some means of education, but he was pretty destitute now, and was much on the streets. Hassan said he was 'a bad man' and that I should not trust him. But he wasn't. He only wanted some company. He showed me around the town and told me where to eat. He never asked for a thing and indeed it was hard to press even a tea on him. One day, when I was in need, Hamud lent me his

184

smart black shoes. It was quite a wrench for him, as they were about all he had; but then he lent them freely, and was there next morning to retrieve them.

My hotel was in the busiest part of town for transport; as in most African cities, transport in Mogadishu was a predominant factor. Africans are very sociable, forever visiting relations or going here and there for some reason or another, so one of the most striking things about their cities is the vast quantity of noisy vehicles grinding through the streets. Mogadishu was mainly dominated by the ranks of Aid vehicles with their blue signs. They plied the streets ceaselessly, like a bizarre convoy that had mistakenly latched on to its own tail. Seemingly as a pre-requisite, they generally had a handsome-looking woman next to the driver. They could be found in all manner of places, their occupants going about any type of business. Those who could not secure a 'private' vehicle resorted to the battalions of public ones: Matato pick-ups, carrying a surprising number of people, were terrible and battered but had a certain charm of friendliness and durability; modern mini-buses with people stepping onto and out of them as they moved; and large 'front-line' buses that growled through long, useful lives. Generally they were so full they could not move very fast, but coming to the top of a hill, the drivers would give a helter-skelter smile and, rather like a bowling ball, they would roll down the way, veering to their bias but mostly missing the skittles.

While I was in Mogadishu there were problems of petrol shortages, so those drivers who could not afford government fuel, sold on the black market, spent days on end jamming the road by the petrol station near my hotel, queueing in a solid steely line, three deep, shuffling forward day after day, groaning in the tink and shimmer of street heat. These patient lines became part of the town scene, the drivers and their boys settled down with their faithful metal nags, chatting, dozing across the seats and sleeping in the back. I could see the main bus stop from my window. All day long crowds of people would wait. Whenever a bus hove in sight there was a mad rush for it and before it had come to a stop, they would be fighting and scuffling to get inside. Big ladies with bundles were the ones to be wary of. With grim determination and strong-armed force, *they* would always find themselves a place. Their small children and babies, clinging to their skirts with white-knuckled fists, would be plonked on the lap of next-door passengers. When they were all crammed in, the bus would lurch off, scattering passengers not properly aboard, leaving a trail of them like confetti.

A large proportion of Mogadishans worked in the vast governmental bureaucracy. This cleverly constructed machine could create a lot of work from and for nothing, and could absorb nearly all those who had no taste or aptitude for business. It gave the impression that it was invaluable and permanently busy about important projects, schemes and policies. It certainly managed to keep me fairly permanently busy for about two weeks. My object was to get written permission to travel to the north of the country. The official line was that the Ethiopians, still intent upon upsetting any further plans Somalia might have in regaining sovereignty of the Ogaden, were bombing the cities, and that cholera was rife; so it was a closed area, out of bounds to foreigners such as myself. However, I had heard that this was only part of the story. The north was also closed off because there was much unrest amongst the people there, with a freedom movement fighting to overthrow the southern-based government. And because as an Aid-dependant country, the worse the refugee situation was made out to be, the more Aid would be received. But I was not deterred.

I had come to know the truck drivers who drove north regularly. Their stop was just near my hotel and whenever I walked past them, they would call me over.

'Come, you want to go to Hargeisa on my truck? I can give you a very good place up here on top. You will like the north, it is very different from here in the south,' they would say.

Unfortunately for me, it was not as easy as that. First I had to make my bureaucratic rounds and wherever I went, I was sent somewhere else. I went to police headquarters, a large grey building with long, dingy corridors of anonymous grey doors. In a corner of one of these dark corridors I found a row of sweating men waiting to petition the man I had been directed to see. They stood silent and cowed, waiting for his door to open, and made no fuss when rich, beautiful ladies or bumptious bureaucrats barged in front of them. Inside the cell-like office, with one steel table and one hard-backed chair, was a crowd of gibbering nobodies and one self-important man. He sat in his chair with unpredictable eyes and a bored, pasty face. Confidence and ignorance dripped from him like sweat. He heard out the petitions before turning his eye to me. I tried to draw myself up, apart from the crowd of fearful people, but really I knew it was hopeless: this man was not here to help. He told me my request was none of his concern. If I wanted to pursue the subject I must go to the NSS.

The National Security Service was one of the staples of life in Somalia, one of those things that, on entering the country, become as significant as the tin mug of camel's milk or the evening call to prayers. The term NSS, and all acquainted with it, pervaded the town, hanging around in dark corners of conversation and as explanations to certain events. It seeped into the streets, into houses and into people's lives. It hung over the country like a thundercloud with promise of water for a parched land, but menacing with its threat to strike with vengeance. NSS headquarters was like a fortress, with a tall wall surrounding it. A phalanx of solemn-faced nomads stood round a table in the yard showing identity cards to an officer. The building was filled with sullen, shifty-eyed men who directed me down more dark corridors. The officer I saw wanted to know why I had come to Somalia, what I did for a living and where I lived in England, why I should want to go to the north, and how the hell had I got a visa anyway? My reply that I was merely a pleasure-seeking tourist, the only possible answer, unbelievable as it sounded in the tense and brooding office, seemed to lighten his mood sufficiently for him to tell me to leave. It was out of the question for him to give me *written* permission, he said, adding when I was on my way out, that Somalia was a free and beautiful country and he hoped I had success with my tourism. He suggested I go to my embassy who, he said, could be responsible if I ended up dead; but it might be worth trying the Ministry of Tourism.

I was surprised to learn there was one, myself being about the only visible tourist in Mogadishu, and anyone I asked for directions also seemed puzzled. When I did find the ministry it was a quiet, pleasant building, low, with verandahs and courtyards, screened windows and a dry musty smell. Here I met a series of polite and interested men whom I found doodling at desks stacked high with telephones, and taking tea with their secretaries. They welcomed me into their sociable offices, equipped with sofas, piles of homely, dusty paper, and old colonial maps browning on the wall. They delighted in talking to me about myself and my tourism, but whenever the subject of a pass to the north reared its ugly head they became terribly apologetic. Just as yet they had not constructed any tourist amenities up there, so I would not want to go anyway; but also, unfortunately, the minister from whom I would have to ask permission was away at the moment, visiting the Hotel Touristique in Kismayu. Now *there* was a fabulous tourist hotel, full of interest and beauty. Why didn't I go there? Later on, after discussing all the merits of Somalia, they told me there was a man in town who might be able to help. He had been brought in especially by the President. He was an expert on tourism but he never came here, to the ministry, so they did not know what he got up to.

I found Mr Sampath in residence at the Grand Hotel Juba. He appeared at his door on the fourth floor in a state of flustered agitation as if expecting another fruitless interruption to his work. When I told him why I had come, he ushered me in saying, 'Yes, yes, do come in. I'm delighted to see you, but really I can't imagine why you were sent to me. Those people in the Ministry of Tourism are so idle and hopeless, I have to do *all* their work for them.' We talked for a long time, Mr Sampath and I, as he let loose a flood of pent-up thoughts and frustrations to someone to whom he felt at last he could speak freely.

Poor Mr Sampath. He had been in Mogadishu for two years,

alone in his room, trying to create a structure for tourism against all odds. The President wanted foreign investment but would not build roads or import buses, he told me. The fleet of ministers and aides completely lacked interest in the subject, except in so far as they intended to see that Mr Sampath did not upset the present system whereby all the big hotels in town were government-owned and all the profits went to their own pockets. Besides, the general policy at the moment was set against having too many foreign eyes in the country to see what went on.

'But,' he sighed, 'I shall try for a while longer. They pay me quite well.'

His professional advice was not to go to the north, but he would quite understand if I still wanted to try. He would see the minister tomorrow, and ask if I could have permission. Perhaps I would come with him?

The interview with the minister, a big, well-fed man, was short. Mr Sampath, bespectacled and carrying sheaves of paper, wrung his hands. The minister would have nothing to do with it and suggested I go to my embassy. Mr Sampath and I shook hands violently, like best friends or conspirators, and he wished me the best of luck.

My rounds went on a while longer, as the British Embassy personnel, it seemed, could do little to help. But eventually they gave me a piece of paper whose main merit was its grandeur. It merely stated that I was a tourist travelling north.

The day always started early in Mogadishu. Shortly after dawn the streets stirred into activity and all morning long remained full of people about their business. By one or two o'clock, though, the official working day was over and the streets emptied, as though a plug had been pulled. Only the grime of dust and dirt was left, with scraps of beggars and cripples here and there. They slept deeply on shaded doorsteps and under carts, rags pulled over their heads to keep off the flies. The beggars were usually wild-eyed, crooked-mouthed men who roamed the streets in worlds of their own madness, spared the torture of padded cells and electric shocks. The cripples were

189

remarkable people. It was almost as if what they lacked in their bodies, they made up for in their faces. Legs and arms might be shrivelled things tucked away but their faces glowed with a sweet gentleness, filled with humility and nervous from the barbs of pity. They chose quiet, unexpected spots to sit in, where they stayed all day long, not moving for the sun. They smiled at me when I passed them, their unpressing demands for alms virtually unnecessary as I already wanted to share that communion with them.

Life only returned to this sun-bleached scene when the shadows became long and the cooler evening air beckoned everyone out of their homes. As in Kismayu, the most pleasant evening occupation was to sit at one of the many pavement cafés and watch the procession of people. Young men in smooth slick clothes dominated the scene by sheer weight of numbers. They were the 'students'. As I made my evening rounds, they were drawn to me, like children to pricey ornaments. They would ask me if I wanted help or direction, and tell me they were students.

'Oh,' I'd say, 'and what do you study?'

Always the answer was, 'I *want* to study medicine and become a doctor,' or 'I *want* to learn English and study engineering.'

I would ask them when they thought they would be able to do this.

'Oh, soon, soon. I am just waiting for my application form to a university in America.' Or, 'My uncle in Libya has said he will send me some money to go to Italy. I am just waiting for a while.' Or even, 'I have a brother in the Ministry of Education. Maybe he can fix me a place in the university.'

They had so many reasons why they did not study just now, and most of them always would have reasons instead of a chance. But they did not care because they had hope. They would follow me around for a while, friendly and companionable. I represented that distant, democratic West with its wondrous freedom and privilege: maybe some of it would rub off on them. I was a straw to be grabbed at. They would become my friends, my protectors and my guides for an

190

evening, and take me to the cafés, the cinema or to some friends. But they would not be too demanding. Later they would disappear, not even asking a goodbye. They were sad, these phantom students. They yearned for education and they knew they would not get it, but they continued life with a faint, lasting hope.

My best friend in town was a student but he was also a shrewd, life-wise person who worked hard in an engineering company, trying to broaden his possibilities. He had taught himself very good English, and studied engineering from books in his room. I met him one evening on the secluded patio of a grand hotel, watching the dark, swelling Indian Ocean as it broke against the old Arab fortress nearby and curled in small phosphorous waves on the beach below. It was a quiet and abandoned sort of place in the heart of town, with a huge dry swimming pool deep in rotting leaves. The paving stones were cracked and mossy from neglect. The only people here were people who had come to sit in their boredom, away from the noisy streets, on the wall looking over the sea and in the pure sea breeze. A rhythmic throb came from the hotel disco-thèque. Prostitutes wandered out now and again, equally bored and frustrated by flagging business, to lounge round the darkened patio like gun-fighters looking for action, tempting with aggression. One young man I had not noticed till now called two of them over. He teased them playfully, using their own game of mockery and provocation. It seemed strange, coming from someone looking as friendly and young as he did.

'How much do you think you're worth?' he jibed. 'Look at you, bulging out of your trousers and displaying your bosoms like watermelons in the market. What *would* your mother think if she saw you now?'

They countered, swaying their hips, 'You are only a little boy. What do you know about *women*?'

They seemed to like him, rather like a younger brother, and he seemed to care for them, like wayward sisters. He tried to shame them but they only stroked his face, saying, 'Don't worry, little boy, you will understand one day,' and strolled away.

191

Shugaar and I became friends on that quiet wall. He did not have too many pre-conceived ideas so I did not have to temper and adapt my speech for him. He would question me intensely about the West, not trying to confirm his idea of it but trying to grasp what it was like. His people were nomads living in the arid, inhospitable bush on the edge of the Ogaden. He told me about this determined race of people who eke out a living only by their intimate knowledge of and harmony with their environment. And by their lack of knowledge of such words as 'defeat' or 'despair'. About their ancient traditions of hospitality and hostility; their fierceness and gentleness; their lives and their deaths, how these things work hand in hand with each other, each one invaluable and essential for the perfect and precarious balance of an obscure and tough way of life which nomads will survive where no one else can. Shugaar knew that this system, which embraces camel raids on other tribes, or leaving weak members of a group to die, or blood feuds and vendettas, can sometimes seem detrimental and wasteful to outsiders. But the system had evolved through centuries; it could be, often is, upset and unbalanced by the meddling hands of ignorant people, with their political intrigues, pressures and conflicts. They disregard the importance of seemingly contradictory tenets, where sometimes perhaps hunger is preferable to despair and freedom of movement is as necessary as a drink of water.

I wished I could have visited his family and tested myself by their standards but living so close to the Ogaden my presence there would most definitely not be appreciated by the military and would cause problems for his family. Shugaar told me of his brothers who, in the wet season, would go off into the more distant bush with the family camels for months on end, with only their sandals, ma'awwis and a spear, to find fresh grazing for the herd until the next dry season. They live only for the camels, whose milk is their only source of food and drink, and for whom they would fight and die, since without camels their family would be dead. They are supremely alone out there and only their confidence that they can survive independently as they have always done sustains them. There are no towns to go to as a last resort, no roads to hitch a lift upon, no relief centres with free hand-outs. Perhaps if there were they would no longer believe that they could live unaided. Perhaps the knowledge that their camels were not so important after all, that they could always get free food if they wanted to, would make their hard lives of fighting for those camels' survival seem pointless. Perhaps they would lose their instinctive will to overcome problems, not to give up. They have hard and hardening lives but they are such full and fulfilling lives that they can bear themselves as a proud people. They can have dignity and can laugh at the beauty and trickery of the world because they outwit it in one of its harshest forms.

Shugaar was a nickname. It meant 'soft hair' and he did have unusually soft, straight hair even for a Somali. He had been sent away from his nomadic family because he had been delicate, not suited to the rigours of the life. He would say, 'Look at me, I am tall, but only skin and bones. My brothers are tall, powerful men, nurtured on meat and milk.'

But he was bright and intelligent so his father, a soldier now, had decided to send him to Mogadishu at a young age, to live with his uncle and be educated. He lived in a small wooden shack adjoining his uncle's compound. It was spartan and dank but he was very proud of it because it was his home and contained his few meagre possessions. There was a single naked light bulb that hung down from an invisible ceiling, and no window at all. The walls were faded and sweaty, speckled with the corpses of flies and mosquitoes where they were not covered with glamorous advertisements cut out from rare Western magazines. Handsome cowboys sat on horses smoking Marlboro cigarettes; space-age cars, glossy and unreal, brazened it out with beautiful, modest model girls wearing yesteryear's fashions.

Whenever we went there he would sit me down in his comfy chair and call out for one of the gaggle of girls who hung about in mysterious and unseen hutches nearby, to get us some tea. He would give me his big file of letters and newspaper cuttings to look at. There was a long and dogged correspondence with a German engineering company. His own letters were so honest and naïve that the replies, which might have been starchy and businesslike, were also warmed with feeling. Although they could not offer to train him, they were delighted by his determination and enthusiasm, sending catalogues and dungarees that to Shugaar were a source of immense pride.

He also had a couple of letters printed in the local English-speaking newspaper, written by himself. They were courageous letters, criticizing the government, but again they were so honest and caring, and written in such a clever manner that, he said, the editor risked publishing them. Inevitably it had led to a problem or two with the NSS. Shugaar had a good relationship with the NSS, though. They knew him and he knew them. He played cat and mouse with them and for some reason (maybe he had connections), they let him get away with a certain amount of cheek. He did not seem to care about his tightrope walk of life. He thought the NSS infinitely inferior; if he pushed them too far and they reacted, he almost felt satisfaction. He quite frequently spent stints in prison for missing a patriotic rally or refusing to take part in the sham of voting.

Shugaar's room was near to NSS headquarters, and we would frequently stop off at a café close at hand that was an NSS haunt. He had apparently been warned off from seeing me too much, but he would boldly introduce me to the smart NSS men.

'This is my friend,' he would say. 'He is a tourist who has come to see how wonderful our country is. Peter, this is Mr So-and-so. He is a very important man in the NSS.'

The man would glower but mutter deprecatingly, 'No, no. I'm not so important. But I hope you enjoy our country and my *friend* here looks after you well.'

Then, before we left, Shugaar would be called over to a whispered conversation and would come out grinning broadly at having mocked the men who dogged his steps. But in town he was not so confident. Mogadishu had ears everywhere, he said. We would always meet in different places. Sometimes, when we were talking, he would suddenly whisper, 'The man

194

behind is listening. I know him,' and we would walk off up the street laughing and talking about the weather and how much we admired the President. Shugaar was very cutting about the government and the President. He did not hate them necessarily, he just thought they were a bunch of clowns. 'The President was only a sergeant and comes from an inferior tribe. He's so scared of the Somali people he hardly dares leave his palace. He is more of a prisoner than we are.'

We met every evening in town and would wander the streets, stopping off now and again at cafés endowed with grand espresso machines where he had some friends. He would talk about the things we saw, commenting on them like an old man.

'Look, see that fat man in the Mercedes over there. Wait. He is looking for a woman.'

The car would pull up to the pavement where many elegant, soft-robed women strolled. The man beckoned out of the window to one of them and, quick as a flash, she was in the car and the Mercedes gunned down the street.

'Cars are very important to these people,' he would say. 'You cannot be a real man in Mogadishu without a car. The beautiful women will not look at you. No one can buy a car because even the richer men only officially earn a pittance. All the cars come as bribes or are Aid-donated. That man probably lives in a house like mine. But he will never take anyone there because he is a smart man.'

Two young, gentle-looking soldiers walked past, holding hands, wearing ill-fitting uniforms.

'Look, they are so young,' Shugaar said. 'They are like lost children. They have no education and they have no choice. They are just toys for others to play with. Probably they were taken from their homes almost as children and taught patriotism and pain in camps in the bush.'

There was one mad and naked boy of about fourteen we often saw roaming the streets. His limbs and skin were like a pasty jelly, his eyes glazed. His lips were thick and puffed and froth dribbled from the corners of his mouth. Sometimes he would be in cafés, standing staring at the people with his hand out, mumbling under his breath; other times he would be curled up, like a dog, in the middle of the pavement, fast asleep. He had rabies, Shugaar told me. His family had had to throw him out because he used to bite his brothers and sisters. Now he lived on the streets. They were his home. People were rough with him if he became a nuisance, but they fed him and cared for him as they would a stray dog.

Shugaar was very gentle with him. When the boy started to make trouble, shouting and crying and throwing his body about like a doll, he would go up to him, take him by the hand and lead him off down the street to a quiet spot, and leave him there.

There was an odd mixture in the streets between this homely caring for each other and the slightly tense contempt of the ordinary folk for the régime and its lackeys. It was a mixture of real people going about their lives and the farce of puffed-up officials and military men who lived in a world of precarious power.

Shugaar pointed out the old and venerable men who sat on street corners with their carved and worn walking sticks that were so precious to them – there will always be old men on street corners who watch the comedy of life passing by. One day we saw an old man with wild hair and watery eyes haranguing a cluster of soldiers from his vantage point of senility. He was growing very excited, waving his arms and stick about, spittle flying from his mouth.

'Look, people, look at these men. They think they are so strong and important, but look, they are like the jackals who grovel in the dirt. Ha, ha! Look at them, the jackals. Jackals!' he shouted.

He stood in the middle of the road, defiant, while the soldiers tried to ignore him: they could not banter with a stupid old man. The passers-by stopped to listen and laugh. But they were laughing more with the old man than at him and the soldiers knew it. They were being shamed.

'Go away, old man, or we'll tap you on the head,' they said with nervous bravado.

He grew more and more excited, his eyes bulging. He had an

196

audience and there was nothing the soldiers could do. To touch him would be to demean themselves; after all, he was just a worthless old man, what did *he* matter? So they strolled away nonchalantly to cries of 'Watch the jackals retreat, with their tails between their legs.'

Shugaar did not like passionate shows of emotion; they lacked too much in dignity. But he was smiling because the old man was like the inner voice of his people.

Most evenings, at some stage, we would go to one of the many cinemas in the heart of town. They were open-air shows, a progression of cheap, gaudy films and were comforting, sociable occasions where audience participation was dominant and very noisy. Whenever there was violence they would jump up and down, shouting for the heroes, and whenever there were sexy scenes they would laugh, much to the shame of the voluptuous actresses, I thought.

There was a complex ticket system at these cinemas. Shugaar put me right after my initial mistake of asking the ticket-seller to sell me a ticket.

'You must never ask to buy a ticket unless he wants to sell you one. You must just give him the money and go in without one. If he sells too many tickets, too much money goes to the government. How can the owner afford to run the place? It would have to close down.'

Sometimes there would be power cuts and then everybody would spill on to the darkened streets and dawdle, eating mangoes and slices of watermelon from the carts stationed outside the doors. There would be a whispering and a tenseness; blackouts are often a sign of something sinister. There had been an attempted coup not so long ago, Shugaar told me, and always the first thing to happen in troubles of that sort is a blackout.

I spent nearly two weeks in Mogadishu, meeting Shugaar every night. Though we had nothing much to do, and nowhere to go, we were never bored. We roamed the streets endlessly, just like everybody else, and we talked endlessly.

'Somali women,' he would assure me, with a youthful sincerity, 'are very headstrong and full of pride. You must

197

never treat them too well or they will think you a fool and treat you as such.'

Sometimes we would go and meet some of his girlfriends; he would always be very caring with them. They were sweet girls who brought us dainties to eat and orange juice to drink; they would sit down opposite us, smiling shyly, as we gobbled down their offerings quickly, and then be off again. Women were companions, wives and workers to Shugaar but never just friends, unless they were the brazen sort in the streets whom he would joke with and mock as you only can with friends.

There was not much talk that the long hours of idleness did not drag out of us as we sat amongst the hum and hubbub of people who also sat waiting, waiting, in the street atmosphere fogged with dusty air and vague, abandoned activity, for the coming of some change. Shugaar was like a penned animal but his patience was inexhaustible and his humour gave release to a risky game. He wrote to me a while after I had left:

'I am still in Mogadishu in tiny cage room in Immigration Department, like a bird, and I am in need of little escape to fly out, but unluckily till now I didn't get. I go every day to work very early, and I draw nothing, then I say to myself better be alone than in ill company. BUT, I go next day? Friend of mine, send me the address of volunteers, reliefs and even rich guys that I may get from them an education or a chance to escape from here (good-luck). A letter is half of seeing each other – do write to me soon.'

I would often be warned off Shugaar and people like my friend Hamud from the north, by café acquaintances who were strictly city types and 'concerned with my safety'; and told not to walk the streets at night, but I think this was an indulgent fantasy. Some people liked to believe that theirs was a hardened metropolitan city. They had heard about Nairobi, and so tried to compete. But I never saw anything on the streets or in the people that seemed in any way a threat to me. I saw some thieves one day, though. They were heading down a street at break-neck speed, their faces contorted in grimaces of fear and their eyes started ahead of them, wildly searching for a route. Behind came a wall of running people, a mass of pounding limbs and flying robes; coloured hats bobbed up and down, and a hue and cry was in the air. As the two terrified thieves neared the corner, a boy lounging against the wall simply stuck out his foot and tripped one of them. With a terrible, headlong plunge, he smacked to the earth. In a single second the crowd was upon him, pressing round in a writhing mass. Sticks were brought up into the air but they never descended upon the unfortunate wretch. People shouted, abused and vaguely kicked him in the ribs and after a suitable time they hauled him up and marched him off, but I doubt to much more harm.

The only brutality and raw aggression I saw was that inflicted by the youth brigade, a specially formed government tool, consisting supposedly of a type of boy scout. They looked after registering the vote, organizing patriotic rallies and generally making their presence felt. I used to see them from my hotel room, invading the market streets. They wore traditional boy scout shorts, green shirts and yellow neck scarves, but they also carried sticks. One minute, there was the market thriving as usual, and the next pandemonium had broken out. In stormed the jaunty scouts. They up-turned tables and stalked about, anyone who looked unkempt and undesirable they grabbed by the scruff, shouting at him and hitting him with their sticks. They were truly hateful people. All the enthusiasm and natural aggression in young men had been exploited and twisted. Put together, with sticks in their hands, power went to their heads. They bullied and humiliated the people in the street under the banner of patriotism, and when they thought they had made enough impression, no doubt they went back to their quite ordinary lives.

The main post office in Mogadishu, a spot where I spent many an hour, was a place of extraordinary confusion but it also had a particular charm. It was a large solid building in the centre of town. Outside, the beggars and cripples set up vigil and young men and meeting couples sat on the wall, dangling their legs. Inside there were long, low counters of faded wood. Behind them sat large ladies in beautiful clothes, who went about their business of franking letters and weighing parcels with a languid thoroughness, dabbing at stamps with podgy fingers. In front of them, a confusion of arms and hands, clasping notes, shook like the branches of a wind-blown tree. I had to find a gap in this wall and squeeze my own arm through, note in hand, and shake it to gain attention. Wherever I looked I saw the backs of pressing people, like punters at the races. In one corner was the public telephone system, ancient numbered phone booths lining the wall. From inside came cries of excitement at distant reunions and the careful pronunciations of tall nomads, wary of these unfamiliar machines. There was a perpetual din. Telephones rang unheeded amid cries of 'Booth Number Two, to Nairobi. Number Two, NUM-BER TWO,' and always the background wail of babies swathed to their mothers' backs but ignored now in the fight to obtain a stamp. Everywhere there was a fine smell of mixed mustiness and sweet, sharp scents, and the warm human odour of hot bodies in humid air.

Hoping to find a letter for myself in the Poste Restante, I was eventually directed to a small boy in the mess behind the counters. He led me off with an important air. We squeezed through rooms jumbled with desks at all angles, and people draped all about them; up some wide stone stairs and along corridors of numbered doors, out of which spilled clerks and customers, talking quickly and holding sheaves of paper to their chests.

We arrived in a small back room that was a total catastrophe of letters and parcels. They were everywhere, half undone, sliding off the table, under the table, under the chairs and cupboards, stuffed into little pigeon holes that were long ago full and now formed part of a cascading waterfall of letters to the lake on the floor. The little man in charge appeared in a string vest. When I put forward my request he did not look very encouraging. He picked his way across the floor, though, to a table with many leaning towers of letters and packages on it, and from in between them took out three or four envelopes. His face suddenly showed definite signs of shock, then, with a huge grin, he lunged towards me, pulverizing a few lost packages on the way, holding out a letter addressed to me.

Outside again, I bumped into my mysterious friend on the bus from Kismayu. He clasped my hand and said, 'Ah, Mr Peter, Mr Peter, I'm so glad to see you. Yes, yes, this is very good. I have missed you. I have not seen you anywhere. I wonder if you can help me with a problem? You see, I have no money left. I'm desperate. I'm so poor, I'm on the streets, starving and maybe even dying. Ha, ha! Please give me some money to buy some Marlboro cigarettes.'

'But, my friend,' I said, 'if you are so desperate why do you not buy some food instead?'

'Oh, no, no, no. That would be no good. When one is really desperate you need cigarettes more than food.'

It sounded reasonable to me and I could see that he did not like asking; he affected a jaunty air that did not fit quite right. Remembering that he had bought me some food, I gave him what he wanted. He was profusely pleased and shot off, crying that he hoped he would see me again. I rather hoped he wouldn't.

The beaches at Mogadishu were not as spartan as those down by Kismayu. In the afternoons I would often walk down to them along the long lido road that ran along the coast, past the old port and past the embassy clubs, and the bars and nightclubs where the prostitutes worked. These beaches had a slight veneer of luxury about them but still they were not lined with swaying palms and bronzing sunbathers. Locals told me there were many sharks who took swimmers regularly. Whenever I went out of my depth I had a tingly feeling in my toes as if they were about to be snapped off; whenever I left the water I would do it with a prancing step, thinking that a shark might get me at the last moment. But they were not really very common and, anyway, I always made sure there were people farther out who would, I hoped, be eaten first. When the tide was out the beach was a wide, soft curve; when it came in, the sand all but disappeared, the waves rolling right up to the weathered coral houses and clubs. They washed up against the concrete foundations and buttresses, swirling along their flat tops. They crept up stone steps and lapped at doorsteps, spraying the insides of windows.

On Friday, the Muslim weekend, everybody came down to the beach for a day out, so this was always the best day to visit it. The entire bay became an auditorium of tussling football games: small pitches for small boys, bigger pitches for bigger boys, and grand, full-size pitches for the serious, concentrating grown-ups. The scrabbling clusters of players sidled up and down like little groups of hermit crabs chasing tiny balls. Husbands brought their demurely dressed wives and strolled along the surf, following after their toddling children who slapped and splashed the water. Fully dressed girls waded out, laughing and giggling, their dresses sticking to them like wet rice paper. Further out, the young men in tight, sporty swimming trunks splashed and shouted in the big waves, showing off to each other, ducking under as a wave approached and popping up the other side gasping like goldfish, with happy exhilarated faces. Everybody had fun. This was no relaxed and laid back beach scene: everyone had had enough of being relaxed and laid back in town. They came here to shout and scream, to run and jump, to shake out all those idle hours from their bones. Only a few rich people on exclusive beach patios, happily superior and sensible, lounged about on deckchairs, sipping beer and watching the people who were free to run and jump. As the tide rose, though, the football pitches and the playground were swallowed up and in the afternoon the sun beat down, driving the people away back to town, until the next Friday. Only a residue of supine forms were left, dozing under scattered gorse bushes, and at the besieged restaurants and clubs a well-shod clientèle sipped wine in the soft salt spray.

Most evenings Shugaar and I would wander down to the seafront near the centre of town when the sun had sunk low. Even though it was not attractive, just a dusty patch of littered ground, there was a long low wall to sit on which made it a favourite place at sunset. Football games were played in the open space and rich, proud men with their perfect doll-like families would drive up in their new shiny land-cruisers to see the scene and, of course, to be seen. When I was there, some disgraced captain had managed to founder his vast container ship on the rocks nearby. The ship heeled heavily to one side, towering above the town. It was broadside to the ranks of waves, and slowly but surely their power was grinding it further on to the rocks, splitting the red steel hull. Tall tiers of containers, stacked up and up like Lego blocks, tottered on deck. Now and again, with a particularly vicious wave, a top one would topple off and crack like an egg far below. Many of these containers had expensive cars chained on top and I think everyone, like me, was waiting for one of those precious things to tumble over the side and be wrecked. The progress of the ship's destruction and the futile efforts made to save it were like a play. Each day brought a new scene. Tugs tied to long, water-logged ropes desperately struggled to haul it off, bobbing up and down in the mountainous waves like corks. There were attempts to unload the containers. Another, smaller boat drew up alongside, both vessels jogging and nudging in the swell. The long finger of a crane swung out, a container swaying and swivelling at its end. The crane man juggled with his levers, but still it bounced and scratched off the side of the ship. The attempt was called off. One day oil was pumped out from a hatch down the side of the hull to lighten ship. The black cloud drifted on the waves to the beaches up the coast.

Below the wall upon which the evening crowds sat, the waves of years gone by had carved a playground of jagged rocks. Caves and cauldrons there were, stubborn pinnacles and shelves of rock awash. The people would watch, mesmerized, as the ranks of rolling waves came in from beyond the breakwater across the bay and threw themselves upon the black, puckered rock. It ripped into their smooth sides and broke their solid strength. Dancing and leaping, they fell upon the playground, thudding into the back of caves, giving vent to whistles of shooting, airy spray and streaming from the top of pinnacles in wind-blown, milky froth. The many staring faces watched, always with anticipation, for the next looming wave, swelling up fast, with menace, to smack that first granite outcrop with just the right curve and speed and so instantly be shattered into harmless wreaths of shining crystal drops, to douse and drench the small boys hopping like seagulls amongst the rocks.

15

The Road to Hargeisa

Whenever travelling in Africa one is always told to get to the truck stop very early. So in the cool quiet hours I got up and having said my farewells to my friends in the hotel, I made for the street that served as truck stop for Hargeisa, capital of the north. On arrival I was accosted by many touts, each trying to manoeuvre me to his particular vehicle. The trucks were all laden high and looked grand, if a little top-heavy, and well primed for their 1500-kilometre journey across what was mostly desert. After much bargaining, I opted to go on a truck driven by a tall, sedate man. I followed my bag up to the top of the load, found a comfortable position and sat down to wait.

All morning the mysterious negotiations that must always take place before anything is done, went on. Now and again someone else climbed up and settled down to wait patiently like me. The sun climbed steadily. Everyone was very curious about me. It was not often they saw a European on top of a truck, and certainly not one going to Hargeisa. Innumerable questions came from the friendly crowd milling about below, and many cups of tea were handed up to me.

After a while a couple of trucks further off down the street growled into life and rumbled off to start their journey. My driver started the engine in his truck now and again, revved it for a few minutes, but then stopped and went back to the negotiations. I got drowsy on my perch amid the background drone of talking and squabbling. More people clambered up next to me. Activity around the truck increased then suddenly we pulled out and started to move off. At once it seemed that everybody in the street jumped on to the truck, scaling the side. My heart sagged. I had not realized there were going to be *so* many people for the three- or four-day trip. But of course this was not the start: we only moved off to another part of town where everyone disembarked again, and the great discussions continued under a tree.

By now it was midday and the sun beat down on our exposed truck-top, but the atmosphere amongst my fellow travellers was one of excitement and joviality. We started getting to know each other. Fortunately there was one older man squashed next to me who spoke good English, so he could interpret the questions directed at me.

'Where are you going? Where have you come from? What is your nationality? Where do you live?'

These were all standard questions. Another favourite was whether I was married and when I said 'No,' they offered me Somali women, their sisters or just passers-by. With great merriment they called one unfortunate girl over.

'*Cali, cali*, this white man wants to marry you.' And everyone would rock with laughter as I tried, politely, to decline.

'But is she not beautiful? Don't you like Somali women?' So it went on.

My companions on the truck fell into three different groups. First there were the students, or would-be students, quiet and shy to begin with but later on the noisiest, forever larking about, pulling each other's legs. They travelled with virtually nothing but a sheet and a comb and had the most uncomfortable positions on which to perch or hang. Then there were a few older young men who were more confident, very friendly and helpful to everyone. They were always merry, singing songs freely and unabashed. They were the leaders, the ones who always thought of new things to do. Lastly there were the elders: a few women, not in fact old but they fitted into this category because they were quiet and dignified, and my interpreter, Nuridin. He was a strict but caring man who could be a bit grumpy at times. He had a small boy in tow, an orphaned nephew, who veered between utter dejection and bouncing enthusiasm.

One of the women took a great fancy to my mirror sunglasses when I put them on and asked if I would give them to her. They were the only pair I had and when I showed reluctance she burst out laughing, because she was only teasing me, and said that I should not worry, she would look after me. I felt I had become the responsibility of all on board, that they would go through thick and thin, if necessary, to make sure I reached Hargeisa, just as they would for each other. We were a group and should arrive as such.

So there we all were, on top of the truck, some of us, like me, with small spaces to sit in and others without; but everybody was merry. At last Mohamed, the driver, roused himself from under the tree, fortunately this time leaving behind the horde of hangers-on. Off we set again and after a couple more stops, headed out of town. On the outskirts we came to an army roadblock. A soldier poked around the truck and asked for everyone's papers. When it came to my turn, Mohamed immediately jumped at him.

'He is an International Passport Holder,' he said. 'You must not harass him in this way.'

Everyone on the truck concurred, and the subdued, confused private was not allowed anywhere near my passport. As a consolation for him, Mohamed shouted up to me, 'Show him your bit of paper, the important one.'

I handed down the letter I had obtained from the British Embassy. It was completely powerless and carried no weight at all, but it was printed on such crisp, clean paper, and had so many smart stamps decorating it, that everybody thought I must be terribly important. So I was allowed on my way.

Mohamed was a good, solid man. He had a frank face, kind eyes and a big aquiline nose. He was a devout, quiet Muslim and wore long flowing robes, but belying his simple, almost child-like look I knew he would do what he thought right, come military man, beggar or street swindler. He would be as gentle as a giant or as hard and unmoving as a rock when called for. I was very pleased to have him on my side.

The road we were travelling was very bad. Built by the Italians just after the Second World War, it had become so pitted and pot-holed that Mohamed was forced to swing the truck on a slalom course. All the first morning we drove through greenish countryside following the course of the Webi Shebeli. It meandered drunkenly on the vast, flat plain, turning through slow, muddy bends, a couple of hundred metres wide. Fields of maize and a few flooded areas of rice grew in the hoops they formed. We passed banana and sugar beet plantations, standing out thick and luxurious in the surrounding drier land.

As the long hours passed and the day steadily died away, so did the greenery. Soon it became semi-desert and we passed many nomads herding camels and cows, and little boys and girls looking after skinny goats. The camels moved with slow, purposeful steps.

The departure of the sun was a great relief to me and my companions, who had been stewing in it all day. The splendour of the soft evening light and our exposed high positions gave us a lovely ride through the dusk. All along the road were many little dik-dik, hardly bigger than a hare, that scampered away as we approached, then stopped to look inquisitively after us.

On we went, big sheets and ma'awwis wrapped around us now to keep off the cool wind. The night darkened and we felt cosy and intimate under the clear, black sky. At about nine o'clock we came to a little village where we stopped for the night. I felt completely exhausted. Everyone jumped off the truck and dashed to a little shack restaurant, taking me in tow. We sat down to a delicious meal of big chunks of goat, rice and camel's milk. The Somalis attacked their food with customary gusto, mushing it all up and pouring the milk on top, stuffing it down as if it might evaporate at any moment. I did my best to keep up, but just ended up making a hell of a mess on the table, my face and the floor.

After some warming cups of sticky tea everyone filtered off into the bush behind the restaurant to perform their ablutions with water taken from a big earthenware pot on the restaurant porch. We all slept on the top of the truck except Nuridin, who took his bag and his nephew and made himself comfortable on the porch. One of the young men, Askar, a neat man a little older than the rest, with a close crop of shiny hair, a little goatee beard and a permanently smiling face, settled down next to me and said, 'How do you like travelling in Somalia? It's hard and dirty, eh? After four days of it you'll be as black as the rest of us, ha, ha.' Already by now I was covered in a thin film of grime. A very tiring night of fending off Askar's feet ended at about five o'clock when we set off again.

The second day was long and hard. We seemed to spend at least half the time stopped for one reason or another at the many army roadblocks. Mostly these were just a piece of piping across the road and a shabby little shack from which emerged a few bleary-eyed soldiers. They prodded around the truck for a while and got involved in lengthy arguments with Mohamed. There were also quite a few small villages along the way, quiet and insignificant in the surrounding stretches of sand and shimmering heat. We generally stopped at them too, but it was hard to determine why. No one asked and no one was told. In two or three hours we would travel only fifteen kilometres or so. It was very trying, but the indomitable patience of my fellow passengers wore off on me and I came to look upon the waiting as much a part of the journey as the heat and dust.

209

At most of the stops the men piled off and drank tea in shaded huts with wooden benches and tables. The women were brought tea on the truck since, rather like broody chickens, once settled down, little could entice them to move. When on the move my companions never ceased to be cheerful, keeping up a continual banter and chat, taking it in turns to drop off to sleep for a while. As the day wore on we wrapped sheets round our heads to keep off the sun; we looked like a bunch of multi-coloured washer-women as we rumbled along.

By now the landscape had become completely featureless. The world was split into two glaring white sheets, the land and the sky, divided by the almost indecipherable pencil line of the horizon. Mirage lakes of water, with clumps of trees and gorse floating in them, broke the distance. Only very occasional nomads and camels were to be seen browsing here and there. The camels looked as at home and comfortable as dozy cows, nibbling summer pastures in far-off, gentler lands. The few villages existed only because of the road: they had little tea shops and eating shacks. Their inhabitants, who were of nomadic stock, also had herds of goats and camels. The camels of nomads are mainly only used for their milk, which is the people's staple diet, along with goat meat. Otherwise camels represent wealth and are a family's capital. When you see a whole herd of them, watering at a well, unharnessed, smooth and slick, they look very elegant and beautiful, with a regal air

210

about them. They are revered by the nomads and even by townspeople. When a truck comes upon them on the road, the driver will not zoom past tooting loudly, as he does with goats; he will wait patiently for them to lope out of the way. Only occasionally are camels used for transport, when a man and his family are moving to another place. Then the man leads in front, pulling a tether with the line of camels attached to it, tied from muzzle to tail. The agal, the nomadic house of long bent sticks, hide and grass, is loaded on to them, along with all the other family possessions. If he has a pregnant wife, or an old mother, she will ride, but this is about the only time you see Somalis riding their camels. Behind the camels come the goats, herded by the children. The family will keep up a fast pace for many hours on end, starting well before dawn and finishing some time after midday. Then they build a circular enclosure from thick, thorny bush, to protect the camels at night. After maybe weeks of this journeying they will come to suitable grazing, and there they will make their home until they need to move again.

At midday we came to a village to find all the inhabitants heading off at a run down the arrow-straight road that pointed seemingly to nowhere. We stopped briefly amid frantic chattering, then set off in the same direction as the villagers, many of them clambering up the sides, hanging on to anything available, including the existing occupants. For about three kilometres the road was full of running, walking, trotting people, then we arrived at the focal point. There were so many people milling around, and so much confusion, that I could not make out what was happening. Everyone else had already jumped off the truck and been swallowed up in the crowd, and I was left standing on top alone, looking over bobbing heads. There was another truck under a tree being loaded with awkward-looking bundles. I saw then that the bundles were people covered in blood, with white, pasty faces. I looked round and saw another big truck that had overturned down the bank at the side of the road. A man appeared and told me six people had been killed.

'Don't you want to come and look?'

Curiosity overcame me. 'Yes,' I said, and hopped down.

Under the tree were two very dead people, laid out; my guide proudly lifted up the sheet to show me. Near the upturned truck there was chaos. We had to fight our way through. The truck had rolled quite a distance. At the point of its first impact was a big pile of goods, jumbled up and bloody. Ripped and inadequate sheets covered four more badly mangled bodies. An old man walked up to them and, with great show to the crowd, picked up the shrouds and moaned and grimaced theatrically. There was a general 'day out' feeling. Everybody was over-excited. I reckoned at least 500 people had materialized from the apparently deserted plain.

A couple of soldiers with long sticks and automatics were keeping the hordes from getting too close, but they were having quite a job of it. People were still arriving, some from the road and some appearing breathlessly out of the bush with their goats and sheep. They rushed to stare with happy, entranced faces; it was a child-like fascination, a look at their own mortality. There is something terribly undignified about death. The way the body loses all its poise and elegance, and becomes a piece of awkward, unhandleable meat. And yet, once laid down with limbs straight and a shroud covering the face, some peaceful dignity and respect is regained. One of the corpses from the pile was carefully picked up and carried over to the other truck. The arms dangled down like those of a rag doll. Someone ran along behind trying to keep the head covered, as if the dead face would ruin the party atmosphere. When I returned to my truck, Nuridin and the woman who had liked my sunglasses were already there, composed, waiting for us to depart. His nephew was beaming happily, chattering nineteen to the dozen to his uncle who ignored him. I climbed on board with a certain amount of trepidation. I now realized the potential danger of my position. It was identical to that of the sad corpses by the roadside. The rest of my companions were now reluctantly drifting back and I asked Askar what had happened.

'It's an accident,' he said.

'I know it's an accident, but I mean, how did it happen?'

'Oh, it was just an accident,' he repeated. The reason why or how it happened was immaterial. It was the hand of God.

We moved off again into the sun-bleached afternoon, leaving the crowds and the corpses behind. Everybody was quiet and absorbed in their own thoughts, perhaps savouring the sweet tang of being alive that comes after a close encounter with death. For the next six hours we ploughed on, sometimes chatty and full of life, but mostly lapsed into silence, stunned by the relentless wind and sun. When we came to a village at sunset, we stopped for the night. Again I was in a state of near-exhaustion, but I recovered a bit after an evening of eating and drinking cups of tea. When the time came for sleep I vowed that I would get a decent night's rest: I would not sleep on the front part of the load with everyone else, but would settle down at the back, on top of the canvas. To begin with, it seemed fine, and I couldn't think why no one else ever slept there. About half an hour later I knew why. A strong wind came rolling across the desert and, in my exposed position, it was impossible to sleep. After fighting my sheet for a while, I climbed down and stretched out on the stony ground. By this time I was so tired I slept at once.

The early mornings, before the sun got up, could be very cold, so when we set off in the dark before dawn we all huddled down with sheets and blankets pulled over our heads and slept again, oblivious of the passing, wraith-like world. The sun faintly tinged the horizon, then brought a briefly welcome warmth but when, after some time, we stopped at a village for breakfast, it was already overpowering. Yet this was the pleasantest time of day. People washed and scrubbed their teeth with a piece of fibrous stick; there was food and invigorating tea. You began to feel more alive and prepared to meet the coming day. Spirits were always high and everyone would laugh and joke as we drove on once more. Their capacity for talking and laughing for hours on end amazed me and although I could enjoy their mood, I was sad that I could not understand much of what they said.

At one little village I found an old man who could speak English. To general amusement, he told me all about his life as

213

a sailor in the British Merchant Navy, and about his days of dancing in the music halls of Covent Garden. When he told me he was 50 years old, everyone burst out laughing and, to his great indignation, vowed that he was at least 70. The villagers crowded around me asking questions, inviting me to stay with them for a few days. I wished I could but I was drawing the line a bit thin just by travelling north with no real permission. I would certainly have been in trouble had I stayed in that militarized area. We left, and the rest of the day was dogged by truck troubles. The main problem seemed to be dirty fuel.

All along the stretch of road along the Ethiopian border and the Ogaden desert, there is virtually no life at all. If possible the country seems to get flatter, broken only by gnarled, stumpy trees and clumps of thorn bush. We passed some craters in the road which I was told were recent Ethiopian efforts to cut off communications by bombing. We simply drove around them. Once we rounded the horn of the Ogaden, which is roughly parallel to the Horn of Africa, the dead pan of the desert was broken: small hills and escarpments of red rock started to appear, and with them more habitation. There was fighting here and periodically the Ethiopians bombed little villages and army posts. There were numerous roadblocks, manned by dishevelled-looking people in all manner of dress, so you were never quite sure whose 'side' they were on. We stopped for the night and after another big meal, I had my first decent night's sleep. The little village restaurant rented out mats. I took one and found a good sheltered spot where I slept peacefully until woken in the early hours by the soft mumble of my companions saying their prayers.

In the morning we had many mechanical and military problems. Whenever we stopped at a military post Mohammed had to bargain and bribe, something that was regarded as quite ordinary, but you had to get the right price. It was a question of conflicting wills. Having named his highest price, Mohamed would come and join us sitting in a tea shop. The military man sat across the way, in his little shack. He ignored us and we ignored him. After what could be a considerable time, the soldier would call and Mohamed would casually stroll over to hear his new demands. If he thought the price fair, away we all went, but if it was still too high, we had to wait. In the end a compromise was always made, but rarely very quickly.

After five or six hours, at a place called Sheikh, we picked up an old man who had missed his truck because he was so busy drinking tea. Up he scrambled, full of mirth and chatter. He spoke a little English and plied me with questions.

'Charma, Charma,' he said, 'your name must be Charma. What do you think of an old man like me? Not a penny or a care in the world, just like a child.'

He was a vital old man, who made us all jolly.

'Soon, Charma, you will see our Somali mountains,' he told me. I was a little doubtful whether Somalia had anything that could be called truly mountainous, but he continued to assure me as we entered a low canyon and cruised up to the end. Suddenly, we were at the top of a vast drop of sheer and broken escarpment. It fell away, maybe 700 metres in craggy steps, to an immense low-lying plain that stretched from the hazy foothills to the distant horizon. The sun was low, casting lakes of shade on the plain. The colours were beautiful. The road twisted and turned away from us, dropping down through the mountainous range, cutting its way round bulbous hillsides and disappearing into deep gullies and behind canyon cliffs. Its smooth white surface ran like a tape far, far below. Everyone on the truck became tremendously excited. We all stood up and felt like kings.

'Do you see? Do you see?' they shouted. 'The Somali mountains. The coastal plain. Aren't they truly beautiful?'

The road here was well banked and surfaced so we descended quite quickly, despite the precipitous ledges. A couple of trucks streamed past us, swaying dangerously in high gear; down in the gullies were the wrecks of others. Here and there flocks of goats browsed, chameleon-like against the grey, shattered rock, disappearing into the green gorse and scree-clogged gullies. Small boys sat high up, on cone-shaped pinnacles, watching their charges, presiding like child gods over the vast toy world spread out below.

Slowly the flat plain came nearer, changing shape and texture until, suddenly, we were part of it. We drew up to a truckie restaurant, alive with exuberant people, which sat under the very toes of the range, almost like an offering. Rows of long trestle tables stood under shady lean-tos, crowded with banqueters, their trucks parked nearby at all angles. I was reminded of a harvest festival supper and although I had recently had a meal, I could not refuse to take part in this feast; it was almost a rite to the hills. We stayed for quite a while, enjoying the company, the delicious rice and camel's milk, the juicy pears. Eventually we boarded the truck like a bunch of drunks, full of the joy of life and headed off with our old man still in tow, the greater part of our journey now behind us.

The climate on the coastal plain was quite different from the desert, wet and sticky. Within minutes I was more sweaty and dirty than I had been after three days in the higher land. As we cruised I watched the sandy plain to the horizon. Suddenly I realized that the landward part of the blue sky was not sky at all but the long-awaited sea. After two hours I spied the port of Berbera, sitting low in the distance, an island of habitation, with a sea of water on one side and a sea of sand on the other. When the truck stopped there I realized just how hot it really was; soon all my clothes were dark with sweat. I was thankful not to stay too long and after a cup of tea we were on our way again, out of the town.

Later, like weights on the two sides of a scale, the sun fell, melting into the west and, opposite, the full moon rose, at first an orb of neon red, then a sequin of pure white, casting a crystal light on the distant mountains. The whole kaleidoscope of colours, the dusky waves of plain, my exhaustion and the wind that whistled past me, and the thick, salty air, all combined to give an overpowering sense of unreality; I felt as though I was in an epic dream. It was one of those moments that redeem the hardships of travelling by land. I felt ecstatic.

We were driving in a convoy of Aid trucks by the time darkness was complete, our light searching the road ahead. Each time we overtook one of the trucks my companions would yell and shriek in victory, jumping up and down

216

energetically, chattering non-stop. Each time we were passed, they jeered and booed, and the drivers tried to ignore their antics.

After an hour or so, we came to a village which seemed to consist entirely of milling truckies and their many stationary trucks. I was still half in a different world but the others climbed down and disappeared into the confusion of noise, motion and dark. I started to doze off uneasily, too shattered to go and find something to eat. After a while the three young students returned and dragged me off to a restaurant seething with cats. My friends kicked them from under the table and were very bouncy and talkative, and slowly drew me out.

As we were sitting in the dark, sipping tea, a small, quiet soldier came up and asked me what I was doing there. He asked to see my passport and we walked off to the truck to find it. We had not gone halfway, however, before Mohamed spied us from some hidden spot and came rushing over.

'What is this soldier doing with you? Where is he taking you?' he asked with highly sprung agitation.

When I told him he yelped with indignation and rounded on the little man, towering above him, glowering with a fixed gaze.

'This man is an International Passport Holder and he is my responsibility.'

The unfortunate soldier did not really stand a chance but bravely he stood his ground and repeated that he wanted to see my passport. While they were arguing I went to find the offending article, and by the time I returned, a crowd of about 50 people had assembled, all yelling at the soldier. I quickly realized that this now had nothing to do with me, I was simply the excuse to have a go at the soldier, one of the race that milked away their trade. As for the soldier, engulfed somewhere in the crowd, well, he had a little pride. I handed my passport through and slipped off to the truck, feeling ill with exhaustion, confused and annoyed, wishing that sometimes everybody would just leave me in peace. I worried what my lack of real credentials to be in the north would bring, but later the man came over and handed me up my passport. He was

217

very polite and smiling, apologized for his presumption and said of course everything was in order.

I settled down in a quiet spot to sleep. But not for long. My cheerful young friends soon appeared and settled down beside me, but obviously with no intention of going to sleep. They joked and laughed and talked to me until at last they could get no more response.

The next day we had only a short distance to go. We climbed back out of the coastal plain, up into a landscape of rubble and small broken hills. The climate was again hot but dry. Soon we passed two conical hills beside the road. Askar told me that they were called 'the woman's breasts' and marked the entrance to Hargeisa.

16

Hargeisa of the North

Hargeisa at the height of day is a scorched, harsh place, little different from the surrounding rocky semi-desert. The streets glare and the air is hot and muffled. The buildings crouch. People hurry along the streets, heavily wrapped up against the sun, and gather in drowsy, close-knit groups under the shade of a tree or in a doorway. We, when we arrived, drove up and down the main street, registering with the police and customs. My companions one by one took their few possessions and disappeared over the side. There were few or no 'good-byes'. I found that a bit hard after our days together. But this is their way. Their meetings and their friends are pre-ordained. When I called after them, 'See you again maybe,' in the Western way, they only called back, *'In sh'allah'* – as God wills.

I felt very exposed, sitting on the truck all alone. We turned into some small rough streets leading to the market area and drove slowly through, squeezing between the stalls and carts and people, the truck getting in the way of everybody. Eventually we stopped in front of a small shop. Mohamed called me down and put me in the cab, saying he would soon take me to a hotel belonging to some of his relations. As I sat there a row broke out overhead, on top of the load, about which part of the load was for whom. A thick crowd pressed against the windows. Hands shoved into the cab with oranges for sale. Shouts and cries came from all around. I could now take my first good look at the northern Somalis.

They looked tougher and more angular than the people of

the south, with eagle noses and high cheek bones. They generated an atmosphere that was tense, almost frenetic, but somehow they seemed more down to earth, more natural. For now, that was the only impression I could glean. Mohamed re-appeared and we went off to the hotel where he abruptly left me, with strict instructions that I was not to pay for anything. I was his guest. I had a small room overlooking the street. I took a long shower. Stretched out on the bed, I fell asleep at once, to dream of desert, nomads, mountains and the endless road.

Hargeisa is an intense town, in a way that Mogadishu is not. It is in a distant, little visited corner of the world, where life is in some ways desperate and not a little oppressed. The people are mostly nomadic, or of immediate nomadic origin, and as such they are a comradely lot. To them, just by being there, I was a brother at once.

The hotel I was staying in was basic and functional, in the poor, over-populated part of town, and like most of its kind was a warm, homely sort of place. Mohamed's relatives welcomed me with charm and as an ordinary guest, though I was the first European to visit them, they said.

Mohamed re-appeared in the evening, when I had woken up, and took me down to the restaurant on the ground floor. We sat down in a din of energetic feeding, everyone gobbling down their food as if it were a race and then moving to sit outside, sipping tea with all the time in the world. We were served plates of soft spaghetti that was very messy to eat with fingers, plates of chopped liver in oil, piles of bread and camel's milk. Mohamed ate his food in silence with speed and washed it down with a cup of tea. He paid the bill, refusing to let me contribute, and then left, saying he had more business to attend to.

The street outside was dark by now; it was wide and dusty, still hot and simmering from the heat of the day. There were street lights down the middle of it but none of them worked. Light shone from gas lamps in the many small shops and lay on the pavements in elongated doors. Oil lamps flickered in several pavement cafés, illuminating in their glow groups of men swathed in robes, gathered together on jumbles of chairs. A low murmur of conversation and the clink of tea glasses rose and fell. People pulled chairs and stools out onto the hearthrug street and sat down to watch. Small boys hither and thithered, hung and drifted about, selling the inevitable cigarettes and carrying glasses of tea. Young men strolled arm-in-arm, stopping off to meet friends or duck into a shop. Other men and girls walked demurely apart, and the occasional car rumbled and bumped along the uneven way. The air was heavy with languid watchfulness. The people sat patiently, but on the edges of their seats.

On that first night I sat at first alone in the café outside my hotel, an alien in their midst. People glanced at me with blank, non-committal faces. The gap was not bridged. I drank more tea and my enjoyment of the scene increased. Currents of an unknown but somehow exciting atmosphere wafted around me. The waiter came to ask something or other, and I could not understand what he was saying. Then two men on my left leant over and translated in perfect English. The barrier was broken and we began to talk. Once encouraged, they pulled up their chairs and offered me a cigarette. I was surprised they had not spoken to me before: usually people who speak English will tackle you straight away. But no, they told me they had not wanted to disturb me. They thought perhaps I wanted my 'alone-ness', and they respected this.

We talked for a long time, late into the night. I was subjected to a fast flow of sedition. It came out like a pent-up thing. They talked of 'we' all the time, 'we of the north'. And they talked quite freely, regardless of who might be listening. Very soon other people came over and offered cigarettes. They asked me at once if I was a journalist and why I had come to the north. They told me about their problems and pointed to the street.

'This was once a very good town,' they said. 'We had cars, we had light. The children went to school. Now look at the street. Look what "they" have done. We sit and wait. Wait for that day when again we can be ourselves.'

When the cafés faded away I left my companions and never

saw them again. Upstairs, in the hotel, I stood on the balcony for a while, watching the last lonely forms hurrying home down the deserted street before curfew. Opposite was a small wooden kiosk. The owner, a lad, worked in it all day. Now he shuttered the window and rustled and bumped as he prepared for bed. Shafts of light came through the cracks, flickering to his movements. The light went out. In the silence a military vehicle drove slowly past.

There were a couple of young men on the balcony who introduced themselves. They were students. From them I got another dose of sedition. They wanted to study but they could not because they were trapped in the suppressed north, they said. They had strong faces but to me, in the dark on this strange, intense night, they seemed scarred with the lines of frustration, verging on despair.

That night I shared my room with another Mohamed, a student of the Koran, a quiet, odd young man. The concierge, an old man who slept on the stairs, was his religious minder. At four in the morning he hustled into the room to rouse Mohamed to morning prayers. Moaning and grumblng, he got out of bed, then came back much later and slept until quite late.

The next morning broke bright and hot as usual. Mohamed appeared again, in his silent way, and bought me a delicious breakfast of oily pancakes, chopped meat and tea down in the noisy restaurant. He spoke hardly a word of English and I only the very basics of Somali, and anyway he was a silent man. But I noticed this morning a nervous distraction on his face. I think he still felt responsible for me because he had brought me here and the idea of being alone was for people like him something sad, or even a bit dangerous; though he did not want to be in my way. His particular concern this morning, though, I discovered when I went outside: two officers from the local NSS were waiting for me. I was to accompany them to headquarters. Mohamed was terribly nervous and kept close all the way.

Headquarters, when we arrived, was like a fortress and the men inside looked besieged. The man at the gate jumped out when we approached, waving his gun alarmingly. Scruffy men with shifty eyes lounged about the yard or sat on a verandah. They cradled and fingered machine-guns like an extra limb.

We were taken into an office where a more important man sat behind a desk; by his elbow lay a big black revolver. At first I was ignored while they questioned Mohamed. He was in a state of agitation, sweat on his brow. He was dismissed. Then the official asked to see my papers and studied them with care; unfortunately, he was not quite as uneducated as the people on the road. Putting on a very serious face, he said that I had no permission to be here. It was serious indeed. He would have to send me back to Mogadishu. But I could sense that he was really just trying to make the point. Now, having demonstrated his power and conscientiousness, he became quite friendly. Why had I come up here, he asked, what did I want to do, where did I come from, and so on. We got talking. I was the simple tourist; I had not realized the rules. But having come so far, and finding the Somalis so nice, could I not just stay for a while? We talked about the culture, the land and many other simple things. He waxed enthusiastic. Eventually he said yes. I could stay for a while and then go direct to Djibouti. But he would not give me any written permission to do so. I think no one in his position of precarious power wanted to put their name to anything that could possibly send them straight down to the bottom of the ladder again. But we parted friends, and he told me he did not want to see me again.

Mohamed was waiting outside in the shade of the tree. He looked visibly relieved to see me and took me off round the corner to find a man who spoke good English. Through him he told me his dilemma: he did not know if I wanted him to remain my guardian, the position he felt he had to take. I was touched by his concern for someone who was basically a stranger, and assured him that he need not, that I was allowed to remain and would not be molested. My thanks for his care were brushed aside. We parted amicably, and he turned up at the hotel sometimes to buy me a meal and be silently friendly. It was only after a week or so, and a lot of persuasion, that I could pay my own hotel bill.

In Hargeisa a wide wadi split the town in two. Most of the year it was dry, only filling up with a sudden, short rush when rain fell in the nearby hills. Now it was dry and doubled as public lavatory and watering place: wells had been sunk and every day when I crossed the bridge I could see the lines of women walking to and fro with leaky cans of water balanced on their heads. On the other side of the wadi were the crouched forms of men, their bare bottoms showing. It was not a very hygienic place. The nomads from the bush used it as a thoroughfare to herd their sheep and cattle and long lines of camels to market.

I went to the camel market one day, on the outskirts of town, a big sandy square surrounded by low, earthen houses. All round the edge stood unhappy huddles of sheep and goats, shaking and shivering. They bleated wanly and looked dejected. At the far end were herds of snorting cattle, skinny and unkempt. But in the middle of the square stood the camels, about twenty healthy-looking beasts with sandy-coloured coats, calm and arrogant. They had sturdy, shortish legs, and wispy black hairs down their spines and concentrating on their humps. They stood there silently looking down their noses, stock-still, only their tails whisking rythmically back and forth and their long eyelashes flickering up and down. Occasionally one would stamp his feet and toss his head, scattering a shower of flies. They were a mixture of males and females and no doubt they were not the finest beasts to be had, as the nomads hate to sell their prize camels. Nearby stood the owners, the nomads, in close-knit groups, absorbed in discussion. Now and again one would walk round a camel, pointing and talking. The others leant on their long wands, one leg cocked like a stork, bargaining and gesticulating with wide, elegant motions. The sheep and cattle were purely business, meat on the hoof. Sometimes one would be brought over and roughly felt, and then ignored. The camels held centre-stage. To the nomads, they were their pride and joy. They could be endlessly discussed and endlessly watched.

The ordinary market in the commercial part of town over the river was very different. The mixture of people, the canopied stalls and wares cluttered in the dirty small streets provided my entertainment. The nomads wore the short ma'awwis wrapped round their waists and rough car-tyre sandals. They always walked with a stick which they often carried laid across their shoulders with their arms draped across either end, like scarecrows. They walked through the crowds as if they were walking in the empty desert, taking long, loping, purposeful strides. They had penetrating eyes and an air of durability and self-contained survival in their angular, bony frames. They would sit in the cafés, or in the shade under a tree, gathered around each other like flocks of birds.

Nomadic women, large and sturdy, wearing well-worn patterned dresses and cloths wrapped round their heads, planted themselves on the ground like sacks of potatoes. Whole alleyways were devoted to them and their wares. A sharp and pungent aroma drew customers in. I picked my way through, bending down to inspect the miscellaneous piles. There were herbs and spices, nuts and beans, coloured powders and coloured beads, all wrapped in leaves and plastics, in sacks and in bags; there were pieces of dried flesh, snake skins and hair; unusual necklaces, leather thongs and finely carved wooden spoons. Some of these items were healers, some warded off the evil eye, some caused coughing and some just added a taste. The women sat patiently throughout the day, cross-legged like buddhas with thick, muscled arms.

The town women looked the most incongruous among the crowds of rougher people. They sauntered in twos or threes with their soft, silky robes billowing out behind in wisps of scarves and head-dress trails. They sailed along with an easy, proud bearing, upright and determined like flagships. Their faces were unreadable, with a Mona Lisa slant to their lips, maybe sometimes a smile, sometimes a mock. I remembered Shugaar's words.

The streets in any part of town, but especially the market place, were a playground for the children. This was where they grew up and learnt the tricks of life. Babies squatted in the gutters. Boys played in the dirt. They polished shoes, they ran around and they salvaged the scraps. Older ones pushed carts selling oranges and bread. The hard-working men and women in the market, looking toil-stained and rough, passed speedily through the crowds carrying boxes between them or piled on top of their heads. They worked back and forth, pressed for time to make their meagre wage. Squadrons of nimble donkeys trotted lightly past with cans of water strapped to their sides, their ragged owners running along behind.

All the shops and doorways were crammed with sacks and boxes of food, stacked up to the ceiling and tumbling out into the streets. Lines of staggering men seemed to be almost continually re-supplying them from large trucks. All announced themselves as 'Aid', in big black print, upside down.

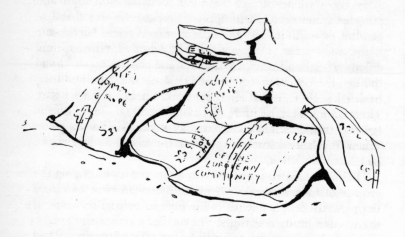

Down by the river, the blacksmiths, tinsmiths and metalsmiths, crouched in the dirt surrounded by their scraps of hardware. They were a race apart, these men, from a tribe that always took up this trade. Normally a blacksmith's work is prestigious but in these parts such people were regarded as inferior. They did not seem to mind and worked quite happily, surrounded by their well tapped kettles, pots and pans. There

226

was an area of cobblers who worked in cave-like rooms with their shoes and lasts hanging all over the walls. Then there were streets of tailors with ancient sewing machines and areas of camel's milk sellers with their thick lumpy milk that sold better the further it had turned.

Everywhere there was an atmosphere of cohesion and brotherliness. All the faces carried the distinguishing mark of the nomad, a lean, alert quality. Always I felt a potential aggression beneath their dignified exterior. Perhaps it was a nomadic trait, the trait of people who have often had to fight for their survival. They were in strong contrast to the people of the south, with their more willowy, easygoing ways. It was a contrast that added a certain air to the place, that drew it out of the ordinary.

On the market side of town there were many soldiers and other gun-clad people who lounged in the cafés or walked in groups, their pride and power stemming entirely from the weapons they clasped. They always looked the most unpredictable. Now and again a truckload of them would roar down the main street, siren screaming, the soldiers bouncing in the back clumsily trying to load and cock a heavy machine-gun. Then they looked comical and unprofessional. The nomads ignored them completely; it was as if they were not there. When they hauled someone off they would just sit and watch in silence, glowering ominously.

There were many madmen, or at least partially mad, on the streets. Like most madmen they were not that different from the ordinary people but just expressed a concentration of all the troubles more controlled in everybody else. Surprisingly, many of them were well educated. They spoke English and had once been professionals of one sort or another. On the street near my hotel there was a doctor who used to wander up and down almost naked, crying and calling to the sky and earth. Other lost souls would come up to talk with serious, fixed faces. But soon they would boil with the effort of stopping their minds running wild and always they ended up spurting out frustrations and froth. People were generally kind to them, telling them off with gentle smiles, leading them away. But

227

they would laugh at the clowns, the ones who purposefully mocked themselves and all around them.

Every evening throughout Somalia, but especially in the north, life came to a stop at seven o'clock. Radios were brought out and placed in the cafés or on the shop counters. Traffic thinned as drivers and pedestrians converged. They gathered round the radios, man, woman and child, with rapt, serious faces, attending to the crackling and hissing and the clear-cut accent from across the world:

'This is the BBC World Service broadcasting from London on its Somali service.'

The rest of the broadcast was in Somali and told of happenings elsewhere and affairs within Somalia. In those far-off, alien streets it was impressive, almost moving, to see the crowds of people with different faces, different cultures and beliefs, wrapped around with sheets and colours, bundles on their heads and babies on their backs, stopping and listening so intently. Always when I asked why particularly the BBC was so important, I would be told: 'With the BBC we can hear news of our country and the outside world that we *know* will always be the truth. With the other services we may hear the truth, and we may hear propaganda. How can we know which is which? This is our only way of finding out what passes in our country and what might be in store for us.'

When the broadcast was finished, life returned at a slower pace. The men remained in the cafés, talking about what they had heard. They had gained new confidence from this recognition in the outside world. They were not alone.

Because of the BBC World Service, and because the north of Somalia had once been British Somaliland, I sometimes found myself being treated almost as a celebrity. It did not suit me particularly well, but it suited the people. The British to them were a yardstick by which to judge the world. They had a deep trust and respect for the British because of the fair-handed and firm way the colonial service had treated them in this part of Africa. The men who had worked here then were still remembered; even the younger men knew their names. And so I was cast into this role of the ideal British man. When old men in

228

cafés learnt I was British they would buy me teas and give me cigarettes. They would tell me all about their lives under the British and ask me innumerable questions about England and the world, listening to my answers with an unnerving trust and belief. Sometimes the whole café would gather round, nodding their heads in agreement at anything I said. They would ask me penetrating questions about myself, my aims and the point of my life. And they never showed any sign of contempt or superiority if my answers did not live up to their own strict codes.

I made one good friend who ran a small shop just up the street from my hotel. He was called Jamal. His shop was the same as almost all the shops on all the streets: a single small room with a long wooden counter, almost at chest height, dividing it in two. The walls were painted green or brown, but were faded now, damp and peeling in places. A solitary bare bulb hung overhead and gave off a warm yellow glow when the small communal generator was working. When it was not, a roaring gas lamp on the counter threw its ugly light around, illuminating dark corners that should have been left dark. Red steel double doors at the front of the shop were thrown back and tucked behind two slim benches against the street wall. Friends and passers-by stopped and sat on these, chatting. The counter was bare except for a modern food blender in one corner; sweet cocktails of milk powder and baby food were mixed in this, to be consumed as a treat by those with some spare cash. The walls behind the counter were covered in rickety metal shelves that stretched up to the ceiling, stacked with the usual assortment of items: milk powder in towers of 'Bonet Rouge' tins; plastic-coated packages of soap cakes and leaky packets of Kenya tea; cans of baby food for grown-ups; tins of Aid-donated corned beef and blank exercise books. Shoe laces dangled on nails and an especially smart belt was pinned along a shelf for all to see. Nail clippers, dried dates, cheap pen-knives, sweets and matches and cigarettes all had their place. Jamal sat on his tall stool in the corner behind the blender. My eyes would wander along the shelves, past the

229

blender, under the counter and over the sacks of sugar and rice squeezed in amongst the débris in the corner, along the disused freezer, always hoping to find something new. But they never did. There were only standard supplies available up here in the north. They were used in many imaginative ways, but there was never anything different.

The shop was Jamal's home. Under the counter he had a big suitcase full of clothes and a box overflowing with books and all the odds and ends that constituted his wordly possessions. He was determined that one day he would be a doctor, so he was teaching himself English from ancient grammar books. When he had finished learning English from these he would be able to study from his *Basic Biology for Beginners* book. Jamal ran his shop with efficiency and hoped one day to have saved enough money to send himself to medical school in London. His life and his hopes surrounded him in his little inconspicuous shack. He sat there all day long and most of the night, serving the children sent along by their families. Their woolly heads and small hands clasping grubby notes would appear over the counter accompanied by peremptory shouts of '*Baris*' or '*Caano lo*' – rice or milk.

I first met Jamal when I went into his shop to buy some incense coils. (I had been unnerved one night when I asked my room-mate Mohamed where I could get one to ward off the mosquitoes. Mohamed said he would go and find one, and slipped out onto the street. It was after curfew and I was alarmed at him taking this risk, just for an incense coil. But when he came back he told me it was no problem: the soldiers only shoot if you cannot pay them something.) Jamal invited me behind the counter and I found beneath it a cosy little gathering. I was placed on a low stool and given one of the sickly cocktails from the blender. I went every night after that. They were great meeting places, these shops, where people of all descriptions would come to buy something and stay for a while to chat and listen. Very quickly I became part of the scene, accepted as just another person passing the hours. Only the children peeked round the end of the counter with wide, inquisitive eyes.

There was an old man who shared the shop as a home with Jamal; he had a bed of sacking under the counter. He was the guard and proudly showed me his bandit-bashing stick. Both his legs were crippled but somehow I felt he would deal with any bandits quite thoroughly enough. He used to enjoy telling me how he had been crippled when valiantly charging the Ethiopians across the desert during the Ogaden war. Another man was always there, huddled up beside the guard, wrapped in sheets and blankets. He only spoke in short aggressive bursts but everyone laughed at him, telling me he was just a fool and an addict. He chewed qat, a small, green succulent plant with many leaves which, in the same way as mira, acts when chewed as a mild stimulant that strengthens the more you chew. He chewed perpetually at a huge golf-ball in his cheek, like a cow chewing the cud; his face was a pasty grey, his eyes dull. They were a great contrast, the amiable old guard with a laughing gleam in his eye, and the dull, brittle qat addict, but they were friends. Neither seemed to resent the other's way of life.

Tall, quiet men came in sometimes. They stood behind the counter talking with Jamal in serious tones about the price of business, or happenings in town. Well educated but frustrated men came in, who would spew out their egos and ideals to me and then leave. Young men came in just to be there and contribute a laugh here or a word there. I asked Jamal what all these people would be doing in normal times.

'Many would do the same slow, idle business, but many also would go to Saudi Arabia for a while to earn money so that they could set up a good business back here. And many would trade with them, with goats and cattle. The people would all find something to do. Some way to make money. This is how our friend here under the counter can afford to eat qat all the time. He made lots of money in Saudi Arabia, but now it is very difficult to go or even trade with them, so he just sits and eats qat instead.'

Time slipped by very easily in Jamal's shop. No one did anything, no one demanded anything. Everyone was just there to be amongst a group of people, to add their bodies to the hub of communal existence, to share each other's proximity. The late broadcast of the BBC would always be turned on and the shop would fill. They listened and cursed and laughed. Jamal would walk me back the short distance to my hotel before curfew. Sometimes he would come up and look at my few books. When he left I would say, 'See you tomorrow.'

'*In sh'allah*,' he would answer shortly.

It seemed sometimes as if he did not believe I was quite genuine, as if next day I would be gone without saying goodbye. Europeans were benefactors, teachers and administrators, but rarely ordinary friends. Or so his limited experience of them probably told him.

Being in Hargeisa I could not help but learn something of the SNM – the Somali National Movement. They were freedom fighters who fought from the Ethiopian side of the Ogaden desert, although they could be found all throughout the north of Somalia, hoping to overthrow the military régime based in the south. It was a difficult aim they had, against high odds. Geographically Somalia is hard for such a force to overthrow, and the Somali army is large and well equipped, first by the Russians before they were thrown out and now by the Americans. The SNM did not have full support because they were a northern group. Some people thought they wanted an independent north and some thought they were communist.

One day, when I was walking out of the hotel to go down to the market, an older, cultivated-looking man who was sitting on a stool in the street called me over. There seemed something pedantic and chippy about him. He spoke to me in an arrogant yet defensive way, and said he would be very interested to talk to me; he would like me to come and have tea with him that evening. His attitude annoyed me and although I said I would come, I made a point of being late; I had other friends who were more amiable. When I arrived he was waiting in the same place with an extra stool and a small table in between. The street was dark and crowded as usual, humming with its customary subdued and secretive air. He called out to me as I approached.

232

'Peter, I could not think what had happened to you. I was worried for your safety.' He offered me the other stool. He was smiling warmly and seemed genuinely very pleased that I had come. I felt ashamed.

'Won't you have a glass of tea?' he said, in his clipped English accent.

'Here, come here,' he called to one of the boys hanging round. 'Now, go and get two glasses of tea from that café. No, not that one, the one over there. And be quick. These poor urchins,' he continued. 'They are so ill looked after. They are incapable of getting anything right. Their parents let them roam the streets like dogs and, as I am sure you know, there are no schools to send them to. This hopeless government seems to have done away with them all. Quite hopeless. What do you think of the Somali people, Peter? We're a curious bunch, aren't we? Ha, ha.'

All this was said in a great rush as he settled on his stool, moved the low table a couple of inches and looked about him as if searching for me somewhere in the air.

'Now, here comes the boy with the tea. Do you like this tea? It's *terribly* sweet, but we like it that way, you know. Ha, ha. Look around you. See all the people just sitting and drinking tea. It's a national pastime. It's our whisky. We're all terribly lazy. In fact, this is a lazy town. But, of course, we have no other choice. That terrible government,' he repeated airily.

'Look at all those street lamps. Don't they look grand? But they don't work. Ha, ha. And the road is a joke, my boy, a joke. You know, Peter, not so long ago this was a wonderful town. Quite something to be proud of. Everybody had something to do. The streets were well lit. It was run properly. It's because we were trained by the British, you know. They trained us well. I was sent to England. I used to . . .' and on he went. He seemed to be trying to prove himself to me, to show that his lowly position as a nobody in a nobody street was quite out of character.

'Yes, and under the old President I used to be the prefect in charge of whole towns, until the coup, when they made some quite false allegations against me and put me in one of their damn jails for ten years. Ten years of my life they took. *Such* a waste.'

Gradually he calmed down as his confidence grew, and I started to understand the frustration and pent-up anger which made him so jumpy. He led a very simple life now, being banished from any position of responsibility.

'Not that I'd want it, though,' he'd say, 'under *this* government.'

He had a small shop selling electrical supplies but even this, he said, was pointless: business just could not survive without the necessary goods and they were not available. Export and import of anything but essentials had, in practical terms, been stopped in the north. Still, he carried on the best he could, just to keep himself busy and sane.

'I shall just sit on my stool and drink tea, waiting like everybody else for the time when this government falls.'

Abdul Sheikh Ali, as he was known, was very vehement about the Somali Government and held it in complete contempt, though always talking about it in an airy way as if he refused to be perturbed by people whom he scorned so much. I would come and sit with him every evening for a while, sipping tea and smoking cigarettes. He smoked in an affected, debonair way and used to say, 'I'm not really a smoker. I never used to smoke before, but what can one do? I am driven to it.'

He would tell me about the people in the streets. Pointing out the mad doctor he said, 'That poor man used to study with me in London. He has been driven quite mad by frustration. They put him in jail, took away his practice and turned his brilliant mind in upon himself.'

Of another madman who used to come up to us occasionally and try to have serious talks, which always ended in disaster, he said: 'And that man was very rich. A brilliant businessman. He went to Saudi Arabia and became a drunk on whisky. It was too much for his brain. Now he is reduced to this.'

The two NSS men who had taken me to their headquarters on my first day used to sit outside the hotel sometimes, in the café; they had told me they would keep an eye on me, for my own safety, of course. Sometimes they would come over to

234

Abdul and me. They would talk about the weather and other polite things, but always with a sly smile on their faces that said, 'We know this man, he's harmless. You can't get up to any mischief with him.'

When they were gone, Abdul would say, 'Oh, they're all right. They're harmless. They're more scared of their own organization than of us. They would never get involved in anything serious. It pays them to get along smoothly with both sides. Oh, they're such an ignorant bunch, you know. Hand-picked from the lowest tribes. People from the President's own area. It's amazing that they survive, but of course they have the Americans backing them up. I get furious, sometimes, you know, when I think of the potential in this country. We could do so much. But we must sit waiting and watching these people messing around. We are good waiters, though. We can wait.'

As he finished, he was smiling and talking slowly, almost to himself. Suddenly he roused himself back to reality; the street, the darkness, our little table. 'Yes, we can wait, so have some more tea while we do. Ha, ha.'

Occasionally friends of his would come to join us. Abdul would disappear into his shop, flustered, to find more chairs. He would arrange them in a neat little semi-circle around the tea table.

One of Abdul's friends was a doctor who owned a small chemist shop down the road. His business was also flagging due to lack of supplies, and because he held the wrong political views, he said. He was a depressed man but full of forced, carefree chatter. Sometimes he would give it up and sit looking at the street with his elbow on his knee and his chin resting on his hand, with a pensive, far-off look in his eyes. Another friend who dropped in now and again was a chubby ex-police captain in neat civilian clothes. Fallen from power now, being on the wrong side, he had an air of resignation and subjection. He did not say much but always looked friendly and smiled a lot, nodding his head vigorously in agreement with every remark. All three of them kept up a wonderful display of dignity and the niceties of etiquette. Politics were rarely discussed when Abdul's friends were there except occasionally in passing, and maybe for my sake.

'Look, Ahamed,' he would say, 'look at those street lamps. Isn't it funny how they should stand there all night with nothing to do. They're rather like us. Isn't the government ridiculous, Ahamed? Ridiculous.' And his friends would nod their heads in unison like professors remarking on the childish behaviour of a student.

He also had some acquaintances who were not so nice and relaxed as these two. Men who had been driven *too* far by their misfortune and were now full of aggression and fanaticism. The sort of men who can destroy the viability and honesty of opposition movements.

Abdul and I would talk of other things that were nothing to do with politics. Just up the street was a small cinema where kung-fu films and Indian melodramas where shown. When they finished all the young people would walk back home past us. Sometimes a boy and girl would be holding hands, and Abdul would remark on this.

'See that? That is a new concept for us. A boy having a girlfriend. It is not a good thing,' he maintained.

'If a girl gives herself to a boy that way it will end up with them sleeping together. Oh, I know in your society the young people are promiscuous. I myself used to so much enjoy going to the dance halls with a young lady. But look at the result. Men and women get married at the drop of a hat, and so often the result is divorce. Then the children have unbalanced lives, and so their children, and so on. Don't you agree?'

I tried to explain that I thought it was not as straightforward as that. But Abdul, despite all his Englishness, was still most truly Muslim and of a different world. He held strong beliefs and they could not be dented.

'We have a crazy system in a way,' he admitted. 'You know, a man will not marry a girl who is not a virgin. But then all the young men want to sleep with girls before they are married. So we have prostitutes. The ones who have fallen. The rest of the women can stay intact, with dignity. Then they can find husbands because the young men can easily differentiate

236

between a good woman and a bad one. As a result we do not have divorces such as you do. Our children grow up unaffected and happy. It is a strange system but it works. Even the harsher sides of it are necessary. Without them it would not work. The circumcision of young girls, the harsh penalties put on thieves. All are necessary parts.'

Abdul was never fanatical and never attempted to convert me to Islam, as many others had. He always talked of things with an academic air, almost as if they were abstract.

'Yes, yes, how interesting,' he would interrupt, 'but now do tell me what you think of . . .'

He also had a great sense of humour. He would laugh heartily, shaking in his chair, over some of our impasses and about the comedy of life. He was a person who loved life and the world; he found it all immensely interesting. He was an academic, an administrator, not a politician, but of course he had to get involved in politics. He could not ignore something which affected his life and his country so dramatically. He had made his decision and he chose the way of opposition.

On one of my last days in Hargeisa, Abdul took me into his shop: he had something very important to tell me. Intrigued, I followed him in. He turned and asked me if I would contact his son in England, when I got back there. The boy had been born there but Abdul had had no contact with him for fifteen years because his mail was intercepted, he said. He asked me to tell the youngster about himself and his situation, to tell him that he still loved him and that one day, when circumstances were better, he hoped he would come out and make his life in Somalia. On the wall a different Abdul looked down from a picture frame. A beaming, clear-faced young man with a group of friends in Trafalgar Square, feeding the pigeons. Next to it was a picture of a small boy, shy and faded – his son.

He took a deep breath and went on. 'I must make sure you understand about us, about the SNM. We are not communist,' he implored me to believe. 'How could we be? Most of the top men were trained and educated by the British in the colonial era. They are fanatically against communism. But mainly we are not communist because we are Muslims and if anybody

237

knows anything about Islam he would realize that its concept of life is exactly opposite to that of communism. We took arms from Ethiopia because we had to have weapons to fight with and no one else would give us any. Now the Americans think that if we succeed in overthrowing the régime we would invite the Russians back. If only the Americans realized we would not and stopped bribing the government with their ubiquitous, unlabelled Aid packets. That alone would be enough to ensure the downfall of this evil régime that is making millions of people's lives pointless and hopeless. Do they not realize that most of the people in the refugee camps are political refugees as much as hunger refugees? Do they not realize that this government actually likes to have refugees, even encourages them, because the more they have the more Aid they can claim? This country's economy rests on Aid money. The refugees are hungry, yes, but it is because they cannot make their nomadic lives work when their animals are stolen and they are bullied and restricted in movement by all the various warring parties in their land, because the Americans and the Russians have made it another of their battlegrounds.'

I knew the Horn of Africa was strategically an important place, close to the Gulf and the shipping routes. The Americans had naval bases in Somalia and did not want to lose them. Russia holds Ethiopia and the relative proximity of the Ogaden to the Gulf made it a place worth fighting for. Abdul turned about the little shop, staring at me hard. 'You must understand. For the Ogaden people it is terrible, because their lives become unbalanced. They lose harmony with their environment, their belief in themselves and their capability to survive independently is destroyed. They must become a broken people in the camps. They have to accept free handouts. They can do nothing for themselves, which to a nomad is like cutting off his manhood. And for us here in Somalia it is equally terrible. The people are becoming so used to cheap Aid food. They are beginning to expect always to be given things without having to work for them. Soon they will forget *how* to look after themselves independently. Africans are great oppor-

238

tunists, you know. Hold out a hand and of course they will take. But we shall cease to be a proper people and become a country of slothful puppets.

'I don't know why I tell you all this,' he continued. 'I suppose just because I can tell you and because I want to tell you, even though you probably know most of it. Many people in the outside world know all these things but no one speaks or cares. But I feel sorry sometimes for the little old lady in Liverpool, the sort of people I have known, who gives a pound or two of her meagre pension to go to Aid when so much of it is misused and ends up as a nut or bolt in some fat politician's Mercedes or a trigger on someone's machine-gun. I feel sorry for her and I feel sorry for all the pawns in the game because the little old lady is deceived, the tax payer is deceived and the voters are deceived in *your* countries.' Abdul stopped for a minute.

'I know I am ranting a bit, but I feel I must say these things. You, I know, have nothing to do with all this and would probably prefer to be left out of it. But you are the only outside ear I have had access to for a long time. Please excuse my exploitation of it.

'All the people here want to do is to educate and advance themselves. We are not primitive people. We were a developed and intelligent people long before the British or the Italians even knew about us. They have helped us, and for that we are grateful, but now the developed nations must stand back and not interfere too much. They must even let us make mistakes. One must be able to make one's own mistakes. It's essential. But now, because of international meddling, we here in the north are a shut-off people. We are being suffocated like fish on dry land. We cannot move, we cannot trade, we cannot educate our children, we cannot build, we cannot fight. We have gone backwards. Some of us nearly despair, that lowest of low emotions. Even the belief and trust that the elder people hold for the British is wearing thin. Where are they? Why does the British Ambassador not come up here from Mogadishu and at least give us some books to put in our library? Why do people we believed to be believers in truth not speak out? They

239

want to save refugees' lives? Well then, expose the reason for most of the hunger. It is not only drought. In some areas, yes, it is terrible, but in others it is compounded by the wars. And the wars are part of the struggles and whims of developed nations. We have lived through drought before, believe me. We are a tough people. But we have done it without your Aid and your wars in the way. What has become of the people in the West? Are they so advanced that they have forgotten about natural man? Do they no longer believe that he is more good than evil? Can nothing be left to destiny any longer? There is reason behind our saying *"In sh'allah"*: Allah knows that we are capable of living without everything being arranged and pre-organized, controlled and directed by ourselves. He does it for us.

'I shall stop boring you now, Peter, and only ask you to remember the one thing I told you at the beginning. Write to my son and tell him I still love him.'

I only saw Abdul once after that evening. He was strangely elusive and polite. I think he felt he had given too much of himself away. He was a Muslim sheikh, and Muslims rarely, and never to foreigners, lower their dignity and perhaps induce pity. Abdul kept himself wrapped up in a rigid frame. He tried to keep his emotions under control in order to stop himself becoming like the naked doctor in the street.

The nights were always long in Hargeisa, at least in my hotel they were. Though the curfew came down on the streets at about eleven o'clock people did not go to bed until much later. All along the passages wandered a selection of young men. I could never quite determine what they were doing in a hotel, but many were permanent guests, I thought. Late into the night they would socialize from room to room, talking around candles, and forever preening themselves in front of mirrors. They were very meticulous washers and at almost any time of the night or day could be found combing their hair through and through, and wandering about half-naked as though perpetually in a hammam. But Mohamed, the boy I shared a room with, was different from the rest. He was trying to learn English, but without much effort. Sometimes I would give him lessons, and he would teach me Somali in exchange. He was supposed to be the hotel register keeper, in return for which he lived rent-free. If all the beds were taken he slept in the corridor near his religious mentor, the nightwatchman. But Mohamed was very apathetic. He carried the register around with him always, like a burden, but never actually filled it in. The staff downstairs in the restaurant were fed up with him; they told me he was a useless, lazy boy. Mohamed told me they were mean, stupid men and so it went on. Only once did I see Mohamed moved to action and eloquence. There were some shots fired outside the hotel one evening. He leapt off his bed as if it were he who had been shot, and rushed downstairs and out on to the street. Later, when he came back, he told me in detail how two boys had thrown a stone at a soldier who was walking with a woman; the soldier had drawn his revolver and fired over their heads. He talked about it for a long time with an animated face. Later he got the sack and I did not see him again.

Throwing stones was a popular game of the small boys: never the girls because they live much more protected and secluded lives, even from an early age. But the boys threw stones at each other and at anything unusual – madmen, old ladies, and, of course, me. I would walk down a small shanty street with the usual scattering of small boys, and they would become silent and watchful as I passed. When I was far enough away, with my back to them, a stone would come whistling past, quite lethal. Depending upon how I then handled things, there might be a shower of stones or no more at all. I discovered the best way was to turn round slowly and stand stock-still, staring; the culprit was anonymous amongst his silent friends. We would stand facing each other until their nerve eventually broke and they would filter off amongst the shacks and alleyways. The worst reaction, as I found to my cost once when a stone had caught me on the head and infuriated me, was to retaliate. Then they thought, 'Hey, he enjoys this game too,' and stones tenfold came pelting back. Once a man I knew was seriously stoned; he escaped on his bicycle but was badly cut and bruised. The children gained confidence and mindless aggression from their numbers; they went wild. It is a bad habit which the adults seem to make no effort to check. I wondered when the transition comes from these little horrors, as I sometimes thought of them, to the sedate and respectful men their fathers seemed to be. I hoped they were not a new breed, this generation born of frustration and aggression.

17

Ganet Refugee Camp

There was a refugee camp on the outskirts of Hargeisa called Ganet. I spent several days visiting it with a team of Médicine Sans Frontières people who worked there. To reach Ganet I had to walk out of town through a mixed quarter of jumbled shanty homes and big walled-in houses belonging to Aid organizations and politicians. The rough, broken track then wound into barren landscape of cracked red rock and heaps of litter. It went through a neat graveyard of piled stones into a small valley of precarious patches of green maize and browsing goats, past a dilapidated Aid encampment with frayed, yellowing tents nudging in the breeze and modern Toyotas rotting on bricks because the wheels were gone, and up between two small hills. Then, like an arrow, it bore across an immense sun-baked plain to the dark rumble of mountains on the horizon.

Standing in the cleavage of the two hills I had a spectacular view of a wide blue sky and infinite golden plain. Down below me, where the hills met the plain, I saw something that looked at first like a thick furze of boulder-strewn growth spreading out in a circle like grey mould, blemishing the smooth surface. Then I saw that this close-knit mat was really thousands of dome-shaped nomadic agals, blurred with a scanty covering of sticks and grasses. Paths of clear yellow sand wound between and wide, white thoroughfares divided the circular grey mass, crumbling bits of hut and mess on either side.

This was Ganet Camp. A haze of smoke hung above it, fed by

unseen cooking fires. Bits of shiny, wind-blown plastic and scattered tin cans glinted in the sun, winking at me. From my vantage point the dead silence gave the camp a feel of detachment and unreality, only disturbed by sharp gusts of wind that carried a strong, musky smell. As I walked down into the camp the sense of stillness remained. I was in an enclosed world of spacious sand and huddled agals, slowly drifting or sitting people, and only a low ebb of tinkering, casual noise. There were people everywhere. They seemed wholly idle and relaxed. Their limbs were languid and their faces blank. They looked slightly different from the Somalis. Most of them were from the Ogaden. They were smaller and lighter-boned, with softer, rounder, chocolate brown faces and wild haloes of frizzy hair. They appeared to be simple folk, with a natural, loose carriage. Most of them were wearing tattered cast-off trousers and shirts, but here and there some wore white robes and white caps, congregating in little patches of cleared ground surrounded by stacked bushes and pieces of wood and plastic. These served as a mosque. The Muslims would sit there for a long time in the day, praying and talking. On the main thoroughfare there were a few stalls in makeshift huts where people sold a few cigarettes, some cakes of soap, matches and one or two other very basic items. One man sold some old, fly-blown meat; there were one or two oranges. These were the things people bought as luxuries when they had made a bit of money selling Aid food in Hargeisa. Men and children hung around, talking and doing nothing. The women did a bit of work, pounding maize with big, heavy pestles in wooden bowls; thump, thump . . . thump, thump . . . They did a bit of washing and a bit of cooking, but mostly they sat in gaggles, bored, passing the time.

The camp was split into segments, some much more populated than others. Here and there a new agal was being built. Precious sticks gathered from the barren surrounding area, rapidly becoming more barren, were bent and fitted into a dome-shaped grid and tied down with strips of bark. The lower half of the 'walls' was packed with mud inside and out. The top half was covered with anything available, from an empty

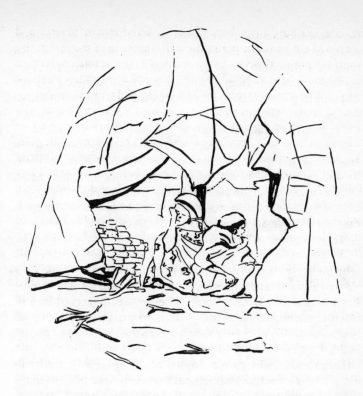

sack to shreds of shirt. The work was all done by the women, as they would traditionally, leaving the men free to care for the herds of camels and goats and to defend their families. But of course there were no herds to tend and no defending to do, so the men were idle and useless. They did not stay near the agals during the day, like the women. They wandered the camp.

On the whole the people looked reasonably healthy. They were not starving, just malnourished. They smiled easily and were very gentle, but their eyes looked sad. There was an air of peace and tranquility which was very nice, but it verged too close to despondency and despair. Deep in their bones they were nomadic people; tough, vigorous and fiercely independent. They knew they had given this up and so they had given up completely. They no longer cared or wanted. They took their free food and survived, that was all. The only energetic activity to be seen in the camp were the queues and squabbles round the water tanks and the feeding centres. There were two big water tanks at either end of the camp; all day long women and children with plastic containers walked to and from them. Twice a day the feeding centres were packed with people collecting their rations.

A complex social system had evolved to allow all these people to live together without too many fights. Many of them held different beliefs, had different traditions, and all of them were unused to living sedentary lives in such big communities. Here their traditions and beliefs became almost unimportant in the strange new world into which they had been drawn. A camp worker, a Swedish nurse, talked to me about it.

'You have to be very patient. It is hard dealing with people who no longer really care, and have no incentive to do so. They just go through the motions of survival; eating and sleeping. Beyond this they do not think. When someone gets ill he will often remain in his agal until we find him. His relations will not think to tell us. Many times we are too late and the person is dead when we do find him.'

There were many such examples of the nomads' inability to grasp their changed circumstances. For instance, nomads know nothing of pit latrines. So there was none, because nobody had instructed them in their use or dug any. As a result the camp was littered with the excrement of people who were either too weak or too apathetic to walk outside the camp. They neither understood nor trusted modern medicine. In the bush they have natural if obscure ways of treating the illnesses they get there. But in the camp there were different and terrible diseases and their treatments did not work for these. To them modern medicine was almost like magic; more importantly, it belonged to the camp, the camp which gave them the illness in the first place. There were many other, smaller difficulties. Their beliefs and traditions would not work for them here. Annika, the nurse, voiced their main concern. 'These are all problems which of course must arise in refugee camps. And, most importantly, the refugees are fed.

246

But I cannot help wondering, when I see these ghosts of people, if it is enough. Out of all those millions and millions of dollars given to countries such as this, is this all that can be done? Cannot governments be a little more responsible and instead of giving huge Aid packets carte blanche, as it were, to obviously corrupt régimes, actually take it in hand and use it to its maximum potential? In Hargeisa, a couple of kilometres away, all day long the streets are crammed with Aid vehicles of one sort or another. It is truly impressive. There is a lot of personnel and energy being used up there. But look at this camp. How many vehicles do you see here?'

In my three days in the camp, other than the small group of MSF, an entirely independent organization, I saw only one other vehicle, obviously not about the right business, and no other personnel.

'This place virtually survives alone. The people are given enough to stop them starving, but that is about all. If that is as far as the money will stretch, okay. But it is obviously not. These people will die of despair as readily as they will from starvation. They are not quite allowed to starve. Starving people can become dangerous. Malnourished people don't.

'No, these people need to be educated, instructed in how to live in communities such as this, given new incentives to try. For each million pounds of misspent money, one qualified worker could do so much. People seem prepared only to feed the refugees. It salves their consciences and they think it is enough. But without the necessary support of instruction and help, it is soul-destroying and cruel. These people need to be more than just leeches. Many of the people here are primarily political refugees, so the responsibility should be more than just to feed them.'

This small group of MSF people could have done with a bit of support. They were a high-action, spearhead team who jetted into crisis areas to do one specific job. They had arrived at Berbera with all their medicine and supplies with them, having learnt not to expect to receive it through the proper channels. As it was, a large proportion of the stuff they brought got 'lost' between the airport and the camp. They were a team of six, some doctors, some nurses. The extreme pressures of their job demanded that they concentrate only on the job they were sent to do: to cure and to save lives. Their job was not to question or to get involved with other problems. Needless to say, of course, those other problems were obvious to them in and out of the camp, but they tried not to become too emotionally involved or else it would affect their efficiency.

They worked as a tight-knit group with little help from the local authorities or the government: in fact one of the group spent his entire time battling against them, trying to get the things or the permissions they needed. For example, Ganet, which had been in existence for some time, was not recognized by the government as an official refugee camp. Because of this, the MSF were not meant to do any sort of surgery there at all, or to treat certain diseases: patients should be sent to the local hospital.

The team used to laugh at this for two reasons. First, the hospital in Hargeisa was a place where patients were not treated but were left to die. They described it as a horrendous tomb with no equipment, uncaring staff, flies and infection. They could not in conscience send anyone to the hospital. Second, the local authorities would not give them the extra petrol needed to take patients there anyway: they could not spare any from the merry-go-round of Aid vehicles in town. And, of course, those vehicles were 'far too busy' to actually venture into the camps.

Being with the MSF volunteers was an enlightening experience and a great pleasure to me. The pressures of their job, both emotional and physical, were immense, but they loved their work and were deeply conscientious about it. Wherever they were in camp they brought an air of confidence and happiness. They laughed and smiled a lot and their group of unofficial helpers gave loyal support. But their numbers were hopelessly inadequate to deal with all the varying problems confronting them. The helpers were all refugees themselves who had fled university or town lives in Ethiopia because of political intimidation. They were all completely untrained and unqualified to do what they did, but they worked alongside the MSF people with deep enthusiasm and commitment, beaming as they went.

There was one wonderful man they called 'Bloody Isaiah'. What he liked most was surgery and now he often undertook minor cases. He would emerge from the scrubby little tent where they had to perform their operations, blood dripping from his hands, with a big grin on his face, laughing happily at accusations that he was a ghoul. The main medical ward was a long frayed tent with patients lying on the ground along both sides. There was no bedding, no light, two chairs and a table. Many of the people there were going to die but there was always a comforting atmosphere in the shabby, oven-hot tent.

The MSF people worked like dingbats from dawn till dusk. There were 20,000 people or more to cope with.

'This is not my job,' they would shout. 'Go and find the camp controller.'

But, of course, the camp controller would not be there, so invariably they would do what they could. The pressures built up. Should we give him this medicine, even if he is going to die? What can we do about the mothers who will not feed their babies properly? How can we halt the malnutrition and scurvy? Sometimes they would be worked up into high states of nerves and exhaustion. They would lose their tempers and argue, but compassionately.

When I was there a conflict of ideals was fought out between two of them. A woman doctor was spending time with the patients when she should have been resting. The leader of the group, the only man, said she should be more detached. If she continued as she was her health would be affected and she would lose her effectiveness.

'How can I let patients die when I might be able to save them?' she yelled at him. 'Is their death less important than my rest?'

'In the circumstances, yes,' he would reply.

But these tough people, who come to the camp for a six-month stint, pulled through and did their jobs well. When they had arrived in the camp, the death toll had been about 35 a day. Now it was down to two or three.

I liked visiting the camp. There, everything was simple and caring. Gone were the tense, brooding streets and the sham of official life. They could not extend here because they were irrelevant. Sad as it was, there was a feeling of pulling together to help, of gentle, vulnerable people, of tranquillity and brotherliness amongst all because everybody was there either to do good, or needing to have good done to them.

My visits to Ganet Camp brought my stay in Hargeisa to a close. By now I had long outstayed my welcome in the north. The NSS came to me, and kindly reminded me of my intention to travel to Djibouti.

18

Through Strange Lands to the Border

The road between Hargeisa and Djibouti was 200 kilometres of rough going. It could take anything from one day to a week by truck. Tea and sugar were brought in from Djibouti, but there was nothing in Hargeisa to trade, so all the trucks going out again in that direction were empty. Now, if you have ever travelled in the back of an empty truck, even on a good road, you will know that it is a thing to be avoided at all costs unless you want to end up badly bruised and shaken, or have to stand the entire journey. Fortunately, Somali trucks were provided with a little metal cradle overhanging the cab, in which were kept tools, tyres and the more prominent of passengers. I made sure I was a prominent passenger. Even so, it was hardly the most comfortable of positions. You were rather like a piece of baggage but without the advantage of ropes to hold you in. All that could be said was that from up there I had the most spectacular view of the country; when the grime and dust of the road became embedded in my every pore I felt well and truly part of it too. The back of the truck was filled with less fortunate youths and large ladies. The youths would from time to time try invading the privileged cradle but were made to feel so unwelcome that usually they gave up. The ladies were well situated on their large behinds, which acted as the truck's shock absorbers should have done, had there been any. They always managed to look comfortable, surrounded by their bundles, baskets and babies, while I became progressively more filthy, tired and aching.

The truck owners are an enterprising breed. They know about bandits and they know their trucks intimately. They know how to deal with the ranks of officials along the routes and at the borders. They must negotiate their load from one place to another, and come out of it with a profit.

On that first day we passed through a silent, eerie landscape of ancient, worn mountains, plateaux and gullies, cracked and crumbled by scorching days and freezing nights. The rock, piled all about, was red and rusty and about as friendly as the pits of hell. It was a land that looked as if, some time in the past, an unknown colossus had vandalized it. The track wound tortuously through the destruction, squeezing between boulders, ducking down over dry, rock-strewn river beds, making no attempt to clear a path for itself but edging shyly round the obstacles. When we reached the plateaux, things weren't much better. Even here the truck had to move at an agonizingly slow pace, crunching and creaking over rocks and into holes, dust billowing like smoke. Twice we made long, treacherous descents down shingle slides into valleys; small secret worlds of fresh green vegetation. A refugee camp was tucked away in each of these. Life in them seemed to tick over languidly, like a badly wound watch. I saw no sign of a vehicle or Aid agencies.

After about twelve hours of this travelling, when night came down, it became a weary business indeed to cling to the lurching cradle. The only distraction to keep me awake and avoid tumbling over the side were the myriad stars. I tried to find constellations I knew, but could not. As we left the higher ground and edged down steep rough tracks, with grinding gears, into the salty air of the coastal plain, we traversed bog and mire and dark reeds decorated with the flicker of fireflies. Our headlights raked the sky and ground as we jolted, like the searchlight of a ship, and our angry engine broke the massive silence, like a baby crying in the night.

Much later, deep in the night, as we crossed a flat plain of soft sand and tufted grass, I saw in the distance the swinging beams of other headlights coming towards us. They were our brother trucks on the journey to Hargeisa. Like ships on a far-off dark ocean we approached each other, slowly creeping across the void. Steadily the groan and rumble of engines grew and as of habit the drivers stopped, engines running, as we drew alongside. Shouts and cries from cab to cab announced greetings and warnings of the road. People tumbled over the sides and dark groups met behind the trucks, mumbling and muttering. Cigarettes were passed around, the flare of a match lighting up grimy, animated faces. A torch was swung from the top of one truck, its beam a tunnel in the swirling dust, illuminating in the other shabby huddles of wrapped-up forms, awkward in the cradles or slumped in the back. There were jokes and laughs, muffled by the immense, overpowering dark, as human warmth united, but soon we parted and once again we settled down, each to his own private thoughts and shudders.

We drove all night with only one brief stop for sleep. Later we watched the yellow glow of dawn seep slowly into the black sky, swallowing the stars as it spread, pushing the night away over the other side. We stopped at a small village on a plateau for breakfast. That first stretch of limbs, that first sip of tea down dry, dusty throats were pleasures not to be forgotten. There were many other trucks and people doing the same, and many little cafés where we sat, slowly regaining consciousness.

Six hours later we reached Seylac (pronounced Zeila), the last town of Somalia before Djibouti. Once it had been an important Arab town, a capital and a port from where their armies could enter what is now Ethiopia on jihads, holy wars, and to capture trade in frankincense. It was surrounded by a huge plain of salt-water ponds, dried up to crystals, and banks of soggy sand and coarse, wind-swept grass, like a tidal lagoon. It seemed that any larger than usual wave could roll on and on for hundreds of kilometres before it met any sizeable obstacle. How the Arab armies marched across it I don't know, as it was cruel with heat. Were it not for the road built from rock the truck would not have been able to make it to historic Seylac. Unfortunately, though, as the rock for this road consisted of historic Seylac, on arrival there was not much to see except for

a few modern, makeshift shacks. Several places have been described as the last place on earth – the border post between Mali and Algeria in the middle of the Sahara is one I know – but Seylac must have capped them all. There was a sense of being nowhere. The heat was staggering, the land fetid and pointless, and the sea, swirling past the spit of land, was heavy and sullen. When the tide was out it was hemmed by mud banks and stinky deltas hopping with mud flies, and when it was in, by an unexciting procession of ripples urged into life by the continuous fierce wind.

The village had only two functions. It served as customs, military and NSS post, and as a dormitory for all the trucks delayed by these posts. Every official here seemed of a particularly disagreeable disposition, as I suppose anyone posted here would be. They could read neither English nor Somali, so did not understand my papers. Luckily the truck driver was much better educated and translated them. At one point I was nearly arrested for photographing a pile of rubble that had once been the old Arab mosque. The official had red bleary eyes and a grubby bandage round his head, and was only persuaded not to arrest me for being either a Russian spy or an American journalist by repeated translations from the truck driver. No one minds tourists because they always have lots of money.

Nothing happened in Seylac during the day because it was too hot to move about. In the evenings everyone sipped tea.

The hotel dormitory I stayed in was run by a voluptuous mamma from Djibouti. She spoke French in that marvellous drawling, sing-song way of the West African woman and ran the place like a despot. She was very large and round, with active, sausage fingers enveloping gaudy rings. She swayed rather than walked, her long, flowing robes hitched up, tucked under her arm, to give her more manoeuverability. She had an entourage of wretched-looking women who cowered and cackled in her presence; they cooked all day in between sleeping and eating. All the other work in the place was done by a couple of unfortunate boys who were bullied and shouted at all day long.

Two days later I made the short journey to Djibouti, once again perched in a cradle but on a different truck. The land we passed looked almost as it if had been pickled and set in salt. Everything was white and glared with increasing pain as the sun reflected in millions of tiny salt crystals. The heat was a real force. Everything was a uniform blank, and the searing air could only be breathed in muffled gasps. With sheets and scarves wrapped round me, exposed on my gibbet, we crossed the salt pans, winding our way among salt-saturated, stumpy trees. After a couple of hours of this the road lost its thread and split into vague tracks criss-crossing in all directions through trees and bushes. Now we raced along, scattering occasional herds of goats, until we reached the border post. Here, of course, there was a long wait resulting in a judicious 'fine' that allowed me to cross into the Republic of Djibouti without a visa, which the embassy at Mogadishu had assured me I did not need anyway.

19

Djibouti

I approached Djibouti with a certain amount of apprehension. It is the smallest country in Africa and very little known. Whenever you mention that you happen to be going there, you are warned not to.

'Why should you want to go to Djibouti? It's one of the hottest places in the world. It's horrendously expensive and it's a trap.'

Djibouti is surrounded to the west and north by Ethiopia, except for the small southern section where it meets Somalia. On the east is the Gulf of Aden. The heat gets trapped there, and so do travellers like myself. It only gained independence in 1977, from the French, but they still run the place like a colony, or rather a military and business appendage. The population is made up largely of Afars who are ethnically Ethiopian, and the Issas who are Somali by breed. Even if all else turned out to be terrible, this, to me, would be one redeeming factor.

The mini-bus that took me from the border was modern, a far cry from the rack of a truck. As it slewed along the sandy roads, I felt already I had left the Africa I had been engulfed in for the last few months, since Nairobi, yet it was almost impossible to believe that I was now very near to a modern city of skyscrapers, street lights and nightclubs. There was none of the usual city paraphernalia, no tarmaced roads, commuter suburbs, hoardings or petrol stations. But sure enough, before long, I saw there in the distance the tracers of street lights, swimming in the blackness like landing lights. We moved towards them steadily, veering sometimes but always coming back on a beeline. Then, seemingly in a matter of minutes, from the familiar, deserted desert we bumped up on to a tarmac road and delved into a sprawl of shanty town.

The street ran straight. On either side were row upon row of tin shack alleys, disappearing to points like irrigation ditches. They flicked past like parked cars on either side. The air was thick and damp as if it were steadily solidifying. I felt an urge to get out, to go back to the clean, clear desert. The pavements surged with people in string vests and shoddy clothes. Faces in every angle of animation and expression flew past the windows. The mass of moving forms spilled off the pavements on to the road, in and out of buses, crowded round trestle tables and chairs. The concentration of humanity was like a liquid jig-saw puzzle. It went on and on, without break or space; claustrophobic, suffocating. When the bus could speed along a clearer stretch of road the images were lost in a blur until we slowed, then stopped.

My eye picked out a man across the road, in an alcove of tables laden with food. He had on a white t-shirt and a red bandana round his head and was tossing some spaghetti in a frying pan over a small gas flame on one of the tables. Wreaths of smoke from a blackened lantern crept up his front and through his hair. Sizzling oil spattered onto his t-shirt. His hands darted among piles of food and bottles and baskets of bread, pinching some salt from here, picking sliced tomatoes and lettuce leaves from there, tossing them together, squeezing a lemon and rattling the frying pan. He was an expert, idly absorbed in his work. Sweat trickled down his temples. A circle of hunched, hungry men sat across the tables from him, watching and waiting for their food. It came to them with a quick hand, spinning a steaming plate over the table to stop beneath their chins.

There was a certain smell in the air, a certain remembered scene, like déjà vu, of dank heat and stale air, hundreds of bodies, hundreds of homes. It was not altogether unpleasant. I was lucky enough after much searching to find a small, cheap

257

hotel to stay in, down an alley, round a corner and through the children amongst the litter. I stooped down into a wooden doorway and found myself in an open yard with a passageway of doors running off it and other, taller chicken-coop houses all around. Through the first door I entered a big, curtained room. There was a family in it with a tall father. He was the patron, and a great talker.

'You want to stay? Of course you can stay. It's so nice here, so nice in Djibouti, you won't want to leave. You see, you see, we have electricity and coca-cola and everything. Everything you want. No, not like Somalia, that terrible place. Isn't it bad? Ha, ha, not like Djibouti. You'll love Djibouti, it's so nice.' He had a round, shiny face and stuttered and gabbled like a machine-gun. He also had two wives, six daughters and an old father and mother. The hotel was kept spotlessly clean by this wealth of women and was well equipped with straw mats and towels.

The other guests were a mixture of seamen waiting for ships, broke businessmen waiting for visas, Syrians and Pakistanis and political refugees waiting for brothers or family to bail them out from abroad. They were all more or less permanent residents, surviving on credit, and unable to move until they could pay their debts. But they were a relaxed bunch. There was none of the hustle and bustle of normal hotels. The few rooms, shared by two or three men, were square boxes with cardboard walls, no windows and slow-circling fans. The large French minority in Djibouti lived far away in another part of town, near to the Foreign Legion garrison. That was a different Djibouti, more like a small piece of France. It was neat and smart and intimidating.

These two different worlds met in the town centre, near the port. Here were the pristine white banks of many nations, with imaginative arcades and expensive décor. There were comfortable airline offices and shipping agencies, overseas businesses, consortiums, consolidations and companies, all fitting compactly into pleasing office blocks of strip lighting and air conditioning. There were supermarkets packed with food flown in from France and chic little delicatessens, cold and crisp and smelling of freshly baked French bread. There were Djibouti bijouteries, couturiers with the latest fashions hanging in the windows, and quiet, curtained tea shops. There were café-bars and plush hotels busy with expensive looking young ladies and crew-cut men, sitting at tables reading *Paris Match* and sipping pastis. Outside stood the hawkers and hustlers, with cigarettes and shoe-shines. The streets in between were on a grid pattern but never very full. They ran down to a small square of green grass and shady palms. Around the square went a procession of French army officers, business men and pretty young wives in their super, up-to-date cars and jeeps, looking for parking places where ranks of boys waited to wash the windscreens and guard the cars. The glass doors to the banks flipped to and fro as a continuous flow of suited men went in and out. They had to weave their way to the cars through a barricade of cripples in wheelchairs of home design, or sitting on the ground using arms as legs. They stationed themselves strategically and pleaded and waved their stumps as the men went through. Many of these cripples lived in the arcades outside the banks. On any afternoon, or late at night, when everyone else was home, they could be found in between the imaginative arches, sleeping or sitting up, with bottles of water clasped in their rubbery hands and flies buzzing round their heads.

The small town centre ran down to the magnificent presidential palace: a tall wall enclosed a garden of expansive trees and well-watered bushes and flowers that grew down to the sea. The drunks and beggars found sweet shade under the trees that drooped over this wall. They lay all day long, near to the President, in happy oblivion, cradling their bottles of wine. Next door a long pier ran far out into the bay. At the far end of it, a white building with masts and flags hung like a boat in the deep blue sea. This was 'Le Club Nautique', a lavish affair of elegance and beauty, of handsome people and sundowner cocktails, with boats and buoys downstairs and an open airy restaurant upstairs. Monsieur de Blanc was mine host whom everyone liked automatically for his suave, debonair ways. He spread his attention fairly and accepted the kisses and endearments of his friends with ease. His staff were equally neat and smiled continuously, even when the lobster was not quite right or the wine a bit too warm. They would be the first to notice and whisk it away from the party tables with a light laugh that said: 'Of course, of course, quite naturally.' Everything there was perfect, down to the slight sea breeze stirring the immaculate tablecloths. Bronzed young men jetted down the pier on mantis-like motor bikes, their girl friends stony-faced on the back, to go to 'Le Club Nautique'. There they sat and sipped cool beers and talked yachts and the fun life with Jacques Cousteau look-alikes, men sporting American peaked caps, true blue eyes and sun glasses twirling at their fingertips. Even the few Djiboutians there, who polished the wood and shined the brass of the motor launches bobbing in a line under the restaurant, had an athletic and self-important air.

The club was a long walk from my hotel. I walked all the way back along the pier, past the palace with its perfectly placed balconies peeping through the palms where the President took the air, through the square with all the banks, past the cripples dozing in the terrible midday heat, along the deserted dusty streets that divided the now shuttered shops and down into the market. Here at last there was some life again. The stalls of fruit and vegetables, meat and herbs, did not close despite the heat. And, of course, the Friday Mosque was always open and stirring with activity, as was the big square in front of it. Here at any time of day a fleet of mini-buses revved and waited for custom. They stood in a bunch, edging and fuming, like the start of a Grand Prix. Each bus had a tout who shouted, 'One more place, one more place for Cartier . . .' They fought amongst each other for passengers, pulling them this way and that. Once full, the bus shot out of the inching line with squealing tyres, slewed on to the road, startling pedestrians and donkeys, and disappeared round a corner, flags and streamers flying out behind, arms and legs sticking out of doors and windows, and the ticket collector hanging on outside, like a bobsleigher.

Two factors rule life in Djibouti, apart from the French. One is the heat and the other is qat. The heat, even in October,

260

which was the winter, is something to which you must reconcile yourself. It is the sort of heat that staggers you, as if a volcanic vent had just opened at your feet, the sort of heat that makes the other side of the street seem a long way away and which, when breathed, scorches nose and throat. If it says it is too hot to do anything, then you do nothing. Since for most of the year most days and nights are like this, little is done in Djibouti except by those who work in air-conditioned offices, or those who have no choice.

Most people handle the heat and pass the long hours by chewing the small leaves of qat, which act as an amphetamine. Qat is bought by the kilo anywhere in town from wooden kiosks prominently placed on pavements and at street corners. There is never any problem with supply because an aeroplane is organized to fly to Ethiopia every day to ferry it in. The fresh supply is on the streets by about ten or eleven o'clock. The government knows very well that if it were to fail in this public service, it would be out of office within a day. Many Djiboutians spend stretches of time working in Saudi Arabia or other high-earning countries. When they come back they have enough money to set up small businesses, shops or buses or something else, or alternatively they just live off the money until it runs out. As this is an African Islamic society, those who have no money can be supported by relatives who do; borrowing small amounts from 'brothers' is also easy, so that in this harmonious system everybody can find enough money for a daily supply, one way or another.

The men in my hotel lived the qat routine every day. They rose late, maybe nine or ten o'clock, then made a slow, meticulous toilet. They combed their hair thoroughly and lazed around for half an hour or so scrubbing their teeth with their special teeth-cleaning sticks. Then they went into town to do any of the little things that needed to be done in order to keep their lives ticking over. At about twelve o'clock they returned with their bundles of qat. Mattresses and cushions were laid out in the courtyard against the wall. Thermoses of iced water were filled, bottles of coke were bought and the radio was turned on. They went about these preparations with a seriousness that could verge on grumpiness. At last they could don their ma'awwis, flip-flops and string vests again and sit down to commence their chewing.

Soon the qat had its effect and their spirits went high. They were talking and laughing nineteen to the dozen, ragging each other, joking and generally being merry. As the afternoon progressed, the once clean and tidy yard became littered with discarded stalks, cigarette butts and empty coke bottles full of ash. The men slouched lower and lower as time passed, their legs lifeless and their heads propped against the wall. The big ball of leaf pulp bulged in their cheeks, making them shine white and bloodless. Still they could talk, smoke and sip coke without interfering with it, but they became sillier and sillier, a bit like drunks, and before long one of them would become irritable and fuddled, then all of them. They had reached the height and were now descending. Much later on they slouched uncomfortably, with bored backs and aching limbs, dishevelled and bloody-eyed, disagreeable and silent.

As darkness fell they became fidgety; soon they climbed to their feet and started to clear up the mess. They had a shower, put on their town clothes and went off to eat their evening meal with the relations or friends who were feeding them. When they returned they were more mellow and friendly. They sat or wandered around until they went to bed at about eleven or twelve o'clock.

This is the general routine for many of the people in the town. Not everyone chews qat, but most who live there permanently do. Some chew more and late into the night, and some chew less. The heavy chewers are easily distinguishable. They have vague, blurry eyes and pasty, dead-looking faces. They are continuously fidgety and when they talk they go on and on very boringly, and can become quite aggressive. Most people chew at home, in regular groups, but some chew on the streets. Down any of the tin-shack alleys there were always huddles of chewers. Often they were groups of furtive youths squatting in the dust, or on a shop verandah, desultorily playing cards. They are oblivious of everything; only the cards and their cliques of friends penetrate their consciousness. For them the streets are home, their families forgotten or lost. They sleep like dogs, curled up together in quiet corners. They beg, they thieve and they chew qat. That is all. Many smaller boys and girls roam the streets, wary-faced and dumb with ignorance. They scavenge in and out of the traffic, down alleyways and into secret cubby-holes like wild animals intimate with this, their jungle. They are the unwanted surplus of humanity, orphans, half-castes spawned by prostitutes and then abandoned. The native community is aware of them; perhaps it does not improve them, but it cares for them after a fashion and feeds them from family doorways.

The main boulevard near my hotel was long, straight and very wide, almost like a park in the midst of the close shanties. Every evening the people would spill out on to it, to breathe and enjoy the space. All down the centre reservation, and on the pavements, small cafés and restaurants were set up, simple affairs of trestle tables with plastic cloths and roaring lamps. I spent my evenings sitting in one of these restaurants in the middle of the road. The street simmered humidity, and moved and broke up, fragmenting into the distance like a painting of a foggy night. The atmosphere was like that of a living room. Faces became familiar. The dirty alleys running off the street became familiar. I made many acquaintances. They would come and sit with me or take me off to their friends and alleyways.

Ali was well educated and had worked in Libya and Italy for a long time; originally he came from Mogadishu, though he looked much more Arabic than most Somalis. He lived in a small shack just around the corner with his wife and children. His pride and joy was a smart, pea-green Mercedes. It was untaxed and illegal so he could not drive it very much, but he would take me for surreptitious rides around the bumpy lanes. We would stop here and there to pick up people who would squeeze in and bump round with us for a while, gossiping, then get out again when we came back to the same place where we had picked them up. We would stop outside huts to talk to Ali's girlfriends and beep at the children who got in the way. One of his friends was a tough seaman who chewed a lot of qat.

We used to sit outside his house, playing music and playing with the children. He would get in the car sometimes, dressed up like an Arab with sunglasses and head-dress.

'Open the door for me, my man,' he would call out of the car window. 'I want to buy that lady.'

Ali had another friend who owned a smart bus and we would jaunt with him sometimes, picking up friends from roundabout, and go to beaches or other parts of town. They had Arabian guitars, flutes and drums and would play wonderful music and sing moving songs.

Ali was a kind man and cared for the children of the streets. He would grab a passing urchin and hold him like a doll, squeezing his arms and legs like a doctor.

'You can't even tell if it's a boy or girl, Ga-damn,' he would say, and give it some food. Ali had worked for an American company once and had picked up this expression 'Ga-damn' from them, complete with accent. He used it profusely, especially when talking about Djibouti.

'These Ga-damn people in Djibouti,' he would moan. 'They have no pride in themselves. Look at the way they keep their homes. They just let them rot and stay filthy. They don't bother about their children. They live lazy, pointless lives.'

He was contemptuous of Djibouti and the Djiboutians, but cared because they were his people.

The majority of the people in the alleyways were women, all very beautiful in the Somali way. They wore the same loose robes of thin, silky material and swanned about in the same provocative way. The whole shanty was decorated with their butterfly forms, sitting on boxes like fisherwomen.

'These women are all Ga-damn materialists and prostitutes,' Ali declaimed. 'They have no feeling or warmth. They think only of money, new chairs, freezers and stoves.'

Prostitution is one of Djibouti's main trades. It is an easy game, with the French Foreign Legion and the free port close at hand.

Opposite my street restaurant was a tall building, its top floor occupied by some young girls; they used to come down and chat with my friends and me. One evening we were sitting

264

around in typically casual fashion. Children were playing in the street, jumping rides on passing vehicles. Women were working and men were praying in the mosque. Suddenly a jeep sped up the street slewing from side to side. Inside were three rough and brawny legionnaires swigging bottles and shouting. They stopped outside the tall house and went in. A minute later the street was treated to a display of one half-naked man standing, defiant, at the window at the top. Girls fluttered behind him. Then, bang, he closed the window. The men at the mosque and the people in the street watched in silence this blatant, intrusive act. But soon the scene was forgotten, tucked away in the strongholds of the mind. Ali, though, was openly indignant, 'Ga-damn, Ga-damn, what did I say? The women are all prostitutes, even those young girls. They put us all to shame.'

Ali was a good Muslim. *They* like to keep their prostitutes hidden, out of the way.

Djibouti was like this, a meeting of cultures. The French remained unaffected, expatriates and sure, but the Djiboutians, nomads and Arabs from forgotten times, had become a race apart. Their life was dull and depressed, but well supplied and not discontented. The French had their businesses and their telexes, their military fervour and crew-cut discipline; the Djiboutians had their heat and their qat.

For me a scene I saw on the main street in town on my last day told the tale of this confrontation. In between an office block and the shabby police headquarters, a tall mosque reared up, proudly announcing Islam with a clear white gleam. It was midday and the street was thronged with traffic; the cars and jeeps of Frenchmen returning home for lunch and a siesta, and walking or bussing clerks, happily finished for the day. A tractor pulling a long trailer piled high with cardboard boxes came up the road. On top were perched two Muslims, bare and brown-chested from work, flowing white sashes round their heads. As they passed in front of the mosque, the call to prayers wailed out from the minaret, high up, impaled against the sky. It called, with power and glory, the devout and stringent Koranic verses. They drifted down and around the tractor-trailer which now defiantly displayed its broadside against the radiant mosque façade, tiers and tiers of white, crisp boxes proclaiming *their* verses of 'Johnny Walker Whisky, Johnny Walker Whisky, a fine blend from Scotland.'

I flew from Djibouti to Cairo, having failed to find a boat. In a couple of hours I was translated from the remote lands where I had passed almost a year to a bus in the Egyptian rush hour. I made an attempt to visit the monuments and museums of the Nile Valley but somehow they palled. These were dead things from which I felt too detached. My mind was still elsewhere, still in a different gear. So I bought an ancient bicycle in Aswan and cycled back down the valley towards Cairo, staying in villages, happy to be away from the ranks of tourists and engine noise. Then I visited the delta, was befriended and accepted, and so spent my last week in Africa amongst the kind of people I had sought during my year.

I thought about this and many other things besides as I stood at the rails on the back of the ferry drawing out of

Alexandria. It was a moonless, pitch-black night and a cold wind blew in my face. I watched for what seemed hours as the city's lights shrank until they became only a lace of stars swimming on the dark sea and then at last winked out, and I was left alone, with only my thoughts and a remembered Africa. My solitary reverie did not last long, though. It was broken by a new acquaintance, an Egyptian, fresh and eager for Europe, who shared my cabin. He appeared suddenly at my side.

'Come my friend, come. Don't stand here all alone in the cold. No, no, come with me, for I must go and find a beautiful European woman to melt my heart.'

Lee Langley

Changes of Address

In CHANGES OF ADDRESS Lee Langley paints a fresh and intriguing portrait of India in the 1940s. She evokes the sights, sounds, smells of the bazaars, the bleached beauty of the landscape, the British in India, the outbursts of violence as the country struggled towards independence. Events are seen both through the eyes of the solitary child trying to keep her balance in the wake of her turbulent mother, and through the narrative of the adult she becomes, trying to understand the woman whose effect on her life was so devastating.

'Miss Langley has a fine comic touch, a vivid sense of place and tells her story with subtlety and spirit.'   *Daily Telegraph*

Flamingo

Sarah Lloyd

Chinese Characters

Sarah Lloyd spent eight months travelling through China – on buses, bicycles, boats and trains from north to south to far west of that vast land – seeking out ordinary people in a bid to understand their way of life in a country incomprehensible to most foreigners. During her wanderings she discovered a China always far removed from the image borrowed, as she puts it, from 'willow-patterned plates'.

'A vivid but unsentimental view of a people torn between traditional values, socialist ideals, and Western temptations . . . Hers is neither the China of the revolutionary posters nor of the tourist snaps.'   *Observer*

'A stylish and intriguingly revealing account.'   *Sunday Express*

Flamingo

PETER MATTHIESSEN

Indian Country

Ever since the white man first set foot on American soil, he has viewed the wilderness as something he could shape to his own ends. The American Indians view the land as sacred, and man as one with it. But they are the losers in this conflict, and they have been forced to witness the destruction of their land and their traditions – powerless against the interests of governments, industrialists and profiteers.

Indian Country is a passionate appeal for the rights of the American Indian to preserve their traditions – an eloquent argument for a reconciled world, where the industrial way of life does not obliterate the old.

'This is an admirable, unsentimental book which might cause anyone to think deeply about the true nature of our Western civilization.'

CHRISTOPHER BOOKER, *Sunday Telegraph*

Flamingo

Adam Zameenzad

The Thirteenth House

For Zahid, life is a constant struggle against chaos. His wife confuses him; his sick, silent son terrifies him; his poverty threatens to overwhelm him. In the background, the political and religious turmoil of native Pakistan seems merely to mock his troubled state of mind in cruel mimicry.

But when Zahid finds a new house to live in, he allows himself a flutter of optimism. True, there are rumours about the house, silly rumours . . . but he feels it is a turning point. Soon after moving in, he meets the Sha Baba, a potent and splendid guru who offers him a vision of happiness.

But happiness is not what fate has in store for Zahid, and the comic progress of his life carries him stumbling towards tragedy.

'Fine, narrative wryness of the R. K. Narayan sort. The wryness, though, never once stifles the power' *Observer*

'If ever comedy was black, this is' *Guardian*

'Ghost story, nightmare, vision . . . It transposes the reader from a world where even the traumas of political upheaval and police brutality – however appalling – are at least solidly real, to an insubstantial, shimmering world where nothing is what it seems and where the significance of people, events and things trembles tantalizingly just out of focus . . . A forceful, moving and confident debut' *Times Literary Supplement*

Flamingo

Flamingo

Flamingo is a quality imprint publishing both fiction and non-fiction. Below are some recent titles.

Fiction

☐ The Thirteenth House *Adam Zameenzad* £3.95
☐ Bright Lights, Big City *Jay McInerney* £2.95
☐ Human Voices *Penelope Fitzgerald* £3.95
☐ Offshore *Penelope Fitzgerald* £3.95
☐ Nelly's Vision *Eva Figes* £3.95
☐ The Joy's of Motherhood *Buchi Emecheta* £3.95
☐ Home Thoughts *Tim Parks* £3.95
☐ Sex and Sunsets *Tim Sandlin* £3.95

Non-fiction

☐ The Tao of Physics *Fritjof Capra* £4.95
☐ The Turning Point *Fritjof Capra* £5.95
☐ The First Three Minutes *Steven Weinberg* £3.95
☐ The Dancing Wu Li Masters *Gary Zukav* £3.50
☐ Before the Oil Ran Out *Ian Jack* £3.95
☐ Indian Country *Peter Matthiessen* £3.95
☐ Nine-Headed Dragon River *Peter Matthiessen* £3.95
☐ Chinese Characters *Sarah Lloyd* £3.95
☐ A Journey in Ladakh *Andrew Harvey* £3.95

You can buy Flamingo paperbacks at your local bookshop or newsagent. Or you can order them from Fontana Paperbacks, Cash Sales Department, Box 29, Douglas, Isle of Man. Please send a cheque, postal or money order (not currency) worth the purchase price plus 22p per book (or plus 22p per book if outside the UK).

NAME (Block letters) _____

ADDRESS_____

_____

_____